Welcome to this
QuickBreakthrough Edition
of

10 Seconds to Wealth

"Learn the truth and you will have the power to massively improve your life. I love this book!"

David Barron, coauthor of *Power Persuasion* (www.Power-Persuasion.com)

"Hiring Tom as my media and marketing coach has been the most valuable thing I've done in several years. Learn his secrets in this book!"

Dr. JoAnn Dahlkoetter, author of *Your Performing Edge* & coach to Olympians

Praise for Tom Marcoux's other work

"In *[Be Heard & Be Trusted]*, Tom teaches potent tools for finding your voice and powerfully expressing yourself, essential for getting what you want in life."

Marcia Wieder, author of *Making Your Dreams Come True* and PBS celebrity

"Tom's *How to Heal When Life's Too Much*, helps if you are having a rough time. I'd recommend it to clients, colleagues, and friends."

Shannon Seek, Principal, Seek Solutions, author of *Organic Organizing Matrix*

"In *Online Secrets to Build Your Brand*, Tom [gets you] more cash per click."

David Barron, persuasion expert, coauthor of *Power Persuasion*

"Tom's *How Top Salespeople Double Sales in Half the Time*, provides me with new techniques that I use."

Steven Seitz, Sales Manager, Silicon Valley Conference Center

10 Seconds to Wealth

---

*I help people experience enthusiasm, love,
and wisdom to fulfill big dreams.*

TOM MARCOUX

Personal Mission
Caption

OTHER TITLES BY

TOM MARCOUX

Be Heard and Be Trusted

*Full Strength Marketing:
Use Your Hidden Strengths to Raise Your Profits
(coauthored with Linda L. Chappo)*

Nothing Can Stop You This Year!

Wake Up Your Spirit to Prosperity!

Wake Up Your Spirit to Prosperity for Couples!

Secret Influence to Get You Out of Trouble

Online Secrets to Build Your Brand

Power Time Management

10 Best Kept Secrets of Persuasion Masters

Double Your Sales in Half the Time

Say Yes to Yourself

Personal Branding

How to Heal When Life's Too Much

*Truth No One Will One Tell You:
How to Feed Your Soul, Save a Business, or Get a Job in a Crisis*

*Darkest Secrets of Persuasion and Seduction Masters:
How to Protect Yourself and Turn the Power to Good*

*Empower Your Personal Brand:
Align Yourself for Promotions and Raises*

10 Seconds to Wealth

Master the Moment Using
Your Divine Gifts

formerly titled
Wake Up Your Spirit to Prosperity

Tom Marcoux

America's Communication Coach
&
The Time-Leverage Detective

A QUICKBREAKTHROUGH EDITION

ISBN: 0-9800511-7-7 / 978-0-9800511-7-9

© 2011 Tom Marcoux Media, LLC

All rights reserved, including moral rights. No part of this book may be reproduced without written permission from the publisher.

QuickBreakthrough Publishing is an imprint of
Tom Marcoux Media, LLC

More copies are available from the publisher:

Tom Marcoux Media, LLC
(415) 572-6609
TomSuperCoach@gmail.com
www.TomSuperCoach.com

This book was developed and written with care. Names and details were modified to respect privacy where necessary.

Interviews and substantial excerpts by other authors are copyrighted by those authors and included herein with their permission.

Disclaimer: No fiduciary relationship is created hereby between the reader and author or publisher. The author and publisher note that each person's situation is unique and that readers have the responsibility to seek consultations with health, financial, spiritual, and legal professionals when implementing any advice contained herein. The author and publisher make no warranties of any kind, and shall not be liable for any special, consequential, or exemplary damages resulting, in whole or in part, from the reader's use of, or reliance upon, this material.

Book design by
kunst+aventur
see *Collophon* at rear

Dedication

*this book is dedicated to the
terrific book & film consultant*

JOHANNA MAC LEOD

Acknowledgements

My heartfelt gratitude to all my other team members. Thanks to the guest authors for their voices of great experience. Thanks to Linda L. Chappo, Stacy Diane Horn, and Jill Ronsley (SunEditWrite.com) for editing. Thanks for comments from my father, Al Marcoux. Thanks to my mother, Sumiyo Marcoux, a kind, generous soul. Thanks to Johanna E. Mac Leod for her essential insights. Thanks to Gregg at Kunst+Aventur for the book's cover, design, editing, fact checking, typesetting, and production logistics. Thanks to Higher Power, our readers, our clients, and our enthusiastic audiences.

Contents

Summary Contents

10 Seconds to Wealth 1
Wake Up Your Spirit to Prosperity 45
Make Money Through Your Natural Brilliance 103
Prosperity is Founded on Relationships 137
Wake Up Your Spirit to Prosperity for Couples 155
Create Confidence. 221
Take Action as a Team for Real Abundance 251
Secret Influence to Get You Out of Trouble 283
Influence Through Energy, Poise, & Charisma. 325
Say "Yes" to Yourself 351
Work Effectively with Creditors 375
Give It a Rest. 399
A Final Word. 411
Special Offer for My Readers. 415
Glossary III
Further Reading. IX
About the Author XXI

Detailed Contents

	LEGEND
📖	Contribution by guest author
📄	Form

DEDICATION VII
ACKNOWLEDGEMENTS IX

Contents

Part I

Chapter 1

10 SECONDS TO WEALTH

MASTER THE MOMENT USING YOUR DIVINE GIFTS 1
10 Seconds to Wealth 3
    We'll begin with belly breathing. 4
    10 seconds are crucial to long-term memory. 5
    Condition your brain to be inclined toward the positive. 5

My Epiphany 6
   Existential Plights 6
A Note about Existential Plights 7
Decide (love) 8
   Use love & compassion to open the floodgates of wealth 10
Intuit (humility) 11
   How Healthy Humility Protects Your Energy 12
   Fear or Intuition—How can you tell? 14
Voice (Forgiveness) 17
   How to "Do" Forgiveness 20
      Let the first thought float by and let in a new thought 21
      Use compassion as your compass 21
Inspire (faith) 23
   How do you get this faith or empowering stance? 24
Nurture (grace) 26
   Three Steps towards Grace: Awareness, Openness, & Experience ... 27
   You've been given grace, but may not feel it in this moment 28
   How You Can Experience "Grace Under Pressure" 29
   Other Sources for Feeling Grace in the Moment 30
   How grace can help open floodgates of financial abundance 31
Express (Art) 33
Conclusion to Divine Gifts chapter 36
   Quickly Access Your Divine Gifts 37
   Access Divine Gifts with a Simple Shift in Thought 39
   The Secret to Quickly Access Your Divine Gifts 40

Part II

Chapter 2

WAKE UP YOUR SPIRIT TO PROSPERITY

Seek the Higher View...49
Two Aspects of Your Self 51
How to Move Through Fear 53
    Mike Robbins

        How to move through your fear in a positive way 54
INTENSIFY THE POWER OF WORDS........................56
Program for Abundance 57
Mindsets...58

How to be Positive in a Negative World.......................60
    Dr. Arthur P. Ciaramicoli

        Awareness of Your Story................................60
        The Truth Expands our Vision..........................61
The Power-3 Income Streams 64
Program for Abundance by Asking for Help...................65
Open the door to healing with the God Box 66
Intuit to do it 67
Retreat from Reverse Examples 70
    Avoid Reverse Examples & Seek Out Inspiring Ones............73
Personaltainment™ Branding 81
    Your Spiritual Path to Wealth 81
    You Can Use Personaltainment Branding at Work 83
        Five Personaltainment Branding Questions................84
    How Is Personaltainment Branding Spiritual? 84
    The Foundation of Personaltainment™ Branding 85

Increase Your Abundance Using Personaltainment Branding. . 87
Personaltainment™ Branding 88
   Personaltainment Branding Does Not Require a Fancy Website 91
      Five Personaltainment Branding Questions. 91
Inspire Hope and Faith 92
   Hope and faith bring inner peace. 93
Target the Good of All 96
   The Big Picture Forgiveness Process 97
   The Good of All Means Everyone Profits from a Situation 98
Conclusion of Chapter Two 100

Chapter 3
MAKE MONEY THROUGH YOUR NATURAL BRILLIANCE

Science of the 9-Minute Miracle Breakthrough process 104
Make your True Self a bigger part of your daily life. 105
Momentum Action Plan (MAP). 106
   Question 1: What do you want? 106
Momentum Action Plan (MAP). 108
   Question 2: No. Come on, what do you really want? 108
Momentum Action Plan (MAP). 109
   Question 3: Better yet, what do you want to feel? 109
      Connect with desired feelings with "See, Hear, Touch" ... 111
Momentum Action Plan (MAP). 112
   Question 4: How do I experience goals on a small scale? ...112
Momentum Action Plan (MAP)—Partial Example 114
A Special Note about What You Want 115
Momentum Action Plan (MAP). 116
   Question 5: How can you graduate up levels? 116
Momentum Action Plan (MAP). 118
   Question 6: How can you gain an Immediate Victory? 118
Momentum Action Plan (MAP). 120

Question 7: How can you announce what you offer? 120
Momentum Action Plan (MAP) 126
Question 8: Say: "I want <goal> & my obstacle is
<impediment>" 126
Momentum Action Plan (MAP) 127
Question 9: Ask, "Give me suggestions, leads, wild ideas?" 127
Momentum Action Plan (MAP) 128
Question 10: Write due dates next to items on your list ... 128
Conclusion of Chapter Three 129
Momentum Action Plan (MAP) 132

Chapter 4

PROSPERITY IS FOUNDED ON RELATIONSHIPS

GREAT RELATIONSHIPS EXPAND FINANCIAL ABUNDANCE 137
H—Honor the personality style 140
U—Understand that no humor bit works for everyone 141
M—Mirror the person's humor preference. 141
O—Open the door 142
R—Respect the person and environment 142
30 Secrets for Creating Humor 143
Secret 1: Prepare the Stage 143
Secret 2: Notice that timing is acquired through practice. 143
Secret 3: Gain timing through subconscious modeling. 143
Secret 4: Play with words 144
Secret 5: Use a good setup 144
Secret 6: Base humor on a song pattern 144
Secret 7: Create a running joke based on the situation 145
Secret 8: Base humor on icons, like Star Wars 145
Secret 9: Enjoy understatement 145
Secret 10: Tie-in experiences shared by the audience 146
Secret 11: Choose a good target (perhaps yourself) 146

Secret 12: Remember to use context well 146
Secret 13: The Power-3 (context, structure, imposition) 146
Secret 14: Twist a familiar phrase 147
Secret 15: Set up the last word to have punch 147
Secret 16: Go on a riff 147
Secret 17: Use the Magic of Three 148
Secret 18: Use the magic of the reoccurring joke 148
Secret 19: Carefully use cynical humor 148
Secret 20: Integrate current topics 149
Secret 21: Make fun of a safe target 149
Secret 22: Put in an Act Out moment 149
Secret 23: Tie in the visual 150
Secret 24: Rehearse your choice of words before telling a story 150
Secret 25: Use similar sounds 150
Secret 26: Use rhythm 151
Secret 27: Note goofy items from the newspaper 151
Secret 28: When speaking, use topic-oriented cartoons 151
Secret 29: Use a label as you tell a story 151
Secret 30: Ad-lib in the moment 151
Abundance is Built on Great Relationships 152

Part III

Chapter 5
WAKE UP YOUR SPIRIT TO PROSPERITY FOR COUPLES

Create (Not Compete) 158
My Personal Values and Goals 161
    The Replace Inky Water Method 166
    Refresh your view of the miracles in your life 169

    Aromatherapy & Enhanced Posture for Added Power 170
    The Process to Replace Negative Thoughts 171
Organize for Hope 175
What a Good Life Looks Like to Me 177
    The Power-3 Income Streams 178
    How Ross Perot became a billionaire in eight years 181
    Prospering Couples are Adept with Savings & Budgets 184
        Secret 1: Take the pain out 184
        Secret 2: Reinforce your partner's sense of being adult. 184
        Secret 3: Consider differences in money styles 185
        Secret 4: Separate couple issues from individual issues 185
        Secret 5: Use the Abundance Coffee Cups method 186
        Secret 6: Have some fun each month as a couple 187
        Secret #7: Learn to budget each other's priorities........... 187
    A New Way to Ease into Discipline to Improve Your Life 188
Use Momentum.. 190
    Devoting Time to Relaxation Improves Your Momentum........ 193
Practice Compassion 194
    It helps to really look at and listen to your partner............. 197
    Secrets for Talking Effectively about Money................... 201
Let Go of What's Not Working.................................. 204
    Powerful steps for the Entrepreneurial Partner: 208
    Powerful steps for the Non-Entrepreneurial Partner: 209
    Let go of the Martyr's Badge................................ 210
Energize to Serve... 213
Conclusion of Chapter Five...................................... 218

Chapter 6

CREATE CONFIDENCE

Want it From Your True Self................................ 227

📖 *Self-Acceptance, Self-Respect, and Self-Appreciation* 232
   Elayne Savage, Ph.D.

       What's a Mistake or Three? 233
       Lessons From the Yellow Submarine 234
       Transforming Self-Rejection into Self-Acceptance 234
Adapt. 237
       Set up a Low Mood First-Aid Kit 238
Keep Learning. 241
Encourage Help. 245
Conclusion to Chapter Six. 249

Chapter 7
TAKE ACTION AS A TEAM FOR REAL ABUNDANCE

Take Over the Weak Spots. 252
Encourage Entrepreneurship and Support. 258
       Value both entrepreneurship and support 259
       Express support with the Moment of Appreciation 263
       Express the Positive Intention in Your Conversation. 264
Adapt to Personal Styles 265
       Prospering Couples Flow with the Other's Personality Style 268
       Prospering Couples Flow with the Other's Thinking Style 269
       Prospering Couples Flow with the Other's Pain-Interaction Style .. 270
Make Good Luck. 272
       Use Your Integrity and Courage in Tough Situations. 275
       Networking will Increase Your Good Luck. 276
       Prospering Couples Consider Pulling Together a Team 277
Conclusion of Chapter Seven 278

Part IV

Chapter 8
SECRET INFLUENCE TO GET YOU OUT OF TROUBLE

Restore a Relationship after a Screw Up 283
Inquire 286
   Discover the Offended's Preferred Language of Apology 287
Nurture.. 288
   Method 1: Let a Negative Thought Float Away................ 290
   Method 2: Use Write Down–Rip Up to Handle Anger 291
   Method 3: Use a Pattern-Interrupt to Shift to a Positive Mood 292
Flex Your Options.. 293
   Expressing Gratitude Can Restore a Relationship 294
   Make a Schedule to Take Action 296
   Schedule These Three Actions and You Will Go F.A.R. 297
   How to ask for forgiveness 298
Listen.. 300
   Use Reflective Replies 301
Understand 302
   To Inspire Forgiveness, Give Forgiveness 304
Energize 305
   Enhancing your romantic relationship 306
      Make Every Loving Gesture You Do Really Count! 307
      Words of affirmation 308
      Acts of service...................................... 308
      Receiving gifts...................................... 308
      Quality time 309
      Physical touch...................................... 309
   Enhance a Business Relationship........................... 311
      The five love languages 311

Words of affirmation 312
Receiving gifts. 312
Acts of service. 312
Quality time 312
Physical touch. 313
Principle 313
Power Question 314
Negotiate 314
  Negotiate for time to consider what you will agree to 314
  Avoid fear and gain think-space. 316
  What to do in your next conversation 316
    He makes sure that Janet knows she is winning. 317
    He does not over-promise. 317
    He ends with the positive news. 317
    He demonstrates that he wants to care for her needs. 317
Create (Not Compete) 318
Embrace 321
Conclusion to Chapter Eight. 323

Chapter 9

INFLUENCE THROUGH ENERGY, POISE, & CHARISMA

HOW TO HEAL WHEN LIFE'S TOO MUCH 325
Humor 327
Energize 329
  Create—Create time-pockets 331
  Open—Open to what is unchangeable. 331
  Prepare—Prepare your options 331
  Expect—Expect and focus on the good 332
  Learn to Replace Worry. 332
Act 334
Listen. 336

Life's Lessons & Experiencing Spiritual Awakening 338
Accept Pain that Lights Your Way to the Divine Aha! 338
Talk About What You're Learning 340
Write About What You're Learning 341
Be Gentle with Yourself 341
Forgiveness and Your Happiness 343
    How You Can Work Well with the Offended Person 343
Conclusion of Chapter Nine 347

Chapter 10

SAY "YES" TO YOURSELF

REDUCE STRESS AND INCREASE EASE 351
Step off the Stage 353
    Awareness and action 355
Accept Better Care 357
Yield to Recovery 361
    The Calm-Tai Chi Movement 362
    Quiet time (prayer, meditation, more) 362
Yearn for Energy 363
    Gain Energy through Talk, Walk, Write 364
    Energy, Money, and Healing 365
Encourage Your Best 366
Support Your Team 369
Personality Style 371
    Beaver ("analytic" or "engineer" or "accountant") 371
    Dog ("relater") 371
    Lion ("director") 371
    Peacock ("socializer") 371
Conclusion to Chapter Ten 373

Chapter 11
WORK EFFECTIVELY WITH CREDITORS

GET OUT OF DEBT AND BACK ON YOUR FEET 375
Talk 377
    The Benefit of Making Arrangements with Creditors. 378
    How to Ask for Lower Payments 378
    How to communicate with your supervisor. 380
    Good Debt v. Bad Debt. 382
Understand 383
Right-Size. 385
    To Avoid Impulse Purchases and Handle Your "Soft Spot" 387
Self-Nurture Chart™. 389
Nurture. 391
    The central idea about nurturing yourself. 394
Conclusion to Chapter Eleven 397

Chapter 12
GIVE IT A REST

Relax into It 400
Ease Through. 402
    The Power of Non-Correcting Conversation. 405
Sing 406
Thank Someone. 408
Conclusion to Chapter Twelve 409

Chapter 13
A FINAL WORD

SPRINGBOARD TO YOUR DREAMS. 411

Author Appearances

Glossary
Glossary III

Bibliography
Further Reading IX
About the Author XXI
Collophon... XXV
Book Offer XXVI

Part I

1

10 Seconds to Wealth

Master the Moment Using Your Divine Gifts

Imagine that you can have what you truly want. How? When you unwrap your divine gifts for success, love and great relationships.

Here's how.

Through this book you'll learn to unwrap your Divine Gifts and experience the process of *10 Seconds to Wealth*.

In 10 seconds you can close a sale or begin a healthy new relationship. On the other hand, in 10 seconds you can torpedo that sale or new relationship.

The point is this: Condition yourself to be ready for those all-important 10 seconds—that window of opportunity when you can make a difference.

For instance, we all know the importance of the first 10 seconds when meeting someone new. After all, first impressions last a long time. However, life changes when we least expect it.

Those all-important 10 seconds can come at any time. Always be prepared for whatever might come next.

Do you realize you have hidden gifts that can help you in those crucial 10 seconds? You can:

- Keep your cool in a negotiation or other sensitive situations.
- Feel deep fulfillment and happiness in the moment.
- Inspire good feelings in a friend, colleague or romantic partner.

Recent research has revealed how the brain processes input. We have learned:

- Successful entrepreneurs interpret situations differently than other people.
- Successful salespeople can envision the sale before making an important sales call.
- People who enjoy warm relationships know how to help others feel heard and cared for.

The point is:

*Oftentimes, 10 seconds can be crucial to the outcome of **any** situation!*

Have you noticed that in 10 seconds you can do something powerful? You can:

- Say something that makes a friend feel important.
- Lose your temper and say something that you'll regret.
- Calm yourself down to make a situation better.

10 Seconds to Wealth

The essence is this:

- In 10 seconds you can close a sale or torpedo a relationship.

- Using your Divine Gifts enables you to be at your best during the crucial 10 seconds of any interaction—whether those 10 seconds are at the beginning, middle or end of the interaction.

- 10 seconds may be what's needed to build and enhance positive connections with the people who are the keys to your success and fulfillment.

- The strategy is to condition yourself to be at your best during those all-important 10 seconds (This book includes many methods to achieve that strategy).

- Recent brain research notes that it takes 10 seconds for positive input to impact your long-term memory. This means that memorizing empowering thoughts, rehearsing effective behaviors, and writing positive details in your personal journal all help to physically alter your brain so that it is inclined toward the positive.

- Conditioning yourself for positive change helps you overcome your "default settings."*

~~~~~~~~~~~~

Scientists confirm that you can condition yourself to be positive. How? Through what scientists call "brain plasticity," which refers to the ability of the brain to change as a result of one's experience (the brain is "plastic" and "malleable"). We'll discuss this idea later in more detail.

We'll begin with belly breathing

Here is a simple process to help your mind and body experience peace. Breathe in through your nose while allowing your belly to expand. Hold your breath for a moment, and then breathe out through your mouth while letting your belly to get smaller. Repeat this process ten times. How do you feel now? My clients have reported feeling relaxed and even stronger.

Now imagine practicing belly breathing every day. What happens? You condition your mind and body to experience inner peace. Augment belly breathing with meditation. In its simplest form, you merely sit quietly for six minutes and focus only on your breath flowing in and out. No strain. No effort.

Research has shown that people can learn to be positive in much the same way one learns to play an instrument. Neurosci-

....

* A default setting is something that has been programmed into you at some point in your past. People tend to fall back to their default setting when under stress. For example, people who become extremely nervous when delivering a speech may have had a traumatic experience giving a presentation at some point in the past.

entists Antoine Lutz and Richard Davidson found that people who regularly meditate could physically change their brains. The scientists used fMRIs and EEGs to study how a meditator's brain functions differently. They found that brain circuits used to detect emotions and feelings were dramatically changed in those who meditate regularly.

10 seconds are crucial to long-term memory.

Psychologist Rick Hanson and neurologist Richard Mendius wrote about how the brain is hard-wired to scan for the bad. They note: "Positive experiences are usually registered through standard memory systems, and thus need to be held in conscious awareness for ten to twenty seconds for them to really sink in."

The point here is that you need to condition your brain to be at your best during the crucial 10 seconds of interaction with a client, co-worker or loved one.

Condition your brain to be inclined toward the positive.

People in the habit of regularly writing in a journal about what is going well in their lives actually experience more happiness.

For years I have written in my "Daily Journal of Victories and Blessings," and I feel grateful and happy when it's time for sleep. Researchers have discovered that journal writing makes it easier for many people to fall asleep. I invite you to begin this healthy habit tonight.

Psychologists Robert Emmons and Michael McCullough verified the value of writing in a gratitude journal. Their study revealed that a group of people writing five things for which they were grateful "ended up happier, much more optimistic about the future and physically healthier—and they even exercised more."*

My Epiphany

While teaching a Comparative Religion class, I wrote these details on a whiteboard:

Existential Plights

Death, Freedom, Responsibility, Meaninglessness**

By the mere fact that you're a human being, it is said that you are stuck with the Existential Plights.

I then did something new in the class. I wrote on the other side of the whiteboard:

Divine Gifts

Love, Humility, Forgiveness, Faith, Grace, Art

In that moment, standing at the whiteboard, I was struck with the idea: *These Divine Gifts provide healing as we're faced with the Existential Plights.* How about that!

Now we're going to explore how you can tune into your Divine Gifts and open the floodgates for wealth, financial abundance and warm relationships. We'll use the D.I.V.I.N.E. process.

....

* Research on the benefits of keeping a gratitude journal was reported in the book *59 Seconds: Think a Little, Change a Lot* by Richard Wiseman.

** The Existential Plights are discussed in the classic book *Existential Psychotherapy* by Irvin D. Yalom.

1. Decide (love)
2. Intuit (humility)
3. Voice (forgiveness)
4. Inspire (faith)
5. Nurture (grace)
6. Express (art)

Through this book you'll learn how to experience your Divine Gifts. To obtain the best results, you will need to actively prepare. The next section on love, humility, forgiveness, faith, grace and art is a springboard to condition your brain for more wealth. For the sake of our discussion, we'll hold that wealth includes financial abundance, good relationships and feelings of fulfillment and well-being.

A Note about Existential Plights

The Existential Plights of death, freedom, responsibility and meaninglessness basically give each person an off-balance feeling often called "free-floating anxiety," which is defined as a generalized and persistent fear that is not attributable to anything specific. The following gives an example for each Existential Plight:

Anxiety about death is often felt in the moment as fear for something that is going dreadfully wrong. It can be the fear of saying something wrong or even losing a sale.

People who are afraid of making a wrong decision may feel that their freedom of choice is a burden.

Many people equate responsibility with the burden of blame. On the subconscious level, this can be manifested as an echo of parental admonishments: "You need to be more responsible!" and "You're to blame for this going wrong!"

Meaninglessness can be the burden of feeling "groundless." This happens when one feels disillusioned. Perhaps one feels betrayed by a parent or friend. Perhaps following a spiritual path didn't provide long-lasting comfort.

The blessings and power of the Divine Gifts are that they give us uplifting support in the moment. The Divine Gifts of love, humility, forgiveness, faith, grace and art give you the experience of fullness, which is the opposite of emptiness or vulnerability.

Decide (love)

When have you really felt loved? Did someone give you a gift? Or hug you when you were crying?

Now come with me on a brief journey, which may become a real shift in your thoughts and feelings.

Imagine that you and I stand and say plaintively: "I need love." Do you feel emptiness in your chest? A hole that needs to be filled up? Some people feel the discomfort of "I need love" to be similar to that of overwhelming heat in a desert.

Imagine that you're in a desert feeling stifled by the weather and you're perspiring. Then, a delicious, cool breeze comes along and embraces you. Now you feel relieved and comfortable. Ahhh. You pick up a cool glass of water with ice cubes and take a drink. Ahhh.

Can you imagine that great feeling of relief? It's similar to the relief we feel when we truly experience "I am love."

The state of being when you deeply feel "I am love" is one of comfort, joy, faith and happiness.

My goal with this section is to introduce you (or perhaps remind you) to an essential distinction. Why? So you'll feel better and stronger.

Ready?

Imagine you have a ruler. On the left side is "I need love." On the right side is "I am love."

I ask you: Which of these two sides feels stronger?

Now imagine two cars. (For the sake of this conversation, both cars run on electric batteries.) The car with a fully charged battery can get up and go! The car without the charge is powerless. It's stuck. It's empty.

When you say "I am love," you are fully charged. You have power. Even better than that, saying "I am love" means to many of us that a person is one with a supportive Higher Power.

Love is a Divine Gift.

You, as a human being, have the ability to love as "standard equipment." This is not to say that it's always easy to be loving. It is a moment-to-moment decision.

To get to that "I am love" part of your being is to make a decision.

What decision?

Often, it is to let your first reflex thought (often a judgment) flow by. Instead, find a compassionate thought and action.

Use compassion as your compass.
What does this look like?
You choose loving actions:
1. Restrain yourself from writing an angry letter to a rude relative.
2. Give a surprise gift to a friend to help her feel important.
3. Listen to the same story for the tenth time when an elderly relative tells it.

When you use "I am love" and "compassion as your compass," you can enhance your personal relationships.

Use love & compassion to open the floodgates of wealth

When you work with customers (or a supervisor or co-workers), make each *10 Seconds to Wealth* count. How? Enter each moment with "I am love." You do that by finding a way to express compassion. In particular, notice that there are two (often unvoiced) requirements that your customers hold: a) Show me that I can trust you, and b) Make me feel important.

When you fulfill those two requirements, customers will purchase more and refer new business back to you.

People often spend more for the services that they trust. For example, I have paid for about 18 domain names over the years, although I do not use the cheapest provider. Why? Because I seek reliability. I use two companies that have served me well. I have no complaints with either of them. Neither gives me hassles or reason for concern.

Opportunities often come from people who like and trust you.

So it all comes down to one idea:

Start from a place of "I am love." That's right. Make a decision and then act on it.

And guess what! You start to feel better and you start to feel safer. Why? Because you are now aligned with the good in the Universe.

You are empowered. You are loved.

Remember to focus on "I am love."

Principle

Embrace the idea "I am love."

Power Questions:

Are you ready to enter each situation from a base of "I am love"? Will you look at situations using compassion as your compass?

Intuit (humility)

Do you have a friend who seems to make life more of a struggle than necessary? Have you noticed that he or she likes complaining? Such a person is often inflexible.

But that's *not* you or me. Right?

Life has given me a number of opportunities to learn about something I call "healthy humility."

Healthy humility is a great alternative to being inflexible and holding onto some preconceived notion about how things are supposed to be.

Instead, I've learned to take a flexible stance and flow with life instead of allowing reflexive judgments to cloud my thinking. How? Let's say I find it rude that a relative won't take my phone calls. I let my initial thoughts flow by. I focus on:

- I wonder what I can learn here.
- Maybe this person is not skilled at handling upset feelings.
- What would I rather think about?

The rigid stance of insisting that other people *should* do something can block the flow of your intuition. How? Because nothing new can get in. Your intuition gives you the gift of new ideas.

Your intuition can give you new solutions that are more expansive than mere rational thinking.

Your intuition can also enable you to be at your best during the *10 Seconds to Wealth*. Your intuition can guide you to say the right things to close a sale or enhance a business relationship.

Take action with your new ideas and you may allow an inflow of financial abundance. (Now, wouldn't that be great?)

How Healthy Humility Protects Your Energy

First, holding a rigid stance takes a lot of energy. Stop wasting your energy! Second, when you have access to your intuition, things start to flow the way you prefer. That's right. You can avoid struggle and the wasted energy associated with it!

With healthy humility, you have access to your intuition, which brings amazing opportunities and even joy.

How? Healthy humility gives you flexibility. In essence, flexibility means you can learn from life, your mentors, and even from your friends. You realize that human beings have a limited perception in the moment. It's like a friend warning you about the spinach on your teeth. Before the alert from your friend, you were oblivious to the spinach problem. You say "Thanks," and then remove the spinach.

> *Mistake:* Thinking that humility is to feel less than others.
>
> *Solution:* Deem healthy humility as an undemanding and flexible approach to learning and being in the moment.

Stand shoulder-to-shoulder with others. Recognize that each of us has limited perceptions in the moment.

We get into trouble when we make judgments about how people should act. Should people say "please" and "thank you"? Imagine you step back from a demanding stance and instead focus on your preferences. We all prefer when people are courteous and say "thank you." With healthy humility, you merely step back and just let people be as they are. (Note that there are times when people must step away from abuse and get professional help.)

Healthy humility is also a gift because, in a way, it lets you off the hook. We can't control other people's behavior and feelings. I remind myself with this phrase: "I don't run that show."

Healthy humility helps us live in the moment and feel better. How? We learn to add helpful thoughts:

- I don't run that show.
- I enter each moment fresh.

- I prefer to . . .
- I wonder …
- I wonder what I'm going to learn here.

Here's the secret: The ideas discussed here allow you to be flexible and avoid wallowing in upset feelings for most of the day. People who are flexible are fun to be around, which means that others easily and naturally bring them opportunities.

One of my book editors said, "Wait a minute. Are you asking people to pretend there are no problems?" My reply: "No! I'm suggesting that we become strategic about how we use our limited time and energy." The example I gave her concerned a couple that chose to devote their energy to feeling good when they were together during the week. For some disagreements they chose to say, "We'll save that for our couple's therapy session on Wednesday." This strategy allowed them to enjoy better times throughout the rest of the week.

Try healthy humility. It takes humility to let go and just observe whether you're welcoming intuition or getting tangled in fear.

Fear or Intuition—How can you tell?

Ever been confronted with a tough decision that was torturing you?

Have you thought: Should I do this or that? Will I get hurt? Will I deeply regret not attempting this action?

I hear you.

Many years ago I was confronted with the choice of taking a particular job. I chose to use the Benjamin Franklin Method. I pulled out a sheet of paper and wrote "Pro" on the left side and "Con" on the right side. I divided the sheet by drawing a vertical line down the center.

I quickly wrote nine positive reasons to take the job: good money, good location, and more. After that I wrote down the first two reasons against taking the job. Then, the third reason practically leapt off the page at me.

Boom! My intuition yelled: *Don't take the job.*

Logic would have said: You have more reasons to take the job than to not take the job.

But the one powerful reason against it turned my thoughts. Without my intuition, I probably would have taken the job, and I would have had painful experience.

My sweetheart said, "It's like your one reason against taking the job was a watermelon, and the nine reasons for the job were peas."

I make space for my intuition whenever possible. If I don't need to make a quick decision, I put in what I call "think-space." I'll say something like: "That sounds like a promising idea. I'll need to talk with my team about it. How about I get back to you tomorrow afternoon?"

My clients ask this big question: What's the difference between the voice of fear and the voice of intuition?

Over the years I've talked this over with psychologists, counselors, authors, and spiritually minded people. I learned that the difference is:

- *Fearful voice says:* contract, protect yourself, hide

- *Intuitive voice says:* expand, try something, explore, learn, grow, experiment

Certainly, when you're deciding whether taking a particular action is an appropriate risk to take, it is helpful to have a system. A good system would include a process to observe the whole situation and reduce the chances of bad outcomes. Also, the system would give you time (preferably with writing in a personal journal) to think through the situation and connect with your feelings.*

And it is still helpful to ask yourself:

- What is the voice really saying? Is it saying "fear" or "love"?
- Is this a chance for personal growth and possibility?
- Is the voice connected to fear? Is it connected to success or failure?

So many of my favorite activities in life involve stepping forward even when fear might try to hold me back (writing books, giving speeches, acting in films and more).

There is always the first time. Imagine this: to transform to a butterfly, a caterpillar must let go of fear.

So, make space for your intuition.

We can find our true path when we connect to our true self that is deeper and beyond fear. Your true self is that part of you that is naturally courageous, brilliant and connected with the good in the universe.

••••••••••••••••••••••••••••••

* Discussions on systems to choose appropriate risk are included in my book *Nothing Can Stop You This Year: How to Unleash Your Hidden Power to Persuade Well, Get More Done, Gain Sudden Profits, Command Intuition and Feel Great.* View a free chapter at Amazon.com

You'll need to pull back from the surface noise of fear. Using healthy humility will help you access your intuition.

Principle

Live with healthy humility and welcome your intuition.

Power Questions

How can you devote some time and space *before* you make a decision. How can you welcome your intuition?

Voice (Forgiveness)

"I'm cancelling Father's Day," Mia's father said. Then he went on to shun her for two months. Her father refused to come to the phone when she called. And he would leave the house when Mia visited her mother.

This was breaking Mia down. She was my client and her tears broke my heart.

"He won't forgive me," she said. I asked her what had happened. She said her father hadn't heard her say "thank you" for the birthday gift he had given her, although she was sure she had said it. But the truth was that this was nothing new. I once asked her to draw a picture of what her father was like, and she drew a volcano. Her father would blow up and shun her for months every year, which was a cause of great anger for Mia.

Now, I ask you. Is there someone who has hurt you? Someone you might need to forgive? Or, do you feel that person doesn't deserve forgiveness?

I hear you.

But the truth is: Forgiveness is about freeing *you* from pain.

Forgiveness is a gift to you. It gives you more time to feel good and whole.

How?

I once appeared alongside Dr. Fred Luskin as a guest on a TV show. He said something I will always remember: "Forgiveness is about ending the cycle of blame and suffering. Forgiveness is when you become the hero of your own story."

Profound ideas.

If Mia feels her father is ruining her life, then she is not the hero of her own story. Also, let's face it, her father appears to be self-righteous and seems unlikely to change. So, Mia has choices. Hard choices. Here's what she does:

- When Mia feels angry when her father shuns her, she lets the thoughts come and go. That is, she lets them flow away like leaves on a river.

- Mia reminds herself that her father is unskilled at dealing with his own upset feelings.

- Mia reminds herself that her father has driven away all his friends, and his behavior is no different with her.

- Mia decides to continue visiting her mother, but she decides to visit for only one hour at a time. In this way, Mia limits her exposure to her father's negativity.

Note that none of this is about Mia waiting for her father to change.

How is her behavior forgiving? Specifically, when Mia reminds herself that her father is unskilled at dealing with his own upset feelings, she chooses to avoid sending him angry letters that attempt to straighten him out. She avoids returning negativity for negativity. She avoids trying to fix him.

Within the word "forgiveness" are the letters that spell the word "free."

I ask Mia, "When you have angry feelings about your father, do you sometimes run a vengeful fantasy in your mind?"

"Yes, how did you know?" she asked.

"I have people to forgive. And sometimes I need to forgive myself, too," I replied.

I continued, "The idea is for you to be the hero. Nurture yourself. Take yourself out of abusive situations. Get professional help if you need to. And don't let your father take up too much of your precious mental time."

"But how am I practicing forgiveness?" Mia asked.

"Have you decided to never visit your parents?" I asked.

"No," she replied.

"Then you're allowing your parents to be who they are. Don't forget they're from a different generation. They handle things the way they know how to handle them."

I continued, "This is important. You can forgive someone and not allow them to abuse you. And you can choose to avoid being vengeful toward a mean person."

It took time, but Mia filled her life with being around friendly people. Her pain quieted down. She now makes sure to get plenty of sleep before visiting her parents so that she has ample energy to be patient and helpful.

I shared with her an important part of forgiveness: the difference between judgment and discernment.

Judgment implies taking a superior attitude toward someone—like a judge sitting on the bench high above a lowly defendant.

On the other hand, discernment implies "recognizing." With discernment, you recognize that the other person is doing the best he can, although his hurtful behavior is inappropriate. When necessary, limit your exposure to that person for a time period.

When we decide to let our thoughts flow from condemnation to compassion, we often discover that we ultimately feel lighter and even freer.

This is the tip of the iceberg. The process of forgiveness is a lengthier discussion. I invite you to learn more. It's truly worth the effort.

How to "Do" Forgiveness

So many speakers mention the value of forgiveness. I wondered: What is a tangible action I can do to begin the forgiveness process?

Here is the action: Focus on *Just One More Thought*. This is your step to success, peace and connection.

What's your first thought when you see someone you don't like?

- "Ugh, he's here. What mean thing is he going to say today?"
- "Oh, I wish she would just go away!"

How about with family members?

- "She doesn't care about my feelings."
- "What an angry person. He's so critical."

Here's a simple step that can bring more success, peace and connection to your life:

Let the first thought float by and let in a new thought

Let's look at the above thought: "What an angry person. He's so critical."

What would an alternative thought sound like? How about: "What a frightened person. He doesn't know how to interact well with others."

Some people would take this second thought (frightened person) and feel some compassion for that person.

Use compassion as your compass

The idea here is that many of us have been conditioned to react to stimuli with judgmental thoughts.

With practice, our next thought can be a "discernment thought."

Here's the difference:
- A *judgmental thought* puts you at a distance. It puts you metaphorically on a high-up bench looking down on the person, like you are superior and judging them.
- A *discernment thought* helps you *recognize* that the person is trying to cope the best she or he can.

The transition from judgment to discernment helps you calm down. It helps you become stronger so that you make a positive response. So, how do we make that transition?

We take a breath. We are quiet. We let another thought arise.

When you're stuck in a judgmental thought, ask yourself: "How can I view this with compassion? How can I connect with this person?"

These are powerful questions. They come from a place of compassion in yourself—that is, from your true self. The ego self (often called the false self) is the fragile part of you that feels small and vulnerable.

When I talk about "voice" and "forgiveness," I'm suggesting that we listen to the compassionate voice in ourselves. That's the voice of our true self, which is naturally courageous, brilliant and loving.

Remember, judgment is *not* connection. Judgment creates space and separation from other people.

So remember: Let that first thought flow by as if it were on a river. Take a breath and know that another thought will come next.

You'll be glad to enjoy more harmony.

Principle

Let a judgment thought flow by and welcome a discernment thought.

Power Questions:

How can you recognize a judgment thought? How can you nurture yourself so you can welcome forgiving thoughts?

Inspire (faith)

What's the secret to more success and happiness?

To understand this, you need to have an experience. This doesn't mean just an intellectual understanding of the experience.

What experience are we talking about? An experience of faith. Whoa! Stop! We're not going to talk about faith in the usual way. Let's try something else. Try substituting the word "faith" for "empowering stance."

Why? Because that's what faith gives you. The empowering stance is your springboard to a positive approach from moment-to-moment. And, we notice that faith is important to various spiritual paths.

Have you given up on something? Have too many disappointments gotten you to back off from life? Have you stopped going for your heartfelt dreams? Do you believe only lucky people get to experience the joy of a dream fulfilled?

I hear you. It appears that many of us have allowed our faith to be squelched by doubt. Where does that doubt come from? Disappointment. Pain. Sadness.

I am with you on this. I carry my own painful experiences. And I carry faith, too. A faith that I have nurtured to be bigger than disappointment, pain and sadness.

How?

It's a choice I make moment to moment.

I choose to act from a base of:

- I can learn from everything I experience.
- Higher Power is supporting me.

These two points help my courage, compassion and empathy to grow.

Use compassion as your compass.

Have you noticed that "compass" and "compassion" are different by only three letters?

Faith can serve you as a compass and as an energy source. When you have faith, you try more things and you take appropriate risks.

Why? Because it is worth it!

I have talked with people from various spiritual paths, and I have discovered that they share a few viewpoints in common:

- Everything is for a purpose.
- Higher Power is looking out for me.
- I am not alone. I am supported.

Imagine that you felt these ideas deep in your heart. When you do, you start from a base of faith. And guess what? You likely feel better and stronger.

How do you get this faith or empowering stance?

You decide. Now. This moment. You make a choice. You say, "I want to experience more happy moments. I choose to live each moment with faith."

Even the atheists I know have faith in something. Often it's science and the betterment of human living through the application of reason.

You operate with faith every time you make a left turn in a busy intersection. Really? Yes. You have faith that your car won't stall at just that moment.

Each day we work with a certain level of faith—our empowering stance.

Now consider taking your faith to a higher level.

What's at stake? Your willingness to put more energy to expanding the horizons of your life. I have a friend who places comfort above everything else. He has a college degree that he doesn't use at all. He works in a field unrelated to his true interests. Why? He doesn't have faith that he can—on any level—use his innate gifts and talents. I feel sad when I think about this.

But this is *not* for you.

Try something different. Get coaching. Study books relevant to your goal. Show the world that you can do something. Begin on a small scale. Step forward in faith.

> *Take the first step in faith. You don't have to see the whole staircase, just take the first step.*
>
> Martin Luther King, Jr.

Take your next step. I'll be cheering for you.

Principle

Choose to approach life with faith (the empowering stance).

Power Question

How can you embrace faith and reassure yourself that you are supported by the people around you and by Higher Power?

Nurture (grace)

Have you ever felt overwhelmed? Have you ever been out of personal energy?

How about discouraged and sad?

Take a breath. We're going to cover some solutions that can help you feel peace and comfort in the moment.

I once felt slammed down by life. I sought help from an older friend. In an almost a flippant way, he said, "In life, you do your duty."

During that time, which was emotional and when I hit bottom, I realized that a moral and ethical life calls for self-discipline. But then I realized something else. It took a lot for me to admit this to myself: I do my duty and it's not making me happy.

So, I ask you, what else is there?

Grace. Ever see someone who is graceful? Figure skater Kristi Yamaguchi jumps to my mind. Certainly, she demonstrates great athleticism. But one detail that stands out is the sheer grace in her hand movements. Her efforts plus her talent create her grace. Her grace is a gift—to her and to us.

Physical grace is easy to see. And, many of us have witnessed someone act with grace. It can be as simple as the time I saw a salesperson bring calm to a situation with an angry customer. She said, "Yes. You're right this is a frustrating situation. And I'm listening carefully to you. I will help you with this."

How can you experience grace?

Three words: *Shift to gratitude.*

Many people express that their experience of grace is like a gift from Higher Power. We'll talk about that soon.

Meanwhile, let me share a practical, everyday example of *shifting to gratitude.* Several years ago I visited Disneyland with a friend. I felt terrific to be in a place that celebrates courtesy and creativity. Unfortunately, my friend felt terrible because she didn't have the money to purchase all the souvenirs she wanted.

Although I had less money in my pocket than she did, my thoughts were immersed in joy and gratitude. Just to be at Disneyland was a gift.

What can you do when there is no immediate physical solution?

Make a shift in your perception. Shift to gratitude.

Three Steps towards Grace: Awareness, Openness, & Experience

When is grace needed? When someone close to you says something that feels like a denial of your right to have or experience your own feelings.

Some time ago, a relative said to me: "You have no reason to be upset." This was simply not true in light of the particular situation and the injuries I had endured in the past from that person.

But here's the big shift: I seek to learn from every moment. So I did a "turnaround" with the words: "You have no reason to be upset."

Turnaround: "I have every reason to nurture myself and be around nurturing influences."

Clearly, this relative was someone to step away from for a period of time.

Let's apply the Three Steps of Grace.

Awareness: What are the positive elements of my life? What gifts do I have?

Openness: Will I let the positive elements in my life inspire positive feelings?

Experience: Will I give myself 10 seconds to experience this positivity?

As we covered earlier, recent brain research notes that it takes 10 seconds of focus for a positive experience to impact our long-term memory. This is one of the reasons that writing in a journal every night (and logging good things that happened that day) helps you physically change your brain cells. This is related to what science calls brain plasticity. *If you write in your journal each night, you will literally experience your life as good—and full of grace.*

You've been given grace, but may not feel it in the moment

My Disneyland example is just a small demonstration of the idea of shifting to gratitude. You need to become *aware* of the gifts in your life in this present moment. Then you can shift to be *open* to something positive, and you *experience* the gift of that positive part of your life.

How You Can Experience "Grace Under Pressure"

Imagine you can turn around distress and actually enter an empowered state of being. This happens when you prepare and rehearse. The idea is to rehearse positive patterns so that they become your new and improved default setting when something goes wrong.

When people are under stress they fall back to the patterns and behaviors in their established default settings. Many of us take a distressing thought and, metaphorically, hold it so close to our eyes that we cannot see anything else. At that moment we cannot feel the grace that is actually present in our lives.

Imagine if someone offers you $20,000 to recite 10 good things in your life at this present moment. You could do it. You'd find the gifts in your life—the grace.

My quick list would include:

- I love my sweetheart and she loves me.
- I'm grateful to be sharing helpful methods with you through this book, which I'm hopeful will bring you and your loved ones more peace, comfort and fulfillment.
- I'm grateful for my excellent health.
- I'm grateful for my family, friends, students, readers, clients, audiences and so much more.

To experience *grace under pressure,* you need to train yourself to shift the direction of your thinking. For example, I sometimes get *tired* grading the work of my graduate students. When fatigue overcomes me, I tap my fist on my thigh as I tell myself,

"I can do this!" I have trained myself to respond to this self-designed trigger. My energy revs up and I complete the work.

Here is a trigger you can use to shift the direction of your thoughts: Say, "I am grateful for …" Then express the gifts and the blessings that are in your life.

Other Sources for Feeling Grace in the Moment

As an instructor of college-level Comparative Religion, I note that many spiritual paths emphasize grace as "unmerited favor" from Higher Power. Many people believe that Higher Power gives us inner peace, inner strength and even guidance. They believe that we cannot earn something so grand as Higher Power's favor.

Those who seek to have a fulfilling connection and relationship with Higher Power often engage in practices such as meditation, prayer, spiritual retreats and more. These activities can provide a sense that there is a reason for what they endure, and that benevolent Higher Power is providing opportunities for *growing in courage, compassion and their ability to express love.*

Here is a trigger you can use to shift the direction of your thoughts. My clients say phrases like:

- Thank you Higher Power for the blessings I have.
- Thank you God for my job and for the steady work.
- Thank you Universe for all the good in my life.

Pick what works for you. The point is to acknowledge and then feel the grace given to you from Higher Power.

I invite you to explore a number of practices such as meditation, prayer and spiritual retreats so that you learn to experience grace in the present moment. Grace is a gift you already have. You'll need to look beyond the concerns that the ego obsesses over in order to find the grace within you. The ego, or the false self, is that part of you that feels small and vulnerable.

On the other hand, your true self is that part of you that is naturally courageous and brilliant and feels connected with all that is good. Your true self feels the grace that you have already been given.

> *You are so weak. Give up to grace. The ocean takes care of each wave till it gets to shore.*
>
> RUMI

What do you give up? The obsessions of the ego. Turn your focus to the gifts in your life. On a visible and practical level, find good feelings by *appreciating what you already have*. Also, find the good feeling by *enjoying the journey* as you take action toward your goals.

How grace can help open floodgates of financial abundance

Use grace as part of your business dealings, including for persuasion, sales, deal making and negotiations. How? Use the methods in this book to condition yourself to be at your best during the crucial 10 seconds that will make a difference. The truth is, gaining wealth is often based on your ability to enhance a relationship, which can happen in 10 seconds. In 10 seconds you can win the sale or lose the deal. In 10 seconds you can create agreement or you can create disharmony.

For grace in the moment, you need to start with two things

- Pure intention
- Natural confidence

When I train graduate students in the art and science of persuasion, I emphasize:

Pure intention keeps in mind the benefit to the listener.

That is, your good intention is to do something helpful for the person with whom you're talking.

The opposite is manipulation: pulling strings without concern for the other person's well being.

Now we turn to the second part of grace in the moment: natural confidence.

Natural confidence is expressing your natural brilliance.

The opposite is being phony and being a mediocre copy of someone else.

Pure intention and natural confidence come together to make you *graceful* during those crucial 10 seconds. And when you're graceful, you turn an average 10 seconds into *10 Seconds to Wealth*.

To access your natural confidence, remember to:

- Keep in mind the benefit to the listener.
- Discover what you do well. (Perhaps, you're a good listener.)
- Express your natural brilliance.

As we discussed, many people feel that grace is a gift from Higher Power. Accept the gift while expressing your gratitude. My clients often say, "I'm grateful for steady work."

Want to feel grace in the moment? Say aloud: "I am grateful for …"

Want to take the experience of grace to another level? Say aloud: "Thank you [Higher Power] for . . ."

Principle

Express your natural brilliance, accept the gift of grace, and experience natural confidence.

Power Question

How can you nurture and express what you are good at?

Express (Art)

Ever watch a movie that moved you to tears? That movie is a form of art.

A while back I was in a car accident. My friend Michael stayed with me for hours at the emergency room. He remained with me while I was stretched out in a neck brace and got scanned and x-rayed. And he was there when I confronted the tough question: "How bad is this and what's next?"

Michael was expressing another form of art: the art of friendship and support.

What does art do? It creates. And often it creates feelings.

Unfortunately, many of us forget that every human being is truly an artist—that is, a creator. The mere fact that you are reading these words means you have adapted to all that life has thrown your way so far. Good for you! And it's likely you have needed to be creative on a number of occasions.

Author Seth Godin wrote, "Art is made by a human being. Art is created to have an impact, to change someone else. Art is a gift. You can sell the souvenir, the canvas, the recording . . . but the idea itself is free, and the generosity is a critical part of making art. By my definition, most art has nothing to do with oil paint or marble. Art is what we're doing when we do our best work."

In the book *The Gift: Creativity and the Artist in the Modern World*, author Lewis Hyde writes that, although we may buy a ticket to a theatrical performance, the play is actually a gift that we receive from the artists involved in the production. One of my editors said: "That is so true. I went to a concert of chamber music for the first time. It was such a gift. One piece consumed me and I felt such emotion that I began to cry. It was the first time in my life I ever cried while experiencing the art of music. The piece was by Franz Shubert. I later purchased the CD."

My point here is that you can experience a source of happiness when you *own* your art, that is, when you express yourself. I'm told that there is even an art to making coffee. (That's not my drink. But I know about making a cookies and cream milkshake!)

There's an art to writing a letter to a friend or romantic partner. For example, one of my best moments in life was when I got the idea to write a letter to my sweetheart. It was brief. I wrote: "Thank you for S-t-r-e-t-c-h-i-n-g." (I made the word span 21 inches, two sheets of paper). I was acknowledging how she demonstrates flexibility in regards to my full schedule. She loved the letter and it continues to hang on our bathroom mirror. You see: Art gets appreciated.

I invite you now to look around. Where is life calling you to express yourself? What can you do in an artful (creative, perhaps life-enhancing) way?

Art gives twice: to the receiver and to the person expressing herself.

You have Divine Gifts just by being a person. You were designed (part of your standard equipment) to be creative and to be able to create art. Do not get caught up in the traditional meaning of art or what it means to be an artist. Art is not just a movie, painting or craftwork. I have friends who created a wonderful family life with a loving, supportive home atmosphere. That's important. And that's art, too.

It takes some effort. But when you devote that extra effort, you find that you're really living!

Start today. Start this hour. Find a way to express yourself. Be an artist!

This world needs each of us to give the gift of our natural brilliance. Thank you for contributing.

Now is the time. Only you can express the art that you are on this planet to express.

Principle

Each person can express art because each person has the standard equipment that makes up of his or her Divine Gifts: love, humility, forgiveness, grace and art.

Power Question

How can you express yourself in a giving, artful way?

Conclusion to Divine Gifts Chapter

We have explored the six Divine Gifts in each of us:

1. Decide (love)
2. Intuit (humility)
3. Voice (forgiveness)
4. Inspire (faith)
5. Nurture (grace)
6. Express (art)

The Divine Gifts are your standard equipment. As you learn to express them, you are also conditioning yourself to be at your best during the *10 Seconds to Wealth*. You'll notice that your Divine Gifts help you stay in a positive state of being.

When you express your Divine Gifts you are naturally confident, courageous, charismatic and attractive. You draw in positive people who bring opportunities. Those who express their natural confidence and goodwill are the people who receive many offers and opportunities.

I see this frequently with my clients. When they enter the empowered state of being, and when they express their Divine Gifts, they light up any room they are in. People are attracted to those who shine their natural light. They are the ones who are alive and ready for the next challenge.

> *I don't believe people are looking for the meaning of life as much as they are looking for the experience of being alive.*
>
> JOSEPH CAMPBELL

People who express their Divine Gifts feel fully alive. The energy flows from them in positive waves. People nearby want to have some of that radiance to rub off on them.

Here's a practical example:

I once gave a free presentation to help job-seekers do well in job interviews. One attendee came up and said, "You should speak for ACME Company."

During the speech I expressed my Divine Gifts, and it felt good. I responded to his kind suggestion with *four sentences that brought in $329,067.*

Are you ready for the sentences?

I replied: "Thank you. Who should I talk with? Do you have her number? How about we leave a message for her now."

At that moment the attendee called the person I needed to talk to and left an enthusiastic message on my behalf. Soon I had a meeting with the person. My total income for the presentations I made for the company brought in $329,067.

Do you see how expressing our Divine Gifts brings in new opportunities?

Quickly Access Your Divine Gifts

What do you want? For some of us, that may take a few moments to express. Here's an approach you can try. Answer these questions:

- What's going on in my life that I do *not* want?
- What is it that I would like to change?

To quickly access your Divine Gifts, it helps to ask empowering questions.

- What gifts are in my life right now? (grace)
- How can I connect with "I am love"? (love)
- What am I learning now? (humility)
- How can I express my creativity and kindness? (art)
- How am I being supported now? (faith)
- How can I see the big picture and look on it with compassion? (forgiveness)
- How can I get coaching? (humility)
- How is Higher Power helping me? (grace)

To be at your best in those all-important 10 seconds, which will help you do well in business, consider these questions:

- How can I turn this problem into a chance to enhance my relationship with the customer? (humility)
- How can I express appreciation for my co-worker? (art)
- How can I make this person feel important? (love)
- How can we, as a team, make this situation better? (faith)
- How can I let go of my frustration and support my team members to get back on track? (forgiveness)

- How can I flow with this situation and make the best of it? (grace)

Here's another way to quickly access your Divine Gifts: Focus on *Just One More Thought.*

For many of us, our default setting is to make a judgment for whatever arises. But to be at your best in the *10 Seconds to Wealth*, let that judgment-thought flow by as if it's a leaf on a river. Welcome the next thought. If you're stuck in judgment, ask this question: "How can I look at this with compassion?"

Access Divine Gifts with a Simple Shift in Thought

Imagine that you keep a log of the thoughts you have throughout your day. How many of them would be some variation of "I *have* to do this"? It's likely that you complain a lot to yourself.

Instead, to access your Divine Gifts, simply shift your thought to "I *get* to do this."

For example, a main component of my graduate school teaching responsibilities is to grade student papers. Most teachers complain about this chore. Instead of saying to myself, "I *have* to grade papers," I tell myself: "I *get to* grade papers." How? *I get the chance to encourage each student.* That simple change in language helps me to get excited about the chore. It makes me feel truly connected to my purpose.

My mission: *I help people experience enthusiasm, love and wisdom to fulfill big dreams.*

So, I *get to* encourage my students.

I invite you to transform "I have to" into "I get to." Then ask yourself "How?"

This is your step to accessing your Divine Gifts. Look for the opportunity.

The Secret to Quickly Access Your Divine Gifts

The coaching staff on a successful football team memorizes the plays. There is no time to look down at a stack of paper when the game is being played.

Using this strategy, I invite you to memorize the methods and words that touch your heart as you read this book. This will help you become ready for the *10 Seconds to Wealth*. For example, you could memorize:

- Replace "I have to" with "I get to."
- Remember your Divine Gifts: love, humility, forgiveness, grace, faith and art.
- Think: How can I look at this with compassion?

Pick any method in this book that captures your attention. Remember: *People under stress tend to fall back to negative default settings.*

But this is *not* for you. Your life is *more* important than a football game.

Memorize methods and rehearse using them. Condition yourself to be better today than yesterday. Over and over, my clients say: "Tom, I memorized that method and I had it in mind when I was in the stressful situation. It made all the difference."

Memorize the methods and tools in this book and you can easily access your Divine Gifts.

Expressing your Divine Gifts helps you create a wealth of financial abundance, better friendships, more love and even inner peace.

The rest of this book covers specific topics that help you to condition yourself to express your Divine Gifts.

Let's move forward …

Part II

2

Wake Up Your Spirit to Prosperity

In this section you will learn Seven Powerful Steps to create the life you really want, including an abundance of time and money, spiritual fulfillment and loving relationships.

Ever feel like you're in a financial rut? This section will shine the light on your natural brilliance. Your natural brilliance is like diamonds just waiting to sparkle when you shine a light on them. Your natural brilliance will light your way out of your financial rut.

The difficulties related to climbing out of a financial rut came up recently. My client Stephanie said, "I'm afraid that the higher I go, the further I have to fall."

"We'll find a way to bring your safety net up with you," I replied. I helped her explore alternatives and uncover her hidden talents. As a success coach, I help clients and audiences stretch and nurture their spirits during the process. I can do the same for you.

What makes this book different from others is that I combine both the spiritual and practical approaches to wealth. As a faculty instructor of Comparative Religion, I guide my college students to experience the beauty and power of spiritual paths. I then provide business strategies from my roles as America's Communication Coach and "The Personal Branding Instructor" (as reported by *The San Francisco Examiner*). I guide my clients to take action to gain more money, do well in business, and expand feelings of fulfillment. You will learn secrets I have used and the strategies of 18 people—millionaires and billionaires.

This book incorporates spiritual and practical methods to increase wealth. As you learn these methods, you condition yourself to be at your best in the *10 Seconds to Wealth*.

In a Chapter Two I will share with you the powerful process of Personaltainment™ Branding, a new level of branding I created. Through this strategy my clients increase their customer base more quickly and also enjoy the process.

You can feel inner peace while you experience the ups and downs necessary to increase your personal wealth and fulfillment.

In Chapter Three you will learn practical methods of the Momentum Action Plan™ (MAP), also known as the 9-Minute Miracle Breakthrough. Use this process once a week or at the beginning of your day to target and do the best actions to improve your life. Learn to add zest to your moment-to-moment experiences. You will also learn to use leverage, which is to gain the maximum benefits from the least efforts.

In Chapter Four you will learn how to deepen and warm up your relationships because, as researchers have shown, quality relationships are the basis for great business success and personal fulfillment. You will also learn the 30 Secrets of Humor to bring warmth and laughter to your relationships. Mark Burnett (creator of the TV shows *Survivor* and *The Apprentice* with Donald Trump) wrote, "Negotiation secret: If all else fails, make them laugh."

Enhancing relationships is a spiritual process. *Prosperity is about having more than money. It also includes financial freedom.*

Over the years my perspective has expanded as I enjoyed a number of adventures that required money, contacts and strategies. I am grateful for my experiences connected to prosperity including:

- Directing and producing feature films
- Traveling to various parts of the world
- Speaking at the National Association of Broadcasters Conference (the world's largest media conference) for six years in a row
- Teaching as a guest instructor at Stanford University
- Publishing my business books, music and novels
- Taking fun vacations with my romantic partner, her parents and my parents

From ordinary beginnings, I became the first college graduate in my family. I live with a lot of hope. In fact, a colleague asked me about my experiences of God; and I replied, "Times of delighted surprise."

Your path to enjoy more abundance begins now with this book. For more information concerning the topics in this book, you can reach me through TomSuperCoach.com and my blog BeHeardandBeTrusted.com

The central idea of Wake Up Your Spirit to Prosperity *is to get out of your own way.*

To manifest what you truly want, you need to change your focus and wake up your spirit. Prosperity consciousness essentially means being awake.

Many of us experience great suffering concerning issues of money, prosperity and scarcity. Some don't realize that their financial details are part of their spiritual path. Spirituality includes the process of giving and receiving value. And prosperity is more than just money.

According to Dictionary.com, prosperity means "having success, flourishing, and having good fortune." It also states that prosperity is "an economic state of growth with rising profits and full employment." What we get from this definition is that prosperity is not just about money. Wake Up Your Spirit to Prosperity talks about spiritual growth and full employment of your natural brilliance, that is, your gifts from Higher Power.

For our discussion, we will use the process: S.P. I.R.I.T.

       S – Seek the Higher View

       P – Program for abundance

       I – Intuit to do it

       R – Retreat from Reverse-Examples

    I – Inspire hope and faith

    T – Target the good of all

In the following sections we will dive into the methods outlined with S.P.I.R.I.T.

You can turn your life into a positive adventure that includes abundance. This book shows you how.

Let's continue …

Seek the Higher View

By emphasizing a Higher View, I invite you to make a transition to seeing things from the viewpoint of your Higher Self. You can focus on your Higher Self or remain stuck in the Ego. The Ego is made of fear. When you are stuck in your Ego you feel small, vulnerable and fragile. A number of people, when stuck in their Ego, feel irritable and angry. Anger is fear twisted.

On the other hand, you can focus on your Higher Self, or what I usually refer to as your True Self.

Your True Self is that part of you that is strong, focused and filled with natural brilliance and courage.

To get unstuck from your Ego and seek the Higher View is to make a transition to your Higher Self as fast as possible. When you're seeing things from your Higher Self, you experience a form of peace, even when things around you are chaotic.

In Taoism the idea is to flow with the universe. The Tao (translated as "The Way") is often compared to a stream of flowing water. Imagine how much more effective you would be if you were like a canoe flowing with the stream instead of like a rock, complaining about the water striking you in the face.

That is, avoid complaining about your stagnation and lack of opportunity. Flow with opportunities that appear.

How can you flow with the universe? How can you wake up your spirit? Focus on this Question How can I serve?

Your focus point is better when it goes beyond your personal needs. You need to see how to make a contribution. Martin Luther King, Jr. said, "Everyone can be great because anyone can serve." Where do you serve? Right where you are.

One of my clients said in desperation, "Serve? I can't serve. I'm barely keeping my head above water now." I shared with her that to wake up her spirit to prosperity is to expand her perceptions. Focusing only on one's urgent, immediate needs is like wearing blinders to the possibilities of service and, as a dividend, expanding earnings. The Ego is stuck in fear and is a small focus area.

To help you look beyond the Ego and its small focus area, let's view the differences between the Higher Self and the Ego.

Two Aspects of Your Self	
Higher Self	*Ego*
Abundance	Scarcity
Expansive	Contracting, pain-avoiding, reactive
Creative	Cowering
How many I serve?	What's in it for me?
Serve where you are	Wait for a purpose to come along
Faith	Doubt
Love-mode	Fear-mode

The idea of the love-mode is to focus on being helpful, which is a Higher Self approach. Also, many of us turn to Higher Power (some say "Spirit" or "God") who can guide us.

How do we, stuck in the real world and dealing with our daily lives, stay in the Higher Self? We memorize phrases that shift the directions of our thoughts.

Memorize phrases to shift your thoughts in a positive direction. Here are examples:

- Be still and know that I am God. (The Bible)
- Minds debate. Hearts relate. (Ann Wilson Schaef)
- We must not allow any force to make us feel like we don't count. Maintain a sense of dignity and respect. (Martin Luther King, Jr.)

- You must be the change you wish to see in the world. (Gandhi)

- Do not lay on any soul a load which you would not wish to be laid upon yours. (Baha'i)

- If you want others to be happy, practice compassion. If you want to be happy, practice compassion. (The Dalai Lama)

- You cannot solve a problem on the same level in which it was created. (Albert Einstein)

- Let no come to you without leaving better.(Mother Teresa)

- Our fears must never hold us back from pursuing our hopes. (John F. Kennedy)

Another way to shift your thoughts and feelings is through music. I can change my thoughts by humming the tune and words of an empowering song. And, I recall the exuberant music of *Indiana Jones* or *Superman, the Movie.*

Shifting your thoughts and feelings is important related to fear. We do not want get stuck in fear because that might prevent us from taking appropriate action. Now Mike Robbins guides us in ways to work with fear that may arise.

How to Move Through Fear

Mike Robbins

Fear is something that we all experience, especially on our journey toward deeper authenticity, fulfillment, and success in life. Being who we really are, expressing ourselves boldly, and going for what we want in life can cause a great deal of fear in us.

I get scared all the time - especially when I'm taking risks, doing new things, and putting myself out there. When I was younger I thought there was something really wrong with me because I would get so nervous - in sports, in school, in social settings, and more. I now understand that everyone else experiences their own version of the same basic fears I have (being judged, making mistakes, looking bad, failing, disappointing others, and more). It's just part of being human.

Many of us run away or hide from our fears because they seem scary, uncomfortable, or embarrassing. We also erroneously think we "shouldn't" have them or we're somehow "wrong" for feeling scared. However, most things that mean a lot to us in life don't show up without any fear at all. And as we strive to live with authenticity, it's inevitable that we'll get scared along the way.

The question isn't whether or not we experience fear in our lives (because we all do and always will for as long as we live); the more important question for each of us to ask and answer is, how can I move through my fears in an honest way so they don't stop me from being who I really am and going for what I truly want in life?

HOW TO MOVE THROUGH YOUR FEAR IN A POSITIVE WAY

1) Admit it—Acknowledge your fear, tell the truth about it, and be real. When we feel scared and are willing to admit it with a sense of empathy and compassion for ourselves, it can often take the edge off and give us a little breathing room to begin with.

2) Own it—Take responsibility for your fear and own it as yours, not anyone else's. We often have a tendency to blame others for doing or saying things that "scare" us. However, when we remember that no one else can "make" us scared - only we have that power - we take back the responsibility and the power of the fear and remember that it exists within us, so we are the only ones who can change it.

3) Feel it—Allow yourself to feel your fear, not just think about it or talk about it (something I often catch myself doing). Feel it in your body and allow yourself to go into the emotion of it, even if it is scary or uncomfortable. Like any emotion, when we feel our fear deeply and passionately, it has a way of dissipating.

4) Express it—Let it out. Speak, write, emote, move your body, yell, or do whatever you feel is necessary for you to do to express your fear. Similar to feeling any emotion with intensity, when we express emotions with intensity and passion, they move right through us. When we repress our emotions, they get stuck and can become debilitating and dangerous.

5) Let it go—This one is often easier said than done - for me and many people I work with. Letting go of our fear becomes much easier when we honestly admit, own, feel, and express it. Letting go of our fear is a conscious and deliberate choice, not a reactionary form of denial. Once you've allowed yourself the time to work through your fear, you can declare "I'm choosing to let go of my fear and use its energy in a positive way."

6) Visualize the positive outcomes you desire—Think about, speak out loud, write down, or even close your eyes and visualize how you want things to be and, more important, how you want to feel. If your fear is focused on something specific like your work, a relationship, money, etc. - visualize it being how you want it to be and allow yourself to feel how to ultimately want to feel.

7) Take action—Be willing to take bold and courageous actions, even if you're still feeling nervous. Your legs may shake, your voice might quiver, but that doesn"t have to stop you from saying what's on your mind, taking a risk, making a request, trying something new, or being bold in a small or big way. Doing this is what builds confidence and allow us to move through our fear.

Fear can and does stop us in life—from being ourselves, speaking our truth, and going for what we really want. But, when we remember with compassion that there's nothing wrong with us for getting scared and when we're willing to lean into our fears with vulnerability and boldness—we can literally transform them into something that catapults our growth and fulfillment in life.

> Mike Robbins, CSP, is a best-selling author of *Focus on the Good Stuff* and *Be Yourself, Everyone Else Is Already Taken*, sought-after motivational keynote speaker, and personal growth expert who works with Fortune 500 companies, non-profits, schools, and groups and people of all kinds. He and his work have been feature on ABC news, the Oprah radio Network,

in *Forbes*, and many others. His books have been translated into eight different languages. To learn more about his work check out: www.Mike-Robbins.com

---

Mike reminded us that we can take positive steps related to any fear that may arise. If you feel a touch of fear, realize that this is just a beginning. Now it's time to step forward.

Intensify the Power of Words

Some paragraphs ago, I shared a secret with you—the power of music. Our target is to use the power of your subconscious mind. In an article in *U.S. News and World Report*, writer Marianne Szegedy-Maszak reported: "Cognitive neuroscientists [identify that] most of our decisions, actions, emotions, and behavior depends on the 95 percent of brain activity that goes beyond our conscious awareness." Realizing this fact, I have my clients associate music, body posture, and an image to words they want to memorize.

For example, Phil played the theme music of *Superman, the Movie* while repeating the words from one of my books: "Courage is easier when I'm prepared." He stood up straight and strong as he held in mind an image of himself wearing a hero's cape. This combination of music, body posture, image and words helps Phil make decisions and take action when he is an empowered state of being.

I summarize this process with these words: *You must magnetize what you memorize*. Some magnets are empowered by a strong electrical current. Similarly, power-up your ability to shift to a Higher View by using a combination of words, music, body posture, and an image.

Principle

Shift to a Higher View. Shift the direction of your thoughts by using a combination of memorized phrases, music, body posture, and an image.

Multi-millionaire Anthony Robbins said, "Successful people ask better questions, and as a result, they get better answers." Along these lines, I am including a Leverage Question for each of these sections. Leverage is like using a stick and a small rock as the fulcrum to move a boulder. Through leverage you can support the flow of grand abundance in your life.

Here is our first Leverage Question.

Leverage Question

What ideas do you want to memorize (and repeat to yourself) so you can quickly shift the direction of your thinking? What music, image and body posture can you add to engage your real power?

Program for Abundance

Another definition of prosperity is "a state of being very lively and profitable." It's your choice: You can live in love-mode or fear-mode. To achieve the best results, program your mind for abundance, which comes from the love-mode.

We seek to override the scarcity programming that may have been *placed there by parents or relatives.*

What does scarcity sound like? "We can't afford it." Abundance includes empowering phrases.

Mindsets	
Scarcity	**Abundance**
We can't afford it!	How can we gain more money?
	How can we serve more people?

Train your mind to see the abundance in life. Here's an example—A friend invites you to an event that is too costly. The idea is to reply with something that empowers you. You can say: "My family's budget is going in a different direction at the moment." Remember that your subconscious mind is listening at all times. Train it with thoughts of abundance, rather than thoughts of scarcity.

Budgets are a useful part of life. Budgets help people plan for vacations; and feature films get made via budgets. Learn to let go of your fear of that word. Do some research and find out the numbers before making a decision. For example, one of my clients, an aspiring author, discovered that she can self-publish copies of her book for only $150 through the print-on-demand process. She moved toward abundance and accomplished her goal of publishing, without getting bogged down in fear. The idea is to take a step forward.

For example, the best-selling book *The Celestine Prophesy* was first self-published. Then a major publisher took notice, and subsequently, millions of copies were sold.

Find out the numbers, and you're one step closer to your dream.

It helps to drop "I can't afford it" from your speech pattern. "I can't afford it" puts you in a world of pain. Instead, put yourself into the world of possibility—a world of abundance.

One interviewer asked me: "The reality could be that someone really cannot afford it. What if the person really wants both things, and can only get one thing?" I responded by talking about a time, many years ago, when a friend and I were in a bookstore. I selected eight books but felt the need to put back seven. At the time my funds were needed for things like rent, food, and bus fare. But I wasn't disturbed because I knew that eventually I would have the money to get any book I wanted. However, my friend was upset. She didn't have the mindset that more prosperity was on the way.

One millionaire told me about a mindset that helped him. He had the phrase: "I'm a millionaire. The funds may not yet be in my bank account—but I'm a millionaire."

You need to program your thoughts and actions so that you support *the flow of abundance in your life.*

Now Dr. Arthur Ciaramicoli shares methods for turning our thoughts and feelings in a positive direction.

How to be Positive in a Negative World

Dr. Arthur P. Ciaramicoli

When I was a young boy my father gave me Norman Vincent Peale's book *The Power of Positive Thinking* and told me that after I finished the book I could move a tree if I believed I could. I read parts of the book and was admittingly a bit puzzled. I understood the point about being positive but didn't quite understand how I could actually make myself think positive and move mountains. The instruction book seemed to be missing although I liked the concept.

In today's culture we are bombarded with self help books, motivational speakers and CD's providing instructions of how to be and remain positive. I don't think anyone denies the value of being positive but most of us who follow the simple instructions aren't quite able to maintain this positive state as easily as we are instructed. What is the missing ingredient?

Awareness of Your Story

Negativity is almost always based on inaccurate interpretation of reality. One of my group therapy clients joined our sessions due to being overly stressed and struggling with self consciousness about his self image. Two aspects of his life embarrassed him greatly, the blue collar town he grew up in and the so-called mediocre college he attended. Over time he let us know of his embarrassment. After several months of sessions he has learned that his perception of his inferiority was a distorted view he needlessly carried with him for several years. As he unraveled his negative story so did others.

One woman talked of not being pretty enough, we determined this perception was not true. Another woman thought she didn't speak well, not true. A few of the men talked of thinking their balding hairlines make them unattractive, not true. One man talked of his superior intelligence, also not true. Whether distortions about oneself are positive or negative the truth must be discerned in order to remain positive in life. You can't be positive with consistency if you're not dealing with reality. The foundation of your sense of self has to be solid and stable. Distortions create road maps that take us to the wrong destination with the wrong people.

Over the years of doing group sessions I have heard these types of stories over and over again. The emotional distress of negative thinking is profound and if you don't become aware of where your biases originated you are doomed to continue living in the prison of pessimism.

The Truth Expands our Vision

Knowing the truth about who you are is a process that can't occur quickly or without significant effort. Just trying to think positively won't work for long if your old story is embedded in your psyche. It takes time, patience and persistence to change negative views to more realistic perspectives.

First we must become aware of our biases; of course we need other objective rational people to help us come to accurate conclusions about ourselves. Then the hard work begins. We have to change the view we established early in life for the new view we have come to learn as adults. We were quite impressionable as young people; taking in the views of others later in life is not easy even if the feedback we are receiving is complimentary. It takes time and trust to come to believe that the negative views we held about ourselves may have originated through our relationships with biased caretakers, coaches, teachers and other significant authority figures as well as peers.

Eventually, with courage and determination, the new view replaces the old negativity and we are finally in a position to live our lives with a positive, realistic view of ourselves. The truth has freed us from the past once we integrate new information in our heart and mind. I emphasize heart as many of us know that our negativity is not rational but it persists as it is recorded deep in the emotional parts of the brain. Change means we have to re-arrange ourselves emotionally as well as intellectually, which is why it never occurs quickly or easily. We can understand without changing. Change has to be an active process involving behavior, intellect and emotion.

Once we have done this work the negativity in our environment and in the world has far less impact on our outlook. When we are at peace within we can tolerate the chaos around us without being effected in major ways. We have reached a state of calm allowing us to tolerate the stress outside of us without becoming overly stressed ourselves. We have then become models for balanced living.

> Arthur P. Ciaramicoli, Ed.D., Ph.D., is a licensed clinical psychologist and member of the American Psychological Association. Dr. Ciaramicoli has been on the faculty of Harvard Medical School for several years, lecturer for the American Cancer Society, Chief Psychologist at Metrowest Medical Center, and director of the Metrowest Counseling Center. Dr. Ciaramicoli has lectured at Harvard Health Services, Boston College Counseling Center, the Space Telescope Science Institute as well as being a consultant to several major corporations. Dr. Ciaramicoli is a seasoned media expert, appearing on CNN, CNNfn, Fox News Boston, Comcast TV, New England Cable News, Good Morning America Weekend, The O'Reilly Report, and other shows. Dr. Ciaramicoli is the author of *The Curse of the Capable: The Hidden Challenges to a Balanced, Healthy, High Achieving Life* and

Performance Addiction: The Dangerous New Syndrome and How to Stop It from Ruining Your Life.

His newsletter, blog comments and contact information are available at his web site, BalanceYourSuccess.com

---

Dr. Arthur has invited us to devote the time and effort to discover who we truly are. He wrote: "Change has to be an active process involving behavior, intellect and emotion." And, I encourage you to engage with the insights and methods throughout this book, particularly the questions at the end of each section. Becoming stronger is a process that requires you to take action.

When you are serious about opening the gate to a better flow of financial abundance, consider: *A great idea is to make your work a prayer.*

Mother Teresa said, "Prayer does not demand that we interrupt our work, but that we continue working as if it were a prayer."

To increase abundance, *move beyond patterns that limit your progress*, like trading your time for money.

When you want to make a leap beyond your current level of abundance, you need to get out of the limiting pattern of trading your time for money.

My next example comes from someone I have learned from directly, C.J. Hayden. Her book *Get Clients Now* details a methodology for effectively gaining clients in a way that fosters ease in her reader's life. To guarantee continued sales of her book, C.J. created the Licensee Kit, a program by which personal coaches use her book and methodology for their clients. To use C.J.'s successful program, coaches must ask their clients to buy copies of *Get Clients Now*. At the time of this writing the Complete Package, Training, and Renewable License is priced at $595.

From C.J.'s example, we learn to move beyond trading time for money. As a personal coach C.J. can only make an hourly fee. But the magic happened when she made the shift to being the creator of a franchise!*

The Power-3 Income Streams

We can learn from C.J. Hayden about the process of creating multiple streams of income. But the crucial detail is to avoid scattering your energy. I learned this when a millionaire told me: "I see a lot of activity, but I don't know how productive it is."

I brought this insight into my coaching work. Over the years, I have seen clients who *dabbled in many money-making activities* before they met me. In response, I invited my clients to improve efficiency and reduce the number of scattered activities they were involved in. I introduced them to The Power-3 Income Streams:

- *Income Stream 1:* **Stability (your base).** One of my clients is a teacher, which forms her base. She can take appropriate time to analyze her stream of income opportunities. She is neither desperate nor harried.

••••••••••••••••••••••••••••

*More information about creating a franchise is in my book *Nothing Can Stop You This Year!: How to Unleash Your Hidden Power to Persuade Well, Get More Done, Gain Sudden Profits, Command Intuition and Feel Great.* TomSuperCoach.com.

- *Income Stream 2: **Automatic.*** A number of my clients make money through the Internet—while they are sleeping.
- *Income Stream 3: **No ceiling.*** A number of my clients are creating books, audio programs, and inventions. They know that when something becomes a hit, there is no ceiling on the amount of money they can make.

When creating a product, it is helpful to hear about the trials successful people endured. It often takes more than one product to become successful. For example, Richard Carlson, author of the *Don't Sweat the Small Stuff* series, told me that *Don't Sweat the Small Stuff* was his tenth book.

Another example: The ThighMaster® (promoted by Susanne Somers), which earned $100 million, was the second item on an eight-item plan of inventions. Peter Bieler, the leader of the ThighMaster team, knew that out of eight products some would fail and some would work. The team was fortunate: After the first item failed (and they learned from the process), the second item was a hit. Peter Bieler knew there was no ceiling to their future abundance.

Using the Power-3 Income Streams (Stability, Automatic and No Ceiling) helps you to avoid scattering your energy-and working on too many income streams at once.

Program for Abundance by Asking for Help

Another way to program for abundance is to ask for Higher Power's help. Best-selling authors Jack Canfield and Mark Victor

Hansen (co-creators of the *Chicken Soup for the Soul* series) emphasize the power of asking. In their book *The Aladdin Factor* they describe hundreds of effective ways of asking for what you want.

Open the door to healing with the God Box

When you turn over your worries and cares to Higher Power, you open the door to healing. Write down what really troubles you and place it in a beautiful, small box—your God Box. Do not read the slip of paper ever again. As you place your paper in the box, recite a prayer like: "God, I turn this over to you. This is too big for me. I ask for Your help and healing so I feel better about this. I seek to do my part better. May this situation turn out for the good of all involved. Thank you. Amen."

Principle

Focus on abundance in every situation. Find ways to move beyond trading your time for money.

Leverage Question

How can I serve more effectively and keep abundance flowing?

[It helps to get a personal journal and answer the question posed at the end of each section. Take 20 seconds and write down your immediate thoughts. You'll gain more benefit from this process.]

Intuit to do it

When I talk about intuit to do it, I'm referring to a strategy that taps into your deepest powers. Intuit to do it means using your intuition to help gain energy, direction and the power to keep going until you complete something crucial to obtain abundance in your life.

"What if I'm intuition impaired?" asked a woman in one of my audiences.

"Perhaps, you're referring to the practice of not making space for your intuition," I responded. We all get feelings about things. We just need to acknowledge them and honor them. Dictionary.com defines intuition as "Immediate cognition ... The act or faculty of knowing or sensing without the use of rational processes ... An impression."

Sometimes we get a flash of insight or a gut feeling about something. For example, a woman seeking more customers for her barbershop realized she needed to reposition her business. She listened to her intuition which told her the best way to attract more male clients (her target customer) was to create a sports theme in her shop. She set up her barbershop like a sports bar with sporting events on the television set and sports-related magazines. Her business flourished, that is, prospered.

Researchers note that self-made millionaires follow through on their hunches. Also, a number of millionaires have said, "You only have to be right 51% of the time."

The important thing is to make space for your intuition.

I give speeches on the topic *Say YES to Yourself.* The idea is that you may need to say "no" to some things to create space so you can say "yes" to other things that focus on your top priorities.

I once gained 4 hours in 30 seconds. That is, I deleted four TV shows from my DVR (digital video recorder).

It's about making good choices. To make good choices we need to create *think-space.* When someone asks you to do something, give yourself time to think and, when it's appropriate, respond by saying: "I'll have to check my schedule when I get back to my desk. How about I call you this afternoon to see if I can fit that in?" This gives you the time and space to think about your decision to the offer.

So how do activate your intuition? First, think favorably about your intuition. Remember the times when you listened to your gut feelings and things turned out well. Second, make time for your intuition. Practitioners of Zen Buddhism and Hinduism set up time for daily meditation. Christians set time for daily prayer.

What if I don't have time for meditation?

One meditation guru was asked, "How long do you meditate?" He replied, "Three minutes a day." His point is that three minutes a day is better than planning to meditate 30 minutes a day—and you don't do it.

Will only three minutes do any good?

Yes. Zen Buddhists look for the sudden flash of insight known as satori, or intuitive illumination. A person can connect with Higher Power in just three minutes.

Carry a small memo pad in your pocket or purse so you can write down your insights. For example, some time ago I was riding a bicycle and, zap, I had an incredible idea for a novel or screenplay. This was a Wow! idea. I immediately wrote it down. If you are driving it might be best to pull your car over to the side of the street. If you write slowly, you can carry an audio recorder. Just be sure to capture the idea. The universe has just handed you a gift. Honor the abundance of the universe and write it down.

Mozart captured musical ideas that flowed into his mind. He wrote in a letter: "When I am, as it were, completely myself, entirely alone, and of good cheer—say traveling in a carriage, or walking after a good meal, or during the night when I cannot sleep: it is on such occasions that my ideas flow best and most abundantly. Whence and how they come, I know not; nor can I force them. Those ideas that please me I keep in my memory [by humming] them to myself."

Make plans and take action because the universe bestows great ideas to many, but only a few have the courage and persistence to take action and make their dreams come true.

Make space for your intuition. Be ready when opportunities arise. For example, there have been times late at night when my sweetheart asks me about some future event. During late hours when I feel tired my reflex is to say "no." So I tell her the truth and say, "If I answer now, I'll say no. So instead, let's talk about this tomorrow, okay?" This is how I make space for my intuition and subconscious mind, which will ponder the event while I sleep.

Principle

Intuit to do it.

Leverage Question

How can you effectively and kindly respond to people and create think-space for yourself?

Retreat from Reverse Examples

Some negative people say "That's too much trouble." Or, "That will never work." We can look at negative people as Reverse Examples. When you want a life of abundance and joy, you need to run—not walk—away from these people, the Reverse Examples.

I call negative people Reverse Examples because they are not standing still; they are actually going backwards. This is contrary to progress and does not support the flow of grand abundance.

I remember once walking to an appointment in downtown San Francisco. Two men were arguing loudly. In my mind I said a prayer: "Blessings to you both." These two men, through their abusive language and tone, were Reverse Examples. They were not just standing still; they were causing damage to their relationship—and in effect they were going backwards.

When using the term Reverse Example to describe someone, it's important to realize that we are not judging that person, but defining a counterproductive action. No one has less value than any other person. The point here is that we need to value our intuition when selecting people to socialize with or think about. There are times when our intuition informs us that "I don't want to be like that person. She does not have the same goals I have. She doesn't want what I want. And she's not willing to pay the price I'm willing to pay to move forward."

Let's look at a healthy and spiritual way to interact with the people we call Reverse Examples. (And let's realize that a person can be both a good example in some area and a Reverse Example in another area.) People want closeness and competence. If you find yourself engaged in something that is creating space (a separation) and implying that the other person is not competent, STOP. Yes, stop. Even if you need to say, "Excuse me. I'll be right back. I need to go to the restroom."

When you return, identify something that you feel the other person is doing correctly. Also, identify your positive intention. For example, one evening, my sweetheart was watching television while I worked on a book—in another room. When I saw her after her programs, I felt uncomfortable. Instead of saying, "You're not spending enough time with me" which would put her on the defensive, I started with my intention and said gently: "I missed you." That created closeness.

When you want more abundance, watch out for the people who are focused on comfort first. These people don't take appropriate risks. Not taking appropriate risks can be a Reverse Example.

A Native American Elder (as quoted by Ann Wilson Schaef) said, "When the Creator gives you something, don't hesitate. Grab it." From this we realize that we must stretch to create a new phase of life that is different from all we have experienced thus far. To learn how to take appropriate risks, you need to feed your mind and spirit with examples of how people have accomplished the extraordinary. The process of successful and appropriate risk-taking is an important part of my audio-book *Free Yourself for Success*. And in this chapter, we will soon learn about risk-taking and more from selected Inspiring Examples: millionaires and billionaires.

The idea of retreat from Reverse Examples points to spiritual processes. People go on retreats to renew their spirits, minds and bodies. But you can have mini retreats during your normal day. These are moments that align with Psalm 46:10: "Be still and know I am God." Some scholars point out that this means: Relax a moment and remember that God is running the universe.

A mini retreat is a moment you take for yourself when you focus on a positive thought. When you do this you give yourself to Higher Power and offer up your stress. For example, when you walk to the restroom during a busy day at work, you can say a prayer in your mind—and have a mini retreat.

The idea of "Be still and know I am God" and taking a mini retreat ties in with something called the Activity-Recovery Pattern. Researchers have found that the most effective people do not work fast and constantly and without breaks. The most productive people use an Activity-Recovery Pattern that includes times of rest and recovery. For example, my morning often includes an intense period of writing. When I am done I get up from my computer or notepad and take time to exercise. My mind recovers while my body moves.

With my audiences, I emphasize take breaks or be broken. Pace yourself and use an Activity-Recovery Pattern.

Some people combine prayer and exercise. I know people who pray and walk on a treadmill for five minutes—three times a day for a daily total of 15 minutes. A landmark Harvard study noted that a mere 15 minutes a day for a total of one or two hours a week will improve a person's health. Those who do this have a 50% better chance to avoid a heart attack, and reduce the possibility of heart surgery. This is terrific news. In just 15 minutes you can combine exercise with prayer or meditation to achieve a healthy body and a healthy spirit.

People who procrastinate are Reverse Examples. On the other hand, people who enjoy abundance do not procrastinate. They take action. Here is a powerful tool I use everyday: The Morning 8. Every morning for eight minutes I take action on whatever issue is crucial for my success. I find it helps to take on these challenges in the morning, when my mind and body are still fresh.

The Morning 8 is when you do what you don't like to do first thing in the morning, when your mind and body are fresh and free from the stress of the coming day.

For example, people who are buried in clutter might devote eight minutes each day to clearing their desks. Over a year (that is, 5 days a week for 51 weeks), that would add up to 34 hours. Imagine how your life could be free of clutter when 34 hours or almost a full work-week was devoted to eliminating disorder.

Avoid Reverse Examples & Seek Out Inspiring Ones

Reverse Examples have quick, easy answers to many new situations: "Don't do it; you'll get hurt" or "The odds are against you getting what you want."

The important idea is to move away from Reverse Examples and their limited patterns of thought. Seek out Inspiring Examples, that is, those people who have done the extraordinary!

Let's learn from fourteen millionaires and four billionaires about their processes to create financial abundance:

1. **Oprah Winfrey:** "Though I'm grateful for the blessings of wealth, it hasn't changed who I am. My feet are still on the ground. I'm just wearing better shoes." She also said, "The key to realizing a dream is to focus not on success but on significance—and then even the small steps and little victories along your path will take on greater meaning …. For every one of us that succeeds, it's because there's somebody there to show you the way out. The light doesn't always necessarily have to be in your family; for me it was teachers and school …. My philosophy is that not only are you responsible for your life, but doing the best at this moment puts you in the best place for the next moment …. You get in life what you have the courage to ask for." She also said, "Always continue the climb. It is possible for you to do whatever you choose, if you first get to know who you are and are willing to work with a power that is greater than ourselves to do it."

2. **Bill Gates:** "I think it's fair to say that personal computers have become the most empowering tool we've ever created. They're tools of communication, they're tools of creativity, and they can be shaped by their user." He also said, "It's a lot easier to connect to the story of the one person or the five people …. I know [that] there's 3 million kids every year dying of things that

are completely preventable with the technology we have today." And he said, "Your most unhappy customers are your greatest source of learning."

3. **Donald Trump:** "What separates the winners from the losers is how a person reacts to each new twist of fate." He also said, "Find the right person, and second, monitor his or her progress …. Only a great contractor can make ten parties happy …. Never accept a contractor's first bid …. Never, ever accept a first offer …. It's moronic to be too proud to save money …. It is important to let people know about your accomplishments …. The best way to impress people is through results …. It doesn't matter whether the success is a small one or a big one—you have to start somewhere and build on it."

4. **Mark Victor Hansen** (co-creator of the *Chicken Soup for the Soul* series): "You control your future, your destiny. What you think about comes about. By recording your dreams and goals on paper, you set in motion the process of becoming the person you most want to be. Put your future in good hands—your own."

5. **Jack Canfield** (co-creator of the *Chicken Soup for the Soul* series): "My life purpose is to inspire and empower people to live their highest vision in a context of love and joy." He also said, "You only have control of three things in your life—the thoughts you think, the images you visualize and the actions you take [your behavior] …. You cannot improve your life, your

relationships, your game or your performance without feedback …. Slow down and pay attention."

6. **Marty Rodriguez** (Century 21's top real estate agent): "Many people become our friends and like to hang around here …. Clients bring their friends …. One time my husband asked, 'Why do you do these things? You don't have to do these things.' I said, 'That's what makes me different.'"

7. **Anthony Robbins** (top motivational speaker and author): "A real decision is measured by the fact that you've taken a new action. If there's no action, you haven't truly decided." He also said, "One reason so few of us achieve what we truly want is that we never direct our focus; we never concentrate our power. Most people dabble their way through life, never deciding to master anything in particular." Also, "The only limit to your impact is your imagination and commitment."

8. **Liz Claiborne** (founder of Liz Claiborne, Inc. who directed the company's designers): "[When I started the company] the goal was to clothe the working American woman. I was working myself, I wanted to look good, and I didn't think you should have to spend a fortune to do it …. I'm a great believer in fit, in comfort, in color. And I listened to the customer. I went on the selling floor as a saleswoman, went into the fitting room, heard what they liked and didn't like."

9. **Brian Tracy** (author of numerous bestselling self help books): "I've found that luck is quite predictable. If you want more luck, take more chances. Be more active. Show up more often." He also said, "Successful people are always looking for opportunities to help others. Unsuccessful people are always asking, 'What's in it for me?'" He said, "The more you seek security, the less of it you have. But the more you seek opportunity, the more likely it is that you will achieve the security that you desire." Also, "All successful men and women are big dreamers. They imagine what their future could be, ideal in every respect, and then they work every day toward their distant vision, that goal or purpose."

10. **Warren Buffett** (listed by *Forbes* magazine as the second richest man in the world): "I only buy what I understand." He also said, "It's better to hang out with people better than you. Pick out associates whose behavior is better than yours, and you'll drift in that direction."

11. **Suze Orman,** (#1 New York Times best-selling author, known as "America's most trusted personal finance expert"): "People first, then money, then things ... To choose [to be] rich is to make every penny count, every dollar count, every financial choice count." Also, "In all realms of life it takes courage to stretch your limits, express your power, and fulfill your potential ... it's no different in the financial realm." She wrote, "Truth Creates Money, Lies Destroy it."

12. **Robert G. Allen** (best-selling author): "Don't let the opinions of the average man sway you. Dream, and he thinks you're crazy. Succeed, and he thinks you're lucky. Acquire wealth, and he thinks you're greedy. Pay no attention. He simply doesn't understand." He also said, "When you're doing what you love to do, the money comes naturally. Maybe not at first, but eventually … if you stick with it. Do you think Bob Hope started out with a goal, 'I want to become a millionaire by making people laugh, then I'll retire to do what I want'? I doubt it. He just did what he did best. And the money came."

13. **T. Harv Eker** (best-selling author of *Secrets of the Millionaire Mind*): "Rich people associate with positive, successful people. Poor people associate with negative or unsuccessful people."

14. **George Lucas:** "If you want to be successful … perseverance is one of the key qualities. It's very important that you find something that you care about, that you have a deep passion for, because you're going to have to devote a lot of your life to it … You're not going to get anywhere without working extremely hard … years and years of very, very difficult struggle through the whole process of achieving anything … The secret is not to give up hope. It's very hard not to because if you're really doing something worthwhile I think you will be pushed to the brink of hopelessness before you come through the other side. You just have to hang in through that."

15. **Steven Spielberg:** "A good director knows when to say 'yes.' ... The public has an appetite for anything about imagination ... I've found some kind of new color that I never splashed against the canvas before .... I don't need to prove anything to anyone. I don't need to prove anything to myself. I just need to stay interested."

16. **Harvey Mackay** (bestselling author of *Swim with the Sharks without Being Eaten Alive*): "What I'll be doing a year from now [is] undoubtedly based on contacts I made today."

17. **Mary Kay Ash,** founder of Mary Kay Cosmetics (with $2 billion in sales): "When I meet someone, I imagine her wearing an invisible sign that says, 'Make me feel important! ... This is one of the most important lessons in dealing with people I have ever learned." Also, "I believe each of us has God-given talents within us waiting to be brought into fruition." She wrote, "It was not extensive market surveys or demographic studies that created the pink Cadillac [her way to motivate consultants to excel], just [my] pure and simple woman's intuition." She noted: "The desire for recognition is a powerful motivator. Anyone who has attended a Mary Kay Seminar knows we recognize our people's achievement with beautiful gifts and tons of verbal appreciation. Exciting prizes are significant symbols of esteem: I believe both words and things are important." Finally, she said at a Mary Kay Seminar: "Are you ready for the most exciting moment of your life?"

18. **Walt Disney:** "We are not trying to entertain the critics. I'll take my chances with the public." Also, "Disneyland is a work of love. We didn't go into Disneyland just with the idea of making money." "Build the castle first [so the construction crew knows the magic we're making]." He said, "You don't work for a dollar—you work to create and have fun." He noted, "Everyone has been remarkably influenced by a book." Also, "If we didn't have deadlines, we'd stagnate … [To juggle so many things,] I'm always close to projects when we're chewing over the basic idea. Once the pattern is set … I let the staff take over, and I go on to other things …. I have always had men working for me whose skills were greater than my own. I am an idea man …. Courage is the main quality of leadership … usually it implies some risk—especially in new undertakings … It is good to have a failure while you're young because it teaches you so much … it makes you aware that such a thing can happen to anybody, and once you've lived through the worst, you're never quite as vulnerable afterward." Walt concluded, "I hope to stay young enough in spirit to never fear failure."

Wow! There are many useful strategies and wisdom condensed in what you have just read.

By the way, my life purpose is: *I help people experience enthusiasm, love and wisdom to fulfill big dreams.* And I am grateful to be working with you. Here is an important point: You can listen to the wisdom of millionaires and billionaire then go out and make new and powerful connections. In the next section we will see how I pulled together wisdom from effective people as I formulated Personaltainment™ Branding.

Principle

Retreat from Reverse Examples. Pay attention to what you need to learn and where you want to be.

Leverage Questions

Who and what are the Reverse Examples in your life? How can you get away from them or reduce your exposure time to them? Which people (who have already achieved what you want to do) can you focus on as Inspiring Examples? How can you use an Activity-Recovery Pattern?

Personaltainment™ Branding

Your Spiritual Path to Wealth

As I mentioned in the previous section, you can listen to the wisdom of millionaires and billionaires to learn to make new and powerful connections. That's how I formulated Personaltainment™ Branding. Personaltainment Branding can help you do well on the job—in a job interview, sales presentation or in building your own business.

Through Personaltainment Branding, I help my clients gain customers faster—with ease and feelings of personal fulfillment.

Personaltainment Branding is connecting with your prospective customers so they will know you and trust you quickly—and purchase what you offer.

For those of you who do not have external customers, you can still benefit from using the techniques in this chapter. Use these techniques with your supervisor and co-workers, who function like your internal customers. You still need to provide services for them, and you still need to keep them happy.

Let's continue to discuss branding. The standard form of branding is the association of a brand with an idea, like Volvo and safety. Similarly, Disney is associated with family entertainment—and theme parks.

Then there is personal branding (which we will cover in more depth in a later section of this book). Here is an example of a personal brand: Tom Marcoux, America's Communication Coach.

The central idea of a personal brand is to answer the question "What are you best known for?" For example, I use the phrase "When you need to make them go 'Wow!'" to illustrate how I help clients impress audiences, prospective customers and others.

I have designed Personaltainment Branding as a step up from personal branding. That is, when you use Personaltainment Branding, you have an advantage over conventional personal branding. The central idea of Personaltainment Branding is for you to create for your prospective customer an experience that is:

- Personalized
- Entertaining
- Connecting

I call this the PEC Triangle. Now I'll give you a specific example about "connecting."

My client Dr. JoAnn Dahlkoetter (bestselling author of *Your Performing Edge* at DrJoAnn.com) asked for my help on a press release during the 2006 Winter Olympic Games. As a coach to Olympic athletes, she wanted to be interviewed on numerous television and radio shows.

My first thought was that she needed to make her message *connecting* to ordinary viewers of TV and radio shows. The problem is that her clients, Olympians, are extraordinary people. How could she reach viewers? We decided to focus on what all people need: Skills to bounce back after a difficult struggle. I suggested that her press release include the following: "People must become skilled at bouncing back, whether it's crashing on ski slopes or crashing in a boardroom presentation," says Dr. JoAnn.

This was especially relevant because Dr. JoAnn had recently coached one of her Olympians to bounce back and regain confidence after a skiing accident that resulted in a concussion.

Finally, Dr. JoAnn's press release included this phrase: "After Michelle Kwan's withdrawal and Jacobellis' fall, Dr. JoAnn Dahlkoetter can explain how people overcome fear and the strategies to recover quickly from failure."

Dr. JoAnn's press release secured interviews for her on NBC Television, Newsweek on Air/Associated Press Radio, KCBS Radio, Bloomberg on the Air in New York and many others.

You Can Use Personaltainment Branding at Work

These techniques only require a pen and sheet of paper—and the following effective questions.

Five Personaltainment Branding Questions

1. What about this is working for you? (personalized)
2. When did this become fun for you? (entertaining)
3. What's most important about this for you? (personalized)
4. In order for you to know that you have what you want, what has to happen? (connecting)
5. How can we make this work better for you? (connecting)

(Another version of Question 2 is: When could this become fun for you?)

You can use these questions with co-workers, prospective customers and current customers.

How Is Personaltainment Branding Spiritual?

In this book we talk about *how may I serve?* Also, we note that Mother Teresa said, "Make your work a prayer." Many of us seek to find spiritual and uplifting ways to work. Fortunately, the Personaltainment Branding process serves the prospective customer in the following ways:

- Personalized means you are important to me.
- Entertaining is giving the customer an enjoyable experience.
- Connecting helps fill the customer's empty feeling of loneliness.

The Foundation of Personaltainment™ Branding

Now that you've had a taste of the process, let me describe how Personaltainment Branding first occurred to me. I listened to certain ideas from Bill Gates: "I think it's fair to say that personal computers have become the most empowering tool we've ever created. They're tools of communication, they're tools of creativity, and they can be shaped by their user."

I then recalled Anthony Robbins' idea: "We aren't in an information age, we are in an entertainment age." Also, from Johnny Carson: "People will pay more to be entertained than to be educated."

I noticed the difference between Baskin-Robbins ice cream shops and Cold Stone Creamery. Baskin-Robins provides a selection of 31 Flavors. On the other hand, Cold Stone Creamery sells ice cream and the choice of add-ins, like chocolate syrup or fudge brownies. Cold Stone Creamery also provides helpful suggestions about add-ins that go together. One combination is called Cherry Cake Double Take®. The Cold Stone Creamery process is thus personalized.

With the iPod and iTunes, music is personalized. At the time of this writing, the online iTunes Music Store has sold more than 10 billion copies of songs.

You can make a lot of money by providing your service in a way that allows the customer to *personalize how he or she uses the service.*

We do best to move forward and let go of dinosaur thinking. Stubborn individuals who refuse to do so will become as extinct as the dinosaur! Look for ways to get ahead of the curve. Keep current by perusing the Internet (including blogs) to see what is in the global consciousness.

Now is the time of Personaltainment™—the time when prospective customers respond best to gestures that are personalized, entertaining and connecting.

Now we'll look at how Amazon.com customers have experiences that match the Personaltainment Branding process.

EXAMPLE 1: A quick analysis of Amazon.com:

Personalized: Customers are given personalized recommendations based on past purchases and items placed in personal wish lists.

Entertaining: The customer's curiosity and feelings related to suspense are aroused so that she or he returns regularly to see what new items are being recommended.

Connecting: The customer can see lists like Listmania and So You Want To … that are written by other customers who share an interest. This might include advice, books and DVDs to help someone do something like write a book. This strategy develops the feeling of community.

EXAMPLE 2: A quick analysis of Nightingale-Conant.com (a website for personal development):

Personalized: The prospective customer (or prospect) types answers about personal characteristics, into a form and gets a computer-designed Personal Mission Statement.

Entertaining: Receiving the Personal Mission Statement is fun, like seeing a daily horoscope at MSN.com.

Connecting: Having received something (the Personal Mission Statement), the prospect feels a connection to Nightingale-Conant. The prospect will then browse the site to find educational programs that can assist in the realization of her or his dream.

Increase Your Abundance Using Personaltainment Branding

I created a form (visible in the next pages) to help a business owner or salesperson design a prospective customer's experience. With Personaltainment Branding, the idea is to make them go "Wow!"

Personaltainment™ Branding

Make them go "Wow!"

Example of website strategies

1. Personalized

See: Include a questionnaire to find out what energizes the prospective customer about his or her work.

Hear: Not applicable.

Touch: The prospective customer types in his or her responses to the questionnaire.

2. Entertaining

See: Prospect receives the computerized response to the questionnaire—which is like getting a horoscope: ("Oh, look at what it says!")

Hear: Include an audio link of the business owner praising the prospect for filling out the questionnaire. Music is played in the background.

Touch: The prospective customer types in her or his responses to questionnaire.

3. Connecting

See: Set up the questionnaire's response to include the prospect's first name in different places.

Hear: Include an audio link with the business owner saying: "Congratulations on devoting the time to fill out the form and get answers. We have found that highly motivated and effective people like you are the ones who complete the form and participate in the process. Well done. Now we will … "

Touch: Use music. Some music actually gives people a physical, positive response—a tingle along the spine, for example.

© Tom Marcoux

Personaltainment™ Branding

Make them go "Wow!"

Website strategy

1. Personalized

See:

Hear:

Touch:

2. Entertaining

See:

Hear:

Touch:

3. Connecting

See:

Hear:

Touch:

© Tom Marcoux

Personaltainment Branding Does Not Require a Fancy Website ...

When you use the Five Personaltainment Branding Questions, you can devise a compelling experience for the prospective customer in any way you interact with the person—in-person, via email, and on the telephone. Again, here are the questions.

Five Personaltainment Branding Questions

1. What about this is working for you? (personalized)
2. When did this become fun for you? (entertaining)
3. What's most important about this for you? (personalized)
4. In order for you to know that you have what you want, what has to happen? (connecting)
5. How can we make this work better for you? (connecting)

For example, you are connecting when you ask someone, "What's most important to you about this?" The response you receive will give a clue as to how you can personalize your next comment and what you can offer that person.

Here's your opportunity to fill in a blank form to apply these ideas to your own work or service to customers.

Personaltainment Branding is a helpful way to distinguish yourself in the marketplace. It is a powerful tool to give the prospective customer a Wow! experience that leads to becoming your customer faster. Personaltainment Branding also builds trust quickly. Everyone wins!

Furthermore, Personaltainment Branding is part of your spiritual path to wealth. It helps you wake up your spirit to prosperity. It helps you see things in a new light. It will give you a new perspective on how to serve people in the way they prefer to be served: personalized, entertaining and connecting.

Principle

To serve effectively, give the customer a Personaltainment™ Branding experience that is personalized, entertaining and connecting.

Leverage Question

Review the Personaltainment Branding process. How can you apply it to your work and use it to inspire prospective customers?

Inspire Hope and Faith

To experience a Higher-Self-mode of living, it is important to focus on hope and faith. Rabbi Harold Kushner wrote a book called *When All You've Ever Wanted Isn't Enough*. That's a powerful title. The truth is that many times what we thought we wanted is truly not enough. For example, a huge amount of money is not enough to bring inner peace. Johnny Carson said, "The only thing money gives you is the freedom of not worrying about money."

Hope and faith bring inner peace

At Dictionary.com, faith is defined as "a confident belief in the truth, value, or trustworthiness of a person, idea, or thing" and "a set of principles or beliefs."

So what do you believe? When you want more abundance, consider these beliefs:

- I learn from all experiences.
- Higher Power has a plan for me. Higher Power is watching over me.
- I am safe.
- I am worthy.
- Money is a tool I use well for the benefit of all.
- I easily gain money because I lovingly serve others in effective ways that attract money.
- To those God has given much, God enjoys their enjoyment.

This last comment, "God enjoys their enjoyment," relates to Psalm 118:24: "This is the day the Lord has made; let us rejoice and be glad in it." It is appropriate and honorable to be grateful and rejoice. And *rejoice* means to feel happiness or joy—and to express great joy.

To express appreciation and joy is respectful of Higher Power. Be a fountain of positive energy, and your energy will bless the people around you.

Note that suffering is not the only road to wisdom. Misery not only loves company; misery creates company.

When you are feeling down, you can use a process to switch the direction of your thoughts: Take out a piece of paper (or just think this through in your mind) and write "I am grateful for … " Then complete the sentence with ten examples. Instantly, your perception is expanded.

In my Comparative Religion college classes, I talk about *healthy humility.*

Healthy humility is acknowledging that *our ego often clouds our perception*, and we often do not know what supports our highest good.

Since we often do not know what supports our highest good, an effective prayer includes an ending of "this situation or better." My client Sandra wants a particular agent to represent her books, but then she remembers to add to her prayer: "this agent or an agent that would be a better match for me and my material."

We need to be humble. We don't see the whole picture in a given moment. Author Tama J. Kieves wrote: "The path of inspiration defies navigation. We arrive by way of revelation."

We live in hope and faith. And we live to witness revelations in our lives. Our search for personal truth goes like this: We receive a bit of guidance. We climb to a peak. We see more. Then we start up to a higher peak.

Joe Karbo, author of *The Lazy Man's Way to Riches*, took such a journey. Joe was deeply in debt. He consulted four lawyers and a judge and learned the extent of the law and how to interact with creditors to gain agreement to reasonable payment plans. He wrote a book based on his experiences that sold 100,000 copies, which significantly reduced his debt.

To create abundance, many people learn to solve a problem—and then teach others how to solve that problem.

To increase abundance, focus on hope. Mary Kay Ash, founder of Mary Kay Cosmetics (with $2 billion in annual sales), said, "Give yourself something to work toward—constantly." Write down what you are looking forward to. For example, one goal can be to earn extra money for a family vacation.

Also, when you design a product or service, have it serve people's hopes. Author Peter Nivio Zarlenga said, "In our factory, we make lipstick. In our advertising, we sell hope."

The important point to remember is that we can choose beliefs that support our path of abundance. We can believe that we have natural abilities and that Higher Power will help us to serve many people, and as a dividend, earn financial freedom.

Principle

Choose beliefs that build up your spirit and personal energy.

Leverage Question

Which of your beliefs support your path toward abundance?

Target the Good of All

One definition of prosperity is tending to favor or bring good luck. When you target the good for all involved, you align with the goodness of the universe. And this helps you attract good luck.

Let's begin by talking about forgiveness. In his book *Forgive For Good*, Dr. Fred Luskin talks about forgiveness as the process by which one ends a personal cycle of blame and suffering. We learn to become the hero of our own story instead of being a victim. One of my clients said, "My brother always beat me up when I was young." Imagine the power that emerges with the following substitution: "This is when I learned to value protecting myself. I asked my parents for karate lessons."

Choose this belief:

I can use everything to help me grow and serve more effectively.

When you focus on this belief, you can support a grand flow of abundance in your life. Learn to forgive—to free up your energy and create more abundance.

This section is about targeting the good of all. By all, I mean include yourself, your family, friends and your Higher Power.

Targeting the good of all is really about forgiveness, which is defined here as "seeing the big picture." The big picture is a more helpful definition of the word forgiveness than its more traditional meaning—pardon, a word that locks us into seeing a guilty person only as one who avoids punishment.

On the other hand, viewing forgiveness as the big picture allows us to go through the process of letting go of our painful feelings. For example, my client Marina received a huge disappointment. For months she helped her friend Janet organize a conference. Marina assumed she would be rewarded with an opportunity to give a presentation at the event. Marina's speaking business was just starting, and she really needed a break. Marina had expressed to Janet her desire to give a speech.

At the last minute Marina discovered that she was not included on the conference agenda. It broke her heart. How could her friend Janet be so unfair and cruel?

I guided Marina through the Big Picture Forgiveness Process. Using the four-step process, Marina began by acknowledging her personal truth, which was that she felt deeply hurt. She overcame her disappointment by expanding her perspective.

The Big Picture Forgiveness Process

Step One: Acknowledge the pain. Marina said, "I'm really disappointed and hurt that Janet didn't give me the opportunity to serve her audience—especially after the help I gave her with the conference preparation."

Step Two: Take care of yourself. Marina treated herself with warm baths, relaxing music and time to write in her journal. She also processed her feelings as we talked through the situation.

Step Three: Examine the situation from the perspective of a metaphorical helicopter—to gain objectivity. In time, Marina was able to say, "Janet didn't include me on her list because she was only including speakers who already had a long list of fans. Janet was only focused on making her conference a success. I can understand that. But I still feel that she could have included me in some way. Since it was a spiritual conference, perhaps I could have led the prayer at dinner time."

Step Four: Become the hero of your own story. Marina eventually said, "When Janet didn't include me in the conference, it became a warning sign that I need to change my perspective. I need to have faith that God will provide me with other opportunities. Also, I need to step up my participation. I need to intensify my focus. I really want to devote more time to marketing my own speaking career. I can't control what others do, but I can make better choices for myself."

Months later Marina still talks to Janet on the telephone from time to time. Marina's healthy approach to forgiveness has saved a friendship—and perhaps opened the door for her friendship with Janet to deepen over time. The good news is Marina is now free of her painful feelings. Her time and energy have been set free, too.

Within the word "forgiveness" are the letters that spell the word "free."

The Good of All Means Everyone Profits from a Situation

We start enjoying life to the fullest when we have learned to let go of hesitation around the word *profit*. Dictionary.com defines profit as "an advantageous gain or return; benefit." When you put service and Higher Power first, you can create profit in a holistic manner.

Author Harold Kushner wrote: "Our souls are not hungry for fame, comfort, wealth, or power ... Our souls are hungry for meaning."

To unlock the floodgates of abundance, we use this question:

How can you expand how you serve, in ways that are profitable and result in the dividend of abundance?

One speaker said, "Marriage is a place where you go to give—not just go to get." Find out how you can expand your contribution to the people in your life. And don't be shy about looking for profitable ways to accomplish your goals. For example, years ago, when working in a retail environment, I was trained to ask, "So what brings you into the store today?" I learned to say it in a friendly way. However, I would not be encouraging the customer to buy something if I approached her by only saying "How are you today?" I would not be serving both the person and the store.

You can make the interaction profitable for the person and for the store.

To target the good of all is to focus on how we conduct our daily lives. When I was in Japan, I witnessed a festival (known as matsuri) that is part of the indigenous religion Shinto. Shinto includes affirmations for family, tradition, reverence toward nature, physical cleanliness and festivals. The idea is, you can uplift your life when you affirm the valuable parts of it. Festivals, celebrations and rituals of worship that honor the Divine are helpful.

Author Sue Patton Thoele wrote: "Soothe your soul with ritual." Rituals keep spirituality in mind. Rituals remind people they are in a relationship with the Divine, and that relationship requires effort and time.

My client Mary celebrates her gratitude for her writing talent with a ritual, her annual "Joy in Writing Day." She purchases a book (she loves books), and she writes something for fun.

Rituals can be simple, brief and meaningful:

At every meal my sweetheart and I hold hands and say together, "We're grateful. Thank you."

Principle

Target the good of all involved.

Leverage Question

How can you expand how you serve, in ways that are profitable and result in the dividend of abundance?

Conclusion of Chapter Two

We have discussed the process S.P.I.R.I.T. and have examined the principles and Leverage Questions that will inspire you to achieve and support a grand flow of abundance in your life.

- S – Seek the Higher View
- P – Program for abundance
- I – Intuit to do it
- R – Retreat from Reverse Examples
- I – Inspire hope and faith
- T – Target the good of all

I have presented Seven Secrets (to wake up your spirit to prosperity), that include:

- The six methods of S.P.I.R.I.T., plus …
- The process to serve the customer effectively: a Personaltainment™ Branding experience that is personalized, entertaining and connecting.

Author David Kundtz wrote that "Spirituality is the meanings and values by which you live your life combined with, for believers, the way your experience the divine. The combination of God, meanings and values is spirituality."

Walt Disney's brother and partner, Roy O. Disney, said, "Decision-making is easy if your values are clear."

You have the power to choose your beliefs and choose how you live on a daily basis. You can choose to focus on scarcity or abundance. You can remind yourself with "I am grateful for … "

As I mentioned earlier, before I go to sleep each night I write in my Daily Journal of Victories and Blessings. A victory relates to an action I took—like exercising. A blessing is a gift—like talking on the telephone with an extended family member. I go to sleep feeling grateful for the blessings and adventures of each day.

I am grateful for the opportunity to connect with you through this book. I wish you a journey of love, abundance and blessings.

Let's continue with the next section …

3

Make Money Through Your Natural Brilliance

In Chapter Two, you learned how to develop the mindset to expand your prosperity. So now the important thing is to progress forward. This section covers the 9-Minute Miracle Breakthrough. Once you learn the process, you can devote just nine minutes a day or even once a week to identifying what will really move you toward your dreams.

With the 9-Minute Miracle Breakthrough, I help my clients bring the process of prosperity expansion down to daily, individually tailored steps.

In Chapter Three, we will learn how to earn more money. Let's remember that money is a tool. For now, this affirmation is helpful: Money is a tool that I use well for the benefit of all. When you really feel this positive energy, you wake up your spirit to prosperity. We can see this process at work with Oprah Winfrey. Millions of people find her to be genuine and generous. One of my colleagues said, "She makes money by giving it away." And Oprah is the first African-American woman billionaire in U.S. history.

In this section you will create a Momentum Action Plan™ (MAP) as part of the 9-Minute Miracle Breakthrough. When you implement the Momentum Action Plan on a daily basis, you enjoy a new zest in your moment-to-moment experiences. You will also learn to use leverage, which means gaining the most benefit from the least effort.

As a sidenote, I first introduced the 9-Minute Miracle Breakthrough in my audio program (and speeches) entitled *Free Yourself for Success*. My clients have found the 9-Minute Miracle Breakthrough to be more beneficial than standard time management and goal-setting practices. You will learn to use the power that is already inside you.

Science of the 9-Minute Miracle Breakthrough process

Over the years I developed the Science of Emotional Leverage™. The best way to describe leverage is with an image:

Imagine that you want to move a boulder. You place a small rock on the ground near the boulder. The small rock is your fulcrum. Then you use a big stick as your lever to move the boulder. With little effort you get big results. That's leverage.

Emotional Leverage is a strategy that utilizes your emotions to help you get big results with little effort. Emotional Leverage is how you free yourself for success. This strategy also helps you take effective action in the *10 Seconds to Wealth*.

Many people get frustrated and give up when they begin new methods or strategies—only to fall back to old habits. This disappointing situation results from a structural error in traditional training. When returning to old habits, these people are just waving around the proverbial stick and not using the key device, which is the fulcrum (or a little rock in our leverage metaphor).

The fulcrum represents merging with your True Self. Your True Self is the part of you that is naturally brilliant and courageous. On the other hand the False Self (also known as the Ego) is the part of you that is stuck in fear and feels caged. That's why we want to focus on your True Self—to help you free yourself from fear.

Make your True Self a bigger part of your daily life

Merging with your True Self is the process by which you consciously direct your thoughts away from fear and toward the perspective of abundance and spiritual growth. Eventually, like learning to ride a bicycle, you can maintain balance without conscious effort. The more you practice viewing life from your True Self, the more you experience merging with your True Self. Many people express that regular sessions of prayer or meditation help them experience inner peace. Such inner peace is a manifestation of the True Self.

This experience of inner peace is what martial arts masters refer to as being centered. Similarly, when Olympic athletes are "in the zone," they are focused. Creative people like writers talk about how words flow effortlessly. The point is that our emotions serve us to be productive when we merge with our True Self.

Your True Self saves you from procrastination.

Fear leads many of us to procrastinate. We seek to avoid pain. The good news is that the ten steps of the 9-Minute Miracle Breakthrough shift our attention away from pain. We get a new focus point. We do not shutdown because of pain. Instead, we begin with four questions to connect with the True Self.

At this point, pull out sheet of paper, notepad or a journal to write down questions and answers. By participating in the following process, you will form a roadmap to your best life. This roadmap is your Momentum Action Plan (MAP).

To be clear: When you go through the 9-Minute Miracle Breakthrough process, you end up with your Momentum Action Plan.

In the Momentum Action Plan, you will be answering ten questions.

Momentum Action Plan (MAP)

Question 1: *What do you want?*

Choose any area in which you desire something. In just twenty seconds, write down whatever comes to mind. It can be a thing, a relationship, a new job, financial freedom, anything. My clients have written:

- I want a new car.
- I want some new business clothes.
- I want my husband to treat me better.
- I want a career that satisfies my need for more prosperity, enriching friendships and exotic travel.
- I want to get a particular project done.

So write down what you want. Just a few words can be powerful.

This reminds me of a time when my parents and I were vacationing at Universal Studios. It was the first time I could show my parents part of my world as a motion picture director. It was also the first time that I pushed my mother in a wheelchair. Her walking had become limited as the result of a long illness. I felt my heart cringe each time I helped my mother transfer from the wheelchair to a chair on an attraction. Her once strong arms trembled, and her face tensed when she stood on her weakened legs. It was a strange contrast to be with my family in a park built for pleasure, and to be so conscious of my mother's pain.

Actors strolled by portraying characters like Laurel and Hardy, Mae West and The Director, who wore riding pants and boots and held a megaphone. The Director took one look at my mother in the wheelchair and said, "No more stunts for you!"

My mother burst into laugher, and my father and I joined her. It was delightful to see my mother's response. What was real here? My mother's pain and infirmity were real, but in just a moment our perceptions changed, and we enjoyed laughter and connection. Our revised perceptions helped us notice more than pain and infirmity in that particular moment.

My point is this: *It took just five words to change how we felt.* When you write down what you want, remember that just a few words can be powerful. And it's part of connecting with your True Self.

You are connecting with your True Self when you emphasize the good, the blessed and the abundance in the moment. Using a few powerful words gives you a pivot point for your thoughts and feelings.

It's the process of *Align with Your Design.*

Consider that whatever you write down immediately may be just the tip of the iceberg. For example, I might say I want to finish writing a children's book. But there's something deeper to it than that—which leads us to the second question ...

Momentum Action Plan (MAP)

Question 2: *No. Come on, what do you really want?*

Often, beneath our initial thoughts about what we want, there is something even more crucial that we want even more.

For me, what's below the idea of creating a children's book is that I really want to make a contribution to brightening the lives of millions of people—something like the joy inspired by Walt Disney.

And what's even deeper is this: I really want to feel I have accomplished a great purpose and that I've lived a meaningful life.

My clients have said:

- I want a new job. But what I really want is an end to the stress and meaninglessness of my current job.
- I want a closer relationship. But what I really want is to feel safe to reveal my deep feelings to my romantic partner.

You'll notice that we're talking about feelings. And that leads us to the third question ...

Momentum Action Plan (MAP)

Question 3: Better yet, what do you want to feel?

It's important to focus on what you want to feel. Remember the first four questions help you access your True Self. This third question gives us a special insight. What you want to feel is like an indicator light on a plane's control panel. This light reveals what your natural brilliance is.

In Chapter Two, I shared a quote from bestselling author Robert Allen: "When you're doing what you love to do, the money comes naturally. Maybe not at first, but eventually … if you stick with it. Do you think Bob Hope started out with a goal, 'I want to become a millionaire by making people laugh, then I'll retire to do what I want'? I doubt it. He just did what he did best. And the money came."

We can imagine a moment or series of moments in which Bob Hope first made people laugh. He probably had the experience of "Oooh. I made them laugh. This feels good!"

Many of my clients have said, "I don't know what I want to do next with my life." The challenge then is to have them remember when they had an experience of "Oooh, this feels good!" We also need to remember moments of "Oooh, I'm good at this!"

Similarly, it may be time for my client to start trying new things to find out what brings the "Oooh!" feelings. How do you know if you will enjoy writing a song? You try it out.

How do you know if you will enjoy a cooking course? You attend a first class. By the way, I know a vivacious woman who has consistently tried new things and experienced success in different phases of her life. Let's look at her journey:

1. She began as a hair stylist.
2. She then owned her own salon. (15 years)
3. She sold the business and traveled the world.
4. She took an interest in graphic arts.
5. She earned a degree in graphic arts and worked as an administrative assistant in a church, using her graphic arts skills. (5 years)
6. Recently, she completed a program with the California Culinary Academy and has begun a career in the culinary arts.

It's important to know what you like; what feels good to you; what is fun for you. What feels great is often aligned with your natural brilliance. The idea is to *align with your design*. This means that you align with your gifts. Higher Power has given you natural brilliance and talents. It is up to you to experiment, to see how you feel, and then refine new skills.

Write down what you want to feel. Here's how this process goes:

>**Sarah** (a client): How do I know what I want to feel?
>**Tom:** Good question. I'll help with a few questions. What do you want?
>**Sarah:** I want to publish a children's story.
>**Tom:** That's great! And what do you really want?
>**Sarah:** I want to make money using my talents.
>**Tom:** And if you can make money by using your talents, how would you feel?

Sarah: I'd feel ... I'd feel safe. I'd feel like I could always take care of myself.

Tom: Great. Write that down. You want to feel safe.

Connect with desired feelings with "See, Hear, Touch"

Often, when we hear a question, our mind gives us the answer in flashing images, or sounds or a feeling. At one point, I listened to Serena, one of my college students with a major in Motion Pictures and Television Production. She described what motivates her with making feature films: "I see the audience clapping; I hear the audience's laughter; and I feel a warm hug (touch) from my brother as he celebrates the accomplishment with me."

So write down what you want to feel and note your impressions of See, Hear and Touch.

Write quickly. Don't hesitate. It's just you and the paper. Remember your initial impressions are usually on target.

By the way, you can keep your answers confidential. *Often, when a dream is new and fragile, it helps to avoid revealing it.* Some people, even family members, can torpedo a dream.

When Walt Disney wanted to create Disneyland, no one understood it. There had never before been a clean, delightful theme park. Walt's wife and his brother Roy were both against the idea. The Board of Directors was against it. Walt had to cash in his life insurance to fund the initial research and design of Disneyland.

My point is that Walt Disney had an unusual faith in his own judgment, and many of us have not yet developed such a valuable faith. It may be best to keep quiet about our new dream until we have some tangible results in the right direction. For example, a friend of mine who is an associate editor of a magazine has recently completed a course in filmmaking. Two of the four films he made are quite effective. That's an important step forward.

The Momentum Action Plan that you're creating is for your eyes only (until you decide who is a real supporter of your dream). Now, let's continue ...

Momentum Action Plan (MAP)

Question 4: *How to experience goals on a small scale?*

In some of my speeches, I hold up a prop—a heart-shaped box.

What's inside your heart? What do you want to feel?

One of my clients told me she wants to be an Oscar-winning actress. I asked her, "Where is the joy for you in acting?"

"It's being in the moment. Feeling the presence of the audience. Feeling the thrill of being alive and expressing my energy when I'm on stage. I had that experience in a high school production," she replied.

Write down this vital question: *Where is the joy?*

Answering this question helps you break free from previous patterns of thinking.

The idea of Free Yourself for Success is to think in a different way. The goal is to develop an entirely different pattern of thinking.

What you want to find is the element that creates the joy. When you know what creates joy for you, you can start experiencing that joy this week—on a small scale.

This week my client can sign up for an acting class. This week my client can borrow a video camcorder and practice a monologue in front of it.

It's important to get to the heart of the matter.

This reminds me of a time, some years ago, when I was directing a feature film. My cast and crew were on the set, which was an airport runway. This was before the September 11th tragedies, which is why my crew could be on a tarmac without any complications.

The heart of the matter for me when I'm directing is to keep everyone safe—and make a good movie. A stuntman was preparing to jump from an airplane before it left the runway. Everyone was unaware that the wing was headed straight for the cameraman's head. The plane's engines would drown out any possible warning. The cameraman was standing too tall. I had a split second to make a decision because no one else could help. A director is like a ship's captain, responsible for everyone's safety. I made my decision. I ran to the cameraman, grabbed him by the jacket and pulled him down. The wing sliced the air where our heads had been! What I learned that day was to keep a constant vigil and then act on what my intuition tells me. And I learned to keep focusing on the Heart of the Matter.

The first four questions of the Momentum Action Plan help you to access your True Self. To see how these elements fit together, let's look at this example:

Momentum Action Plan (MAP)—Partial Example

What do you want?

To complete writing my children's book.

No. Come on, what do you really want?

To uplift the lives of millions of people in ways similar to what Walt Disney did.

Better yet, what do you want to feel?

To feel really alive. To feel the exuberance, a warm, full feeling in my chest (touch) when audience members laugh (hear) while watching an animated feature film I directed. To see big smiles as audience members rise from their seats at the end of the film.

How can you experience the heart (core elements/the heart of the matter) on a small scale?

The heart of the matter is to enjoy the excitement of collaboration—when people come together and make a "whole" that is better than the sum of its parts. I can enjoy the process of working with the artist, and guiding her to illustrate my story. I can enjoy the happy surprises when she returns with sketches that improve upon my initial ideas!

Now is your opportunity to pull all this together (and write your answers in your personal journal):

Momentum Action Plan (MAP)—so far

What do you want?

No. Come on, what do you really want?

Better yet, what do you want to feel and note your impressions of See, Hear and Touch.

How can you experience the heart (core elements/the heart of the matter) on a small scale?

A Special Note about What You Want

When you consider what you want, take a moment to put aside your thoughts and feelings that hold you back—like putting them into a drawer. Imagine that the Genie from Aladdin is here. You can have anything you want if you just write the details into your Momentum Action Plan.

My point is that once you voice what you want to feel and write it out where you can see it, you have made a major leap forward toward getting what you want.

Unfortunately, many of us will need to counteract our impulses to guard against disappointment and to avoid wanting too much. Please know that life brings disappointment no matter what. Playing small does not safeguard us from experiencing disappointment. But playing small does prevent us from enjoying surges of excitement and feelings of fulfillment that come with pursuing our dreams.

On the other hand, things flow better when you allow yourself to imagine big possibilities, and the universe provides you with some terrific, surprise opportunities. For example, years ago, as I walked down the corridors of the university I graduated from,

I had a sudden feeling of *I want to teach.* Later, the father of one of the actors in a feature film I was directing alerted me to film-related group and website. Through that website, I learned of a possible teaching position at a particular college. At the time of this writing I have been teaching graduate students and college students for a over a decade.

The point of this story is to get in touch with what you want. When you do, you open the door to joyful possibilities.

Now, we are ready for the next question …

Momentum Action Plan (MAP)

Question 5: *How can you graduate up levels?*

First, let's look at an example of my client who wants to be an actor. As a novice actor, she can:

- Take an acting class.
- Participate in Community Theater.
- Get a headshot (photo) made.
- Audition for local commercials.
- Make her own digital film that she can edit using her home computer. Or she can utilize the filmmaking talents of students at a local college.

Someone starting a business can plan out the steps needed to achieve a goal—that is, climb up a step and graduate to the next level. Let's say this person wants to become a professional speaker who sells products on the Internet.

She can:

- *Level One:* Give a free talk to a local association. Record the talk with a video camera and attach a microphone to her collar for the audio component.
- *Level Two:* Take the audio recording from the speech and download it onto a home computer. Make three copies of the speech by recording it onto CDs.
- *Level Two (part 2):* Take the three CDs to the next speech she gives to see if they sell.
- *Level Three:* Make more copies if the initial three CDs sell.
- *Level Four:* Consider writing a book based on the topic of the CDs she has been selling.
- *Level Five:* Write a book proposal to submit to an agent (who will submit it to a publisher).
- *Level Five (alterative):* Self-publish the book.

A person who self-publishes his or her first book is in good company: Deepak Chopra, Edgar Allen Poe, Sigmund Freud and many others have done just that. In fact, author Christopher Paolini, when he was 19-years-old (and with his parents' help), self-published the book *Eragon*. This book was made into a major motion picture.

The idea is to rise upward step by step. The question is *How can you graduate up levels?* If you don't know what the levels are, you can get a coach or listen to educational audio programs. Also, review your answers to Questions 1 through 4 to help you understand what you truly want, and your feelings about those desires. Then create a concise plan that will help you reach your next levels.

In order to make progress you need to stretch your comfort zone a little. But the important thing is to ease into doing new activities, which is covered in our next section …

Momentum Action Plan (MAP)

Question 6: *How can you gain an Immediate Victory?*

The process for picking something that will be your Immediate Victory begins with preparation. Begin by writing down three easy things that will lead you in the direction of what you want. Make sure they're easy.

My clients have written:

- Do a Google search on the topic I'm interested in.
- Go to the bookstore and browse the books related to what I'm interested in.
- Get the book and read it for 15 minutes.

The Immediate Victory is a two-fold strategy: Focus on your successful action and then reward yourself for your accomplishment. When you begin with easy victories and rewards, you feel encouraged to progress toward your goal.

During one interview, the host of a show said her reward was chocolate.

"I suggest that you have a menu."

"Of chocolate?" she replied, with humor.

I'm suggesting various rewards—and definitely some that don't involve calories.

In addition to writing down three easy tasks, write the rewards you want—so you have something to anticipate.

Rewards my clients have written include:

- A hot bath
- A phone call with my best friend
- To read my favorite fiction book
- To listen to an MP3 of my favorite singer

A reward is a wonderful way to encourage you to take more and more steps toward your goal. Starting with something easy prevents you from procrastinating. Researchers note that procrastination comes from fear and the anticipation of pain. Taking easy steps first helps eliminate both fear and concerns about pain.

Ease Into Momentum by starting with something easy. Reward yourself for your success. When you do your inner child says: "YES! This is great. I'll give you the energy to do more of this."

Your inner child is the part of you that feels small and vulnerable and wants to play. I emphasize that a strategy of Emotional Leverage is to make space to take care of your inner child. Find ways to be good to yourself and to include fun as part of your day.

Momentum helps you keep going. *You free yourself for success when you Ease Into Momentum.*

I call this process *The Easy Part Start.* If you want to write a book, you can start with an easy task: writing the chapter titles.

That's what I do. Then I make a list of my anecdotes and a specific detail of research for each chapter.

The idea is to take action. Stop talking, and start doing.

Mother Teresa said, "There should be less talk; a preaching point is not a meeting point. What do you do then? Take a broom and clean someone's house. That says enough."

We are inspired to take a small step forward—The Easy Part Start. This reminds me of the old phrase: To know and not to do, is not to know. Let's take action ... and move on to the next question.

Momentum Action Plan (MAP)

Question 7: *How can you announce what you offer?*

Focusing on this question "How can you tell the world what you offer?" is a crucial step that many people leave out. There are those who would rather keep their heads down and just do their work. A number of artists and engineering-type people would prefer a world in which they just do a good job—and hope magically to get rewarded. But it doesn't work that way. People need to see you doing quality work.

In order to make your dreams come true you need to tell the world what you offer. And, the essence of telling the world is to clearly and concisely express what you're best known for. This is your personal brand.

The center of personal branding is this question, "*What am I best known for?*

When I think of *what am I best known for?* I think of this story Sam told in a job interview:

> "I was hired to be a unit production manager for a feature film. The screenplay called for a bus. But the budget was strained. We needed a public place so that the romantic leads could meet by happenstance. A bus would require rental fees, hiring an off-duty police officer, hiring a bunch of extras, feeding everyone, and getting costly permits. I suggested the solution of having the two people meet in an elevator. Then I suggested that we could build an inexpensive elevator set in a living room using two by fours. The face of the producer lit up with relief. She told me, "Sam, I can always count on you to solve a problem with creativity and to guard the budget. Good work."

So what do you think Sam is best known for? The answer is in the producer's comment. In essence, Sam solves problems with creativity and he guards the budget.

Sharing a story illustrates a desired characteristic, and this is a vital part of your personal brand.

Here are the elements of your personal brand:

- The answer to "what am I best known for?"
- A story that moves emotions
- A label
- A soundbite

Here's how Sam's might fill in his personal brand elements:

What am I best known for?

Solving problems with creativity and guarding the budget.

A story that moves emotions

Sam solves the problem for completing the feature film.

A label

Sam is a creative solution finder.

A soundbite

"Sam, I can always count on you to solve a problem with creativity and to guard the budget."

Find ways to effectively show what you offer. That's what Elijah Wood did when he wanted to play Frodo in the feature film trilogy *The Lord Of The Rings*. He had a friend videotape him wearing Hobbit clothes and doing an English accent. Elijah sent the videotape to the director Peter Jackson. That's how Elijah Wood came to star in the world-famous epic. By the way, *The Lord of the Rings III: The Return of the King* is the first fantasy movie in history to win Best Picture at the Academy Awards!

Remember that other people may influence the things you want:

- There's a job you want.
- There's funding you want.
- There's a movie role you want.

You need to effectively tell people what you offer.

That's the magic of an effective personal brand. Here are examples:

- My personal brand is Tom Marcoux, America's Communication Coach.
- Anthony Robbins calls himself America's Results Coach.
- Mark Victor Hansen uses the phrase America's Ambassador of Possibility.

A personal brand works in job interviews.

In a job interview, one of my clients used the phrase: "At XY Company, I was the go-to person for computers."

A personal brand makes you memorable. In a job interview a person could say: "I was called the Captain of Cost-cutting."

The idea is to give the interviewer the words she will repeat to her colleagues.

The interviewer will say, "Yes, Janet Smith is impressive. You know, she was known as the Captain of Cost-cutting at XY Company."

A personal brand involves a powerful story that moves emotions. For a job interview, plan to tell a story about how you saved the day using your skills or talents.

A personal brand quickly helps people get to know and trust you. It makes you stand out from other people.

Your personal brand improves your website.

In my audio program *Online Secrets to Build Your Brand*, I help my clients create a powerful personal brand that they present on their websites. I teach them to design their websites to provide visitors with a quick overview of who they are and what their services provide.

Websites need to answer the following questions that a web visitor has:

- *Question 1:* Who are you?
- *Question 2:* How can you help me?
- *Question 3:* How can you show you me that you're an expert?
- *Question 4:* How can you show me that you're trustworthy?
- *Question 5:* Why must I take action now? (It's best when you design a hyperlink that entices the web visitor to click immediately.)

Researchers have noted that people decide to leave a website within four seconds after arriving on a webpage—if their interest isn't grabbed immediately. Webmasters need to seize the attention of the web visitor. The above questions help them improve the design of their website—and attract visitors who will stay longer than four seconds. In the Internet world, establishing a personal brand is how to gain the visitor's trust and the person's business. In this way, prosperity can be expanded.

Here's another example of a personal brand: Tom Marcoux, The Personal Branding Instructor, as identified by *The San Francisco Examiner*. This example, which gives much more information about me, is almost similar to an endorsement.

Your personal brand needs to be true.

You need to be able to back up your personal brand with expertise. For example, my website has the domain name TomSuperCoach.com. When I started using that domain name I knew my friends and colleagues in the speaking industry would tease me about it. And they did send emails teasingly addressed to "Hey SuperCoach." Or, "Hello SuperTom."

There is a solution to the teasing: Live up to your personal brand. My domain name, TomSuperCoach.com, has proven to work because:

- I study everyday.
- I put in significant effort to provide helpful, effective coaching to my clients.
- I have a track record of guiding clients, audiences and readers to great results for over two decades.

Another point is the domain name of TomSuperCoach.com solves an important problem when I appear on television and radio. One TV host asked, "How does our audience get in contact with you?" When I replied "TomMarcoux.com," the host asked, "How do you spell Marcoux?" This is why my team came up with TomSuperCoach.com.

Problem solved, and a personal brand was created.

Your personal brand is the method to effectively tell the world what you offer.

Momentum Action Plan (MAP)

Question 8: *Say: "I want <goal> & my obstacle is <impediment>"*

In my workshops, I hear audience members say:

- I want to start a business, but my obstacle is no money.
- I want to act and win an Oscar award, but my obstacle is I don't know anyone in the movie industry.

In some of my speeches I show a graphic with a STOP sign. I change it into a START sign with just three letters: A-R-T. The art of making a breakthrough is to connect with people, ask questions, and get new ideas.

Now it's your turn. Fill in the blanks and write this down:

I want <goal or desire> and my obstacle [to getting what I want] is <impediment>.

The idea is to talk to people about your goal—after you have taken some action steps in the right direction.

When you talk about your goal, you might hear someone say something like: "Oh, my cousin Stephen is an agent in Los Angeles."

One interviewer asked me, "How can I tell people what I want and the obstacle in front of it without sounding desperate?" I replied, "It's a matter of tone and timing. First, you listen to the other person. When you're listening, you're making rapport. Then, when the person asks 'What do you do?' you can reply with something like, 'At the moment, I'm a teacher. But what

I'm really focusing on is moving my writing career forward. My obstacle is that I'm looking for a literary agent."

Here is an example of how connecting with one person can blossom into a big opportunity. When I began making films, many years ago, I didn't know anyone. To get started in the industry, I wrote a screenplay that I showed to a software engineer who passed it to another engineer. It then went to a real estate developer and finally to the California Motion Picture Commissioner. Three years later, when I directed my first feature film, the California Motion Picture Commissioner became my Associate Producer. He secured for me an airport and airplane—for free—for the film's production.

Remember to prepare so you can clearly express:

> I want <goal or desire> and my obstacle [to getting what I want] is <impediment>.

Momentum Action Plan (MAP)

Question 9: *Ask, "Give me suggestions, leads, wild ideas?"*

To ask for suggestions, leads and wild ideas is an important part of getting a breakthrough. We need to get new ideas. We need the input of other people.

Participants in my workshops and seminars learn powerful ideas by sharing with each other.

Ask for input or feedback. *Ask someone. Ask Higher Power.*

The next process is something that I teach to my college students. I use a process I call *Choice Market Testing*™.

To get productive feedback, show someone two versions of something you're working on and ask these two questions in this sequence:

1. Which one do you prefer?
2. What about <the person's preference> grabs your attention?

Ask for help from Higher Power.

Jack Canfield came up with the title for his bestselling series *Chicken Soup for the Soul* by asking for God's help. He asked God to awaken him the next morning with bestselling titles. He woke up with the phrase "Chicken Soup for the Spirit" in his mind.

Remember to ask for help. A number of millionaires have said, "Wealth is a team sport."

Momentum Action Plan (MAP)

Question 10: *Write due dates next to items on your list*

We have now come to the final step in your Momentum Action Plan: Write a due date next to important items on your MAP. This is crucial. Remember this old phrase: A goal without a due date is just a wish.

This reminds me of a time when I was directing a feature film. When I'm directing a feature film, believe me, I'm under timeline constraints.

Here's the situation: I am on the set when a little 8-year-old actress, Kim, is expected to arrive at any moment. While I'm talking with my director of photography, a crew member calls out, "Kim's here."

I turn around, and my jaw hits the floor. There is Kim, with her timid little smile and a HUGE cast on her thumb. Broken thumbs were not in the script! So I tell everyone to Take 5, which means five minutes. I really want to say take five hours because I don't know what to do. So I sit down to rewrite the script. I immediately stand up and pace—trying to figure out what to do. After a while I come up with an idea.

I call the cast and crew to the set. The rewritten scene includes two brothers talking to each other. One brother is the father of Kim's character. The father had left the little girl in the care of his older brother. The older brother, disgusted with his brother's unchecked alcoholism, says, "Just in case you're interested, Kim broke her thumb!" Furious, the father pulls his fist back to slug his brother. Of course, the father is interested in his daughter's health! Just then Kim runs in, broken thumb and all, and says, "Daddy!"

I was relieved that my quick solution made the film better. When making a film, the director needs to adhere to a budget and schedule. In essence, the director has a due date every day in that a certain number of scenes must be filmed each day.

Having a due date makes you get creative. It helps you charge up with energy.

Conclusion of Chapter Three

In Part II, you learned to make powerful plans so your daily steps will help you expand prosperity. Additionally, you applied the Leverage Triangle™ System. With the first four questions you learned to access your True Self. With questions five through ten you implemented the final steps of the Leverage Triangle. The Leverage Triangle is:

- Merge with your True Self
- Strategize
- Act

The Leverage Triangle is the cure for situations in which people try new strategies and then find themselves falling back on old habits.

The problem with traditional training is that it focuses on the methods or strategy first. And the truth is you don't want to start on the outside. It's inside you where the energy comes from. So that's where you begin. You don't start with the method; you start with you. That's the first step of The Leverage Triangle—Merge with your True Self.

Furthermore, by filling in the details of the Momentum Action Plan (MAP), you have gone through the 9-Minute Miracle Breakthrough—although the training process probably took more than nine minutes. However, going forward, now that you know the process you can complete the Momentum Action Plan for your week or month in nine minutes or less. You can make copies of the blank Momentum Action Plan form, which appears after the filled-in example (see the next page).

Momentum Action Plan (MAP)

(An example)

1. What do you want?

To complete my children's book which will lead to an animated feature film.

2. No. Come on, what do you really want?

To uplift the lives of millions of people in ways similar to what Walt Disney did.

3. Better yet, what do you want to feel?

See: *The smiling faces of an audience watching the animated film I directed.*

Hear: *The applause of an audience during the closing credits of the film.*

Touch: *To shake hands with people who buy the children's book that accompanies the film.*

I want to feel really alive. I want to feel the exuberance when audience members laugh while watching my animated feature film.

4. How can you experience the HEART (core elements/the heart of the matter) on a small scale?

The heart of the matter is to enjoy the excitement of collaboration—when people come together and make a "whole" that is better than the sum of the parts. I can enjoy the process of working with the artist, and guiding her to illustrate my story. I can enjoy the happy surprises when she returns with sketches that improve upon my initial ideas!

5. How can you graduate up levels?

Level One: *Complete my children's book and make 25 copies.*

Level Two: *Obtain an agent and seek a publisher to publish a version of my book on a massive scale.*

Level Three: *Prepare for an animated feature—including storyboards and a budget.*

Level Four: *Seek to expand my circle of contacts and leads.*

6. How can you do something easy and gain an Immediate Victory?

Go to Amazon.com and find a book on preparing an animated feature film. My reward can be an hour in a warm bath with soothing music.

7. How can you tell the world what you offer? (personal branding)

Come up with a soundbite to describe the children's book. Come up with a memorable domain name.

8. Say: "I want <goal or desire> and my obstacle is <impediment>." (Tell someone.)

I want to produce and direct an animated feature film. My obstacle is to find funding sources.

9. Ask: "Please give me suggestions, leads, and wild ideas." (Ask someone. Ask Higher Power.)

Contact an association that supports uplifting media projects and ask them for the names of people who help film projects gain funding and support.

10. Write a due date next to an item on your list.

On March 19, 20__, I will contact the media association toward gaining contacts and leads.

The next two pages are a blank form for you to fill in.

Momentum Action Plan (MAP)

To help you stay on track, complete this process on a weekly or monthly basis.

1. What do you want?

2. No. Come on, what do you really want?

3. Better yet, what do you want to feel?

   See:

   Hear:

   Touch:

4. How can you experience the HEART (core elements/the heart of the matter) on a small scale?

5. How can you graduate up levels?

6. How can you do something easy and gain an Immediate Victory?

7. How can you tell the world what you offer? (Give details of personal branding.)

8. Say: "I want <goal or desire> and my obstacle [to getting what I want] is <impediment>." (Tell someone.)

9. Ask: "Please give me suggestions, leads and wild ideas." (Ask someone. Ask Higher Power.)

10. Write a due date next to an item on your list.

©2011 Tom Marcoux, TomSuperCoach.com

4

Prosperity is Founded on Relationships

Great Relationships Expand Financial Abundance

In Chapter Two, you learned the tools you need to wake up your spirit to prosperity. Then, in Chapter Three, you learned to make plans to take powerful daily steps to create more prosperity in your life.

Now in Chapter Four, we focus on how to build and warm up your relationships through inspiring humor and laughter. When you're at your best during the *10 Seconds to Wealth,* you are enhancing relationships, which create the opportunities for wealth you desire. Humor is an important component. "Laughter is the closest distance between two people," said comedian Victor Borge.

The important thing to realize is this: *Real financial abundance is built on great relationships.* We often hear about the "big break," and many times that opportunity comes from a good relationship established years earlier. When you are committed to expanding prosperity, you are committed to improving your relationship-building skills. Here's an example:

On the set of a major motion picture, the Assistant Director was sweating bullets. Any delay meant $100,000 was being lost in wages, equipment rental and crew salaries. The Assistant Director turned to his crew members and, in a light tone, said, "Come on guys, let's pick it up a bit. You've got me looking at the Want Ads." The crew members moved faster, and the filming day was saved. Just the right tone and humorous words did the trick.

Learning to add humor helps you:

1. *Lead a team.* To create more abundance, we often find that we must become a leader of a team. "A sense of humor is part of the art of leadership, of getting along with people, of getting things done," said President Dwight D. Eisenhower.

2. *Inspire people.* Leaders need to inspire people. Great leaders use humor to build a community. "Laughter is the sun that drives winter from the human face," wrote statesman and novelist Victor Hugo.

3. *Improve your daily life.* "Humor is the great thing, the saving thing. The minute it crops up, all our irritations and resentments slip away and a sunny spirit takes their place," wrote Mark Twain.

4. *Enjoy giving and receiving love.* "We cannot really love anybody with whom we never laugh," noted writer Agnes Repplier.

5. *Diffuse anger.* "You cannot be mad at somebody who makes you laugh—it's as simple as that," said Jay Leno.

6. *Become resilient.* "Life is tough, and if you have the ability to laugh at it you have the ability to enjoy it," said Salma Hayek. Also, Albert Camus wrote, "In the depth of winter I finally learned that there was in me an invincible summer."

7. *Create a spiritual connection with people.* "Among those whom I like or admire, I can find no common denominator, but among those whom I love, I can: all of them make me laugh," emphasized poet W. H. Auden.

We can communicate well and create warmth in our relationships when we use humor to support our efforts. Often we hear, "She was a great speaker." Why? "Because she was funny, and she told great stories."

Here are methods to help you use humor. Humor is not merely telling jokes. Often, humor arises when emphasizing certain details in a story. Human beings are built to appreciate stories. An old phrase holds: "God created people because God wanted to hear stories." This chapter is based on my presentation, *Get Connected through Humor*.

Appropriate humor can warm up and deepen a relationship. We use the H.U.M.O.R. process:

H – Honor the personality style
U – Understand that no humor bit works for everyone
M – Mirror the person's humor preference
O – Open the door
R – Respect the person and environment

H—Honor the personality style

Our goal is to create rapport with other people. Before you use certain humor-creating methods, note the personality style of the person you are addressing. Here is an example of a behavior to avoid:

One time at an office supply store, the clerk made a client Stephen wait for a while, and then short-changed him. The manager was nearby and said, "Oh, that's how we get the money to order lunch." His attempt at humor completely broke a possible rapport with Stephen. Neither the clerk nor manager said, "I'm sorry for causing you inconvenience." That would have been appreciated because Stephen was under a deadline and lots of pressure. It would have been better if the manager had been respectful during their first encounter. Although his attempt at humor might have been well-intended, the manager's method of handling the situation was not appreciated. It would have been better to begin with an apology.

Part II, Chapter 4   Prosperity is Founded on Relationships • 141

U—Understand that no humor bit works for everyone

No item of humor works on all people. It helps to have ways to bounce back when the humor does not work. For example, once when speaking to over 300 people, I made a comment: "I wonder how Captain Kirk would handle this. Mr. Spock, raise the 'stress' shields." Some laughter. Still, I felt that my humor bit missed the mark. Then I said, "I guess that one was for the Trekkies." More laughter. That saved the moment. I generated two moments of laughter.*

M—Mirror the person's humor preference

Roger Dawson, author of *The Secrets of Power Persuasion*, identifies five patterns of humor. And I will supply my example for each pattern:

- *Exaggeration:* A friend told me about a time when she was staying in a particular apartment building. She told someone: 'If these cockroaches get any bigger, I'll have to put them on a leash!'
- *Putdowns:* "And then Joe said, 'A martial artist? He couldn't kung-fu his way out of a paper bag!' " (I personally avoid putdown humor because it can cause trouble and hurt feelings.)

----

* Yes, I know that *Star Trek* fans prefer the term "Trekkers." For non-fans and to facilitate the humor bit, I had to use the other word.

- *Puns:* I stand at work. The agony of the feet. (defeat)
- *Silliness:* In The Pink Panther, Peter Sellers does pratfalls.
- *Surprise:* Henny Youngman said, "Take my wife—please!"

Listen to the other person's preferences in humor. I have a friend who is a software engineer, and he loves wordplay. He is the only person I share puns with.

O—Open the door

Listen carefully to how the other person responds to something with a humorous tint. To open the door to humor: In the beginning, try small, gentle humor items. Perhaps, you might share an innocent cartoon from a local newspaper. See if the person chuckles, smiles, or fails to respond.

R—Respect the person and environment

I advise against using profanity. To many people, the only sure-fire environment where profanity usually fits in is a stand-up comedy nightclub. When using profanity outside a nightclub, be sensitive about the environment and the personalities that are present.

30 Secrets for Creating Humor

Secret 1: Prepare the Stage

In my college classes, I say a few things to help the students realize that appropriate humor will be part of my presentations. I mention that "humor will walk into the class at times, and go running out."

Secret 2: Notice that timing is acquired through practice

The secret to creating humor is to practice on safe audiences. Practice your humor on your loved ones and friends. Choose someone with whom you have a high comfort level. It is helpful to practice because successful expressions of humor require smoothness and comfort on your part.

Secret 3: Gain timing through subconscious modeling

We learned to talk through subconscious modeling when we heard our parents talk. Through them we modeled our behaviors.

Now the question is this: How do you get comedic timing working for you subconsciously? Learn from stand-up comedians and by watching romantic comedy movies. When you're watching and enjoying these programs, you are subconsciously modeling the behavior of the comedians.

Secret 4: Play with words

When I visited the Comedy Warehouse in Walt Disney World, I witnessed comedians making up improvised humor. A comedian interviewed an audience member who met her fiancée through the Internet. The comedy troupe sang songs with these phrases:

- In Amsterdam—we'll go Dutch.
- She caught him in her net (Internet)
- You got a male (you got mail)

Secret 5: Use a good setup

At the Comedy Warehouse, the comedy troupe sang improvised songs. We, the audience, were told that the performance was improvised. However, as a comedy writer, I could see the pre-set structures. The performers knew certain music passages. The piano player had to know the pre-set song patterns. Also, the performers were using certain pre-set rhythms that I'm sure they practiced and rehearsed. Still, the audience laughed more and more because it was set up to believe that the performers were performing without a net.

Secret 6: Base humor on a song pattern

Some years ago, a friend and I waited and waited for a table at a restaurant. We were starving. I remembered the song by the rock band, Queen: "We will, we will rock you." Then, I sang to my friend, "We will, we will grovel!" I mimed begging for food.

Secret 7: Create a running joke based on the situation

In the situation when my friend and I were starving and waiting at the particular restaurant, I created three spontaneous bits of humor. The running joke was being hungry. The humor came from my voicing some exaggerated reactions to the hunger.

Secret 8: Base humor on icons, like *Star Wars*

While starving and waiting at the restaurant, I reminded my friend of a situation in *Star Wars: Episode IV: A New Hope* (the first one in 1977). Obi-wan Kenobi, the Jedi Knight, had used the Force to change people's minds. He said, "These aren't the 'droids you're looking for." Succumbing to Obi-wan's power, the Stormtrooper replied, "Uh, these aren't the 'droids we're looking for."

Since my friend and I were still waiting to be served lunch, I made the connection that we wanted the waiter (like a hypnotized Stormtrooper) to bring us our food. I said (like I was Obi-wan Kenobi): "You want to bring Tom and Sarah the food right now." Then, I said, like I was the waiter, "Oh, we're bringing the food right now." And the food arrived within seconds!

Secret 9: Enjoy understatement

At Walt Disney World, I watched a film about the art of animation. One animator who was balding and round said, "I was given Phil (in Hercules) to animate. He's short. He's bald. He's kind of fat. It's a stretch for me." Laughter rose from the audience. It was a triumph of understatement.

Secret 10: Tie-in experiences shared by the audience

At the Comedy Warehouse at Walt Disney World, a woman hesitated giving a book to a comedian. The comedian said, "You've got to give it back. There's nothing free at Disney." The crowd roared with laughter.

Secret 11: Choose a good target (perhaps yourself)

Denis Waitley, the best-selling author of *The Psychology of Winning*, uses himself as the target of humor. He speaks about the missteps he took when young and caught up in his Ego. He talks about when he was a fighter pilot. He says, "I mowed the lawn in my flight suit—so the neighbors knew who they were living next to."

Secret 12: Remember to use context well

"There's nothing free at Disney" works so well because the audience spent (and I do mean *spent*) a whole day at Walt Disney World. This reminds me of a comment bouncing around the Internet: "Disney World is a people trap invented by a mouse." (As a sidenote: I really enjoy myself at Disney theme parks, so my comments are only intended as gentle humor.)

Secret 13: The Power-3 (context, structure, imposition)

The successful use of humor is about using effective patterns. Let's continue with the example "There's nothing free at Disney." *Context:* People spend money all day at Disney theme parks. *Structure:* The last word makes the joke funny. *Imposition:* The audience has feelings about being imposed upon by the pricing of Disney related items.

Secret 14: Twist a familiar phrase

Change a word and you make something funny. "Eat, drink and be merry, for tomorrow we economize." The original phrase is "Eat, drink and be merry, for tomorrow we die."

Secret 15: Set up the last word to have punch

Notice the last word in this example: "Take my wife—please!"

Secret 16: Go on a riff

A riff is a musical solo or a spontaneous improvisation. Here is an example: I was walking through Universal Studios, Florida, when I heard a rock and roll version of a classic Christmas song, "Oh, Holy Night." As my friend Sarah and I were listening to the song's phrase *Fall on your knees,* I said:

"That phrase Fall on your knees is one of the most powerful phrases in music—but not today.

"The melody is here; and the singer's somewhere over there.

"This is Sam's mother's favorite song. If she heard this version—she'd puke."

Let's notice that I went up the scale of intensity. I finished with an extreme word—puke.

Secret 17: Use the Magic of Three

In the above example we see the humor is structured in a pattern of three. The first statement sets up the situation. The second statement continues it. And the third statement twists the situation into a surprising direction.

Secret 18: Use the magic of the reoccurring joke

I once made a good rapport with a participant at a seminar. Because Joe demonstrated a good sense of humor, I made him the focus of some comments. He asked about the 15 judgments, a person makes about another person—which I call the four second barrier. I replied, "Someone meets you and thinks: nice suit, nice tie, needs Rogaine." Through the rest of the evening the comment about Joe's bald head became a reoccurring joke. Later I said, "What are the five forms of humor?" Joe replied, "Vicious"—and got a big laugh. I bowed Joe's way and said, "Forgive me."

Secret 19: Carefully use cynical humor

In the waiting area of the thrill ride Terminator 2: 3D at Universal Studios, Florida, TV monitors show mock commercials for the fictional company Cyberdyne (which, with no social conscience, created dangerous technology that destroys Terminator's world). The Cyberdyne commercial had a slogan: "We care so you don't have to."

Secret 20: Integrate current topics

One year, I witnessed the gruesome make-up show at Universal Studios. A goofy special-effects teacher discussed the then just-released remake of the movie *The Mummy*. He said, "The prince is sealed in a tomb of flesh-eating Pokemon." The audience laughed with glee.

Secret 21: Make fun of a safe target

While standing in line for the thrill ride Terminator 2: 3D at Universal Studios, my friend and I (and the crowd) became tired of waiting. An actress came out and played the role of the public relations person for Cyberdyne, the unfeeling corporation that created the humanity-crushing technology. The actress played the part well. Her character spoke in phony, ingratiating tones—and had a grating habit of saying, "Superrr." At one point she said, "No applause necessary." I said to my friend, "And none will be heard."

Secret 22: Put in an Act Out moment

An Act Out moment is when the humorist acts out his routine instead of just standing and telling the story. A comedian who Acts Out another person will change his voice and posture to help the audience see the character. For example, if I was talking about a conceited CEO, I might perform (Act Out) his character. I would cross my arms, send my nose up into the air, and speak in a haughty tone. I would say: "I am a CEO. I know everything, I see everything, and I get indicted for everything."

Secret 23: Tie in the visual

At the Universal Studios gruesome make-up show, the goofy, special effects teacher pulled out a mannequin that looked like a shark had eaten half its body. He said, "This is Barbie. We have a special on Barbie today—half-off." The audience rocked with laughter.

When on vacation in the South of France, one of my friends heard another traveler commenting on vacationers' tendency to overeat. The traveler said, "If I eat any more I'll have to grease my legs to get my pants on."

Secret 24: Rehearse your choice of words before telling a story

Often a good story sounds better with concise words. Rehearse key phrases. Here is an example:

A man was getting tired of his wife always saying "Turn around, I think I left the iron on" when they were driving away, leaving for their annual trip. The next year, like clockwork, she waited until they were two miles away from home. She said, "Go back, I think I left the iron on." At a stoplight, the man pulled the iron from beneath his seat.

Notice how the story is told with few words.

Secret 25: Use similar sounds

One time on vacation, I turned to my loved one and said, "Ahh, what a sight to see: A flamingo doing the flamenco." She chuckled.

Secret 26: Use rhythm

Rhythm is a helpful component in humor. Here is an example expressed in the book, *The Healing Power of Humor*. Joan, a hospital nurse said, "I'm a body scratcher, patcher, wire attacher and bed pan snatcher."

Secret 27: Note goofy items from the newspaper

An essay contest in England entitled *Buy Britain* gave out prizes: radios made in Japan.

Secret 28: When speaking, use topic-oriented cartoons

When giving a presentation, it's easiest to warm up the room by placing cartoons on an overhead projector at the start of your talk. In this way, you don't have to worry about finding the right joke to set the tone of your presentation.

Secret 29: Use a label as you tell a story

I was coaching a client who wanted to make her story funnier. She mentioned a mean teacher at school who ate wasabe (the Japanese horseradish condiment). I suggested she label him Wasabe-breath.

Secret 30: Ad-lib in the moment

At a hospital, giving a presentation on *Say YES to Yourself: Successful Strategies for Conflict and Change in the Workplace*, I talked about working with a blunt, hard-charging director. In the moment, I improvised this comment: "Tell the bottom-line Director, 'The patients are still alive. It's a good day.' " The audience laughed.

Abundance is Built on Great Relationships

We warm up and deepen relationships with appropriate humor. Becoming skillful with expressing humor is worth every effort you make. For example, for years I have shown a particular film clip to my students of my college course Science Fiction and Fantasy. The film clip is a scene from the feature film *The Abyss*, directed by James Cameron. The lead character "Bud," portrayed by Ed Harris, is introduced while he leads his team. He gently, and with humor says, "Hey Harry. Do me a favor, will ya? Square away this mud hose, get rid of some of these empty sacks. This place is starting to look like my apartment."

Bud uses humor to guide his team members to keep the work area safe.

My students consistently say that they like Bud. And this illustrates my point: appropriate humor warms up relationships. With better relationships, you wake up your spirit to prosperity. For example, this book was completed with editing work from some of my friends. One I have known and trusted for twenty-two years, and the other for twenty-six years. And yes, we laugh together often.

Try experimenting with various forms of humor. Practice on safe audiences.

Part III

5

Wake Up Your Spirit to Prosperity for Couples

How often does your heart whisper: "I want more romance, money and fun"?

In this section you will learn Seven Powerful Steps to create the life you really want, including an abundance of time and money, spiritual fulfillment and loving relationships.

Through my work with individuals and couples, I have noticed that using the right method at the right time is like dispersing the clouds and casting sunlight on your path toward prosperity.

Before working with me, Stephen and Maria argued about money. And Maria had given up hope. By using the methods in this book, Stephen learned to cherish Maria like a princess, and Maria learned to help Stephen feel like a hero. Resentments flowed away, and they became a Prospering Couple.

As a success coach, I help clients and audiences stretch and nurture their spirits during the process. I can do the same for you.

What makes this section different from others is that I combine both the spiritual and practical approaches to wealth.

This section will show you how to get the support you need from your partner. It will also place you both on the same page regarding prosperity. This section helps in these situations:

- You are the proactive partner and you're reading this book on your own.

- You and your partner are reading this book together (or both have a copy and discuss it once a week).

- You are currently single and training yourself to be a good partner in order to attract a suitable mate.

To optimize each of these situations, each section ends with:

- Couple's Action Step
- Individual's Action Step
- Principle
- Leverage Question

These chapter sections are important because this section helps you take action, which is the only way to truly expand the prosperity in your life. During your *10 Seconds to Wealth,* you need to act effectively and that activity requires that you condition yourself to be at your best.

> *Fortune favors the prepared mind.*
> LOUIS PASTEUR

You will learn techniques to see opportunities and refresh yourself to move past tough times.

The couple that wants to get out of a financial rut needs to focus time and attention on their Couple's Prosperity.

Prosperity is more than money; it includes inner peace. MerriamWebster.com defines prosperity as "the condition of being successful or thriving; especially economic well-being."

This book incorporates spiritual and practical methods to increase wealth. Also, in this section, I will guide you to increase the romance and flow of abundance in your relationship.

You can feel inner peace while you experience the ups and downs necessary to increase your personal wealth and fulfillment.

In Chapter Six, you will learn practical methods to create confidence—both in yourself and your partner.

In Chapter Seven, you will learn how to work as a team to make breakthroughs to more joy and wealth in your relationship.

To manifest what you truly want, you need to change your focus and wake up your spirit. Prosperity consciousness essentially means being awake. For example, many of us experience great suffering concerning issues of money, prosperity and scarcity. Some don't realize that their financial details are part of their spiritual path. Spirituality includes the process of giving and receiving value. And prosperity is more than just money.

This section talks about spiritual growth and full employment of your natural brilliance, that is, your gifts from Higher

Power. (Please select the name that you prefer; some readers might prefer the name God, for example).

For our discussion, we will use the process: C.O.U.P.L.E.

> C – Create (not compete)
> O – Organize for Hope
> U – Use Momentum
> P – Practice Compassion
> L – Let Go of What's Not Working
> E – Energize to Serve

The above methods are necessary for couples to achieve prosperity. Each method will be explained in detail in the following sections.

You can turn your life into a positive adventure that includes more prosperity.

Create (Not Compete)

Author Mark Goulston, M.D., wrote: "Most women want to be cherished and most men want to be admired." This can translate into "cherish me like a princess" and "admire me like a hero."

The difficulty is that the longer a relationship lasts, the more likely disagreeable characteristics have surfaced, or events have occurred. The Prospering Couple must devote time and attention to create opportunities so that each partner gets what he or she needs: to be cherished or admired. This creates harmony, which wakes up our spirit.

With my clients I emphasize "Create (not compete)" because, to open the floodgates of abundance, we need to create personal energy. When I say "create," I mean set up situations in which our personal energy is enhanced.

We need energy to do things we have never done before. That's how we'll enjoy more prosperity. And in a couple, the partners need to support each other to create the best person each can become. Toward that end, in my workshops, I have couples complete the *25 Ways You Can Help Me Feel Loved List,* which they then give to their partner. The list reveals how their partner can become more supportive and loving. It also acknowledges that each partner is personally responsible for appreciating the good parts of his or her own life.

At this point, it is good for each partner to fill in a copy of the following list (in your personal journal) ... *25 Ways You Can Help Me Feel Loved List.*

After filling in this list, share it with your partner. This 25 Ways list is a powerful process to increase feelings of romance in your relationship.

Certainly, your 25 Ways list can create good feelings in your partner. But the truth is that we need to take care of our own personal energy. Toward that end, I have clients write a different list entitled the *10 Blessings List.*

You can change how you feel with one idea:

"I am grateful for ... "

Next, write a list of your own 10 Blessings—that is, 10 things you are grateful for. A personal journal is a handy place for your list.

With these two lists you have begun the process to create good feelings on a daily basis.

You can use these two lists by working on a point (or detail) per day. The great thing about the 25 Ways list is that it is like a menu of your partner's preferred dinner selections. It helps to provide what your partner likes—as often as possible.

This simple practice truly increases romance and good feelings.

The Prospering Couple also makes sure to share their values and goals with each other. At this point, each partner fills out the list on the next page.

My Personal Values and Goals

What I would do if I knew I would not fail:

One of the most important parts of my life is … (if this part were missing, it would break my heart):

What I'm working on now to improve my life:

What I have learned from hard experience:

I am proud of myself for:

I am afraid of:

What I want to do to make things better in my life:

What I can do to dissolve some of my fears:

Using the lists you just completed, have a conversation with your partner and share your thoughts and feelings.

The next step is to create a bridge to each other.

Here is a story that illustrates the process …

Legend of the Bridge

A married couple owned a farm that had a long river running through it. Years ago, they had built a bridge in order to connect the sections of their farm.

By habit, it became the woman's job to tend the far side of the farm, across the bridge. And she hated it—although she never shared this with her husband.

But also by habit the couple allowed themselves to be too busy to share their feelings with each other. Inside they both felt like they were drifting apart.

One day the woman was working on a section of the farm across the bridge when a natural dam collapsed. A flash flood crashed down the river and through the bridge—taking most of it away. The man yelled frantically to his wife. He reassured her that he would get help.

The man ran to the Wise One of the village. Knowing his wife was safe because there was shelter and food where she was, the Wise One simply gave the man a saw.

Over the next days the man and woman rebuilt the bridge and moved closer toward each other. As they worked, they talked. One day the woman said, "You know, I hate working on this side of our farm."

"I didn't know that," the man replied.

After four days they completed the bridge and joyfully embraced each other.

They then created a new tradition: They would have a picnic near the bridge each week. During their weekly get together, they shared their feelings, and together they planned their future. They decided to rotate working on the far side of the farm. They felt closer now than ever before.

The Wise One mysteriously appeared and said, "Keep on building your bridge. You do the work of love, and you enjoy love's wonders."

From this "legend" we learn to create the emotional bridge that can bless a romantic partnership. Supportive conversation is needed.

The "legends" in this book are parables that I have authored. I chose the label of "legend" to give us the feeling that the stories have a element of timeless wisdom.

Build or strengthen the bridge between you and your partner. Heartfelt talking and sharing make up the bridge's material.

The Prospering Couple learns to handle competition.

Sometimes, couples find that certain habits of thinking or talking are actually competitive in nature. These competitive habits are destructive toward a relationship.

Now, we're going to talk about competing and how to transform destructive habits.

A number of people say: "I'm not competitive. I never liked competitive games." I have heard my clients make this point. You might recognize the following statements.

- "You don't spend enough time with me."
- "You're ignoring the kids."
- "You always make time for your best friend."

These phrases have an element of competition to them. Note that one partner is attempting to push the other person. One partner is trying to control how the other uses his or her time.

On the other hand, we can be creative and convey the important message in a gentle way.

Transform *you don't spend enough time with me* into this empowering question: "How about I meet you for lunch on Tuesday?"

Transform *you're ignoring little Joey* into this supportive question: "Hey, I had an idea. I can do the laundry on Saturday morning, and you can take Joey to breakfast. How's that sound?"

Transform you *always make time for your best friend* into this empowering Question "I miss you. How about I meet you at your office at 6 PM, and I'll treat you to dinner? Does Wednesday work for you?"

This process of transforming competitive (or controlling) language into gentle suggestions leads toward a more empowered partnership.

When there is discomfort, find a way to be creative.

This is part of what we're emphasizing with the phrase: Create (not compete).

Unfortunately, competing is a Destructive Default Setting in many people. A Destructive Default Setting is a pattern that includes a trigger and a reaction behavior that is set in one's childhood.

For example, as a child, Sam was repeatedly rejected by his older brother and kept out of his older brother's activities with friends. Sam felt deeply hurt by this. His self-esteem plummeted, and each time he was rejected it threatened any self-respect he might have felt. As a child, he learned that he was "not good enough" to be included in his brother's activities. And Sam learned to bury his painful feelings in anger and now reacts by becoming aggressive when he feels threatened in any way.

For instance, at dinnertime, Sam's wife Helen says, "Honey, we still need to fix the screen on the bathroom window." In a huff he gets up from the dinner table and runs to the bathroom to fix the screen. Not having fixed the screen is interpreted by Sam's subconscious mind as proof that he is not good enough and not organized enough. Sam's Destructive Default Setting is to hear his wife's request and then translate it in his feelings as a threat to his self-esteem. Sam does not feel safe because in his subconscious mind, he is only safe when he proves that he is "good enough."

In a couple's therapy session, Sam and Helen realize that this is Sam's Destructive Default Setting.

But just having an insight and then saying a simple affirmation often is not enough to transform a deep-seated pattern formed in childhood.

To solve the problem of arguments that occur because of Sam's Destructive Default Setting, we have two levels of empowering behaviors.

Level One: Helen becomes skillful in how she presents situations.

Helen now gives Sam some time off. She keeps a journal and writes down items that need to be done. She avoids presenting tasks-to-do when Sam is eating and on Sundays. In couple's therapy, Sam and Helen come up with neutral times for discussing household chores. And sometimes, they wait to discuss touchy subjects in their couple's therapy session.

Level Two: Sam learns to facilitate his own healing

The Replace Inky Water Method

Imagine you have bucket filled with water that is mixed with black ink.

If you pour enough fresh water into the bucket the inky water will flow out, leaving you with just fresh clear water.

We need words, body posture and music to make sure we flush out old destructive patterns (the inky water).

Here's how the Replace Inky Water Method works for Sam. Over the years, to feel safe, Sam has adopted the behavior-patterns and thoughts of a perfectionist. Researchers have noted that beneath perfectionism is fear.

Now, he needs more than words to help him calm down.

First, he finds soothing music that he prefers.

Second, he identifies valuable ideas that he wants to make part of himself. He uses one of my phrases: "It's not about perfection; it's about putting one foot in front of the other." He also uses the phrase: "I am safe as I am."

Third, he applies these words to fit like lyrics to his favorite music.

Fourth, he learns to deep breathe—extending his belly as he breathes in and contracting his belly as he breathes out.

Fifth, he places a small pillow behind his back while he is seated. This helps him sit up straight with his vertebrae aligned.

This above combination of techniques helps Sam develop the "space" to make new choices.

Instead of reacting with anger (with the subliminal fear), he can slow down and make better choices. He can choose to respond by writing down the tasks-to-do in his pocket calendar. He can write them on a "holding pattern" list. That is, he can comfort himself by knowing that he has captured the task, and he will place it in his schedule, as appropriate.

The point here is: new ideas need to become part of the person.

The use of words plus music helps the new ideas "fill up the bucket" of the mind. We tend to only focus on one thing at a time. Set a new pattern of focusing on empowering thoughts and feelings. The truth is that no perfectionist can do "all things to feel safe" all of the time. A sense of safety must develop from within the person—not from a reliance on doing external things perfectly. Another idea that goes with "I am safe as I am" is: "I can handle it." Author Susan Jeffers in her book, *Feel the Fear and Do It Anyway,* discusses the transformational power of the idea "I can handle it." A spiritual phrase is "I can handle it with God."

Here's another example of using the Replace Inky Water Method. My client Marlena wanted to expand her prosperity. She said, "I need to gain more sales. But I'm nervous about making cold phone calls to prospective customers." Using the Replace Inky Water Method, she listens to a favorite, energizing song with the lyrics: "You're Simply the Best!" (sung by Tina Turner). She also holds her arms up in the air like an Olympic Gymnast celebrating a perfect landing. These two details help her flood out her nervousness with a new empowering state of being. The truth is that Marlena has the power to shift her state of being. She immediately dials the next phone number.

This Replace Inky Water Method is a helpful part of waking up our spirit.

> *Words are weak, feelings stronger, and actions the strongest—but truth is the best of all.*
>
> AL MARCOUX (Tom's father)

The Replace Inky Water Method is more powerful than mere words.

> *There are only two ways to live your life. One is as though nothing is a miracle. The other is as though everything is a miracle.*
>
> ALBERT EINSTEIN

It is best to use the Replace Inky Water Method so that we remember the miracles in our life. Pause for a moment;

remember how wonderful it felt to have your sweetheart in your life—especially at the beginning of your relationship. Remember the feeling of closeness and how grateful you were to be together. And being together now is still a miracle—it is still a blessing. This is the truth. Over time we can come to let the miracle feel like something commonplace.

Refresh your view of the miracles in your life.

That's how we need to approach filling our minds and our emotions. And that's why we choose to use the Replace Inky Water Method.

We can start with words, representing the ideas we want to focus on. Then we need to go to the next level: we need to engage multiple senses—and in this way we are pouring in more fresh water.

Using music is a powerful way to continue.

I like to recall some music by John Barry. His orchestrations immediately place my body at ease. Then, I think of a few words like: "God relaxes Tom." As I listen to the music I even think of the words as lyrics.

Researchers note that people remember lyrics with ease. The combination of words and music flow easily into our long-term memory. Also, our bodies feel differently in response to words and music. This is why creating your own empowering lyrics to your favorite songs is extremely powerful.

Choose songs that build you up. Earlier, I mentioned the song with the lyrics: "You're Simply the Best!" Those words and music can build a person up. The person's state of being changes instantly.

Aromatherapy & Enhanced Posture for Added Power

Choose a pleasing smell or aroma. Here are some supporting ideas about the power of smell.

> *Smell is a potent wizard that transports you across thousands of miles and all the years you have lived.*
>
> HELEN KELLER

> *Nothing is more memorable than a smell. One scent can be unexpected, momentary and fleeting, yet conjure up a childhood summer beside a lake in the mountains.*
>
> DIANE ACKERMAN

Add an aroma by purchasing things to add to your house—fragrant candles with forest smells, or potpourri with floral scents. You can set up a five minute quiet-time session in which you light a soothing, aromatherapy candle.

Some people even bake a cake to fill their home with that comforting aroma.

The next important element is good body posture. You will feel better when you line up your head to rest over your neck vertebrae. You can do this, as a physical therapist advised me, by sitting up and placing a pillow behind the small of your back—this aligns your body. You're relaxed. Stronger. Peaceful. Ready for life's ups and downs.

Occasionally, when I'm sitting on a train and writing, it helps to place my hands straight up in the air (this is part of a Yoga posture). Then I think of an affirmation like: "Thank you God for helping me serve people." I then add the image of holding my arms up with an audience of thousands of people doing the same. (Sometimes, in my workshops, I lead participants in stretching movements.)

The Replace Inky Water Method is a process in which we combine an image, music, an aroma, body posture and an empowering phrase. We flush out a destructive habit. That is, we overwhelm it with the image, music, an aroma, body posture, and phrase. The combination of these elements helps you create an emotion that empowers you. That is, we overwhelm the negativity with these empowering gestures.

You may have a habit of thinking something like "My partner doesn't do the laundry as much as I do," which is a habitual and competitive way of thinking. Aim to flush out this thought.

Here's how the process goes:

The Process to Replace Negative Thoughts

First thought: "My partner doesn't do the laundry as much as I do."

> Say to yourself: "I want to feel better. I choose (music, an aroma, a body posture) to help shift to an empowering state of being." Then make use of that item.
>
> Add this thought: "My partner does _____, which is terrific." Set these words as lyrics to your favorite song. Then breathe deeply and raise your arms like an Olympic gymnast in celebration.

We use this process to eliminate needless resentment. When our spirit is unhampered by resentment we are in the process of waking up our spirit for Couple's Prosperity.

Resentment and anger shut us down. In a low mood, we literally cannot see the good in our lives. That's the reason we seek to release ourselves from the cage of resentment so we can live on the level of an awake and loving spirit.

One interviewer said, "Wait a minute. Let's go back to that couple and the laundry. That couple really needs to discuss the reasons one partner does not do his or her part with the laundry."

I replied, "True. And our plan here is to balance out the feelings. Resentment is going to make any discussion about laundry upsetting. It could become a full-blown argument."

I continued by describing how a positive conversation could go. In this situation, Miranda wants Erik to do the laundry more often.

Miranda says, "Erik, first I want to thank you for cleaning the windows once a month. That really helps. I feel really good about seeing through clean windows. And I have another detail to discuss. Is this a good time for you?"

Erik agrees, and Miranda continues: "It would help if you'd consider doing the laundry every other week. Since I do the cooking four nights a week, I'd appreciate if we'd balance that out with splitting the work on the laundry. Okay?"

The point of the above scenario is this: If we live in our resentments, our discussions will be strained. The solution is to consciously focus on the positive details.

Use phrases to enhance Couple's Prosperity.

When we memorize words then we facilitate the process of *10 Seconds to Wealth*. In this way, in the golden seconds, we can instantly shift the direction of our thoughts. Here are some helpful phrases:

> *Success is important only to the extent that it puts one in a position to do more things one likes to do.*
>
> SARAH CALDWELL

> *With God all things are possible.*
>
> MATTHEW 19:26

> *In the depth of winter I finally learned that there was in me an invincible summer.*
>
> ALBERT CAMUS

> *If you have faith as small as a mustard seed, you can say to this mountain, 'Move from here to there' and it will move. Nothing will be impossible for you.*
>
> MATTHEW 17:20

> *My strength is my enthusiasm.*
>
> PLACIDO DOMINGO

> *Money is a tool I use well for the benefit of all.*
> TOM MARCOUX

To enhance feelings of closeness in your relationship and open the gate for abundance to flow in, use the Replace Inky Water Method.

Individual's Action Step

Identify something that is negative (the inky water). Use the Replace Inky Water Method by choosing details (image, music, an aroma, body posture, words) that help you move past the negative thought.

Couple's Action Step

List three things that you appreciate about your partner. Share your appreciative comments with her or him.

Principle

When in discomfort, find a way to be creative.

Leverage Questions

What bothers you? How can you find a way to become creative? How can you work with the situation in ways that avoid "competition"?

Organize for Hope

To organize for hope means to make plans that can lead to positive breakthroughs.

> *The success[ful person] always has a number of projects planned to which he looks forward. Any one of them could change the course of his life overnight.*
>
> MARK CAINE

The Prospering Couple experiences hope when selecting projects that may mean a big breakthrough to financial freedom.

Hope actually results from our own personal definitions of success and fulfillment—and then taking appropriate action. Some people do not have hope because they do not see how things can get better. You ask them about how things are going, and they often reply "same old; same old."

On the other hand, I encourage my clients to approach situations with "Make it a game you can win." Here is a definition of success and fulfillment that is obtainable.

> *To laugh often and much; to win the respect of intelligent people and the affection of children; to earn the appreciation of honest critics and endure the betrayal of false friends; to appreciate beauty; to find the best in others; to leave the world a bit better, whether by a healthy child, a garden patch or a redeemed social condition; to know even one life has breathed easier because you have lived. This is to have succeeded.*
>
> RALPH WALDO EMERSON

At this point it would help for each partner to give his or her definition of personal fulfillment and success. Write in your personal journal. Then, when appropriate, share with your partner what you have written.

Each partner might have a different definition of a "better life." The Entrepreneurial Partner may be focusing on: "When our company is serving millions of families around the world."

I define an Entrepreneurial Partner as a person who naturally has a future-focus, has a vision of how things can get better, and is okay with risk-taking.

The Non-Entrepreneurial Partner may have more of a present moment focus and may be more focused on the relationship. The Non-Entrepreneurial Partner might say, "When we have financial abundance, we'll have more leisure time together." Here is an important idea:

My point here is that both viewpoints are valuable.

In fact, it's valuable to focus on sharing time and enhancing your relationship.

> *We do not remember days, we remember moments.*
>
> **CESARE PAVESE**

It is important to find out what your partner really wants. When your partner believes it's possible to get what is desired, he or she will feel hope.

When both partners know their personal goals will be fulfilled, then more energy is available for wealth creation.

At this point, it will help for the partners to fill in this list.

What a Good Life Looks Like to Me

I have time to do these leisure activities:

I enjoy these leisure activities with my partner:

I have money to do these activities:

I have the money, time and resources to fulfill my personal dreams of:

After filling out this list, share your feelings and the items on your list with your partner.

Wealth creation takes strategy.

In a previous section, I discussed the Power-3 Income Streams:

The Power-3 Income Streams

- *Income Stream 1:* Stability (your base). One of my clients is a teacher, which forms her base. She can take appropriate time to analyze her stream of income opportunities. She is neither desperate nor harried.

- *Income Stream 2:* Automatic. A number of my clients make money through the Internet—while they are sleeping.

- *Income Stream 3:* No Ceiling. A number of my clients are creating books, audio programs and inventions. They know that when something becomes a hit, there is no ceiling on the amount of money they can make.

Making big progress toward financial freedom is really about working as a team that is organized for hope. Also, it helps to team up with other people.

> *Success in show business depends on your ability to make and keep friends.*
>
> SOPHIE TUCKER

Sometimes people talk about the "virtual company" in which people who are sole proprietors of their own businesses come together for a big project. For example, Marcia Wieder, author of *Making Your Dreams Come True*, has an executive assistant who she has not seen for a long time. Her virtual assistant Angee Robertson does Marcia's work at her home office in Alabama while Marcia's home base is San Francisco. Marcia wrote: "Angee literally runs my office. More than anyone else, she is responsible for the tremendous growth my company is experiencing. I dream up the ideas, products and events, and she makes them happen."

To illustrate the point of teamwork, here is a story …

Legend of the Way of the Circle

There were two villages beneath a volcano. The village of Lo had people who did the least to just get by. It was common for the people to think only of themselves and look for the easy way out. In business and love, they would solve their conflicts with win-lose situations.

Yet the village of Hy had the Wise One leading the people in the Way of the Circle. The people worked to spread enthusiasm; to step out of their own concerns and join with others for common goals. Conflicts were solved in a win-win way. And the village of Hy learned to work hard—then play with joy.

By closely watching the volcano, the members of both villages knew it would some day expel lava down the mountainside. The lava would travel down two grooves, each directly in the path of one of the villages.

The mayor of the village of Lo gathered his people and said, "We have a problem to solve." A lottery was held, and the "unlucky" winners were asked to push a large boulder up the mountainside to block the lava flow and divert it past the village.

The village of Hy also gathered.

The Wise One stood before the crowd. Wise One raised both hands, and everyone quieted down. Wise One wore a robe with large sleeves. A bird flew out of the left sleeve. Another bird flew out from the right sleeve. As the birds approached a bush, Wise One magically produced a nest in one hand.

The crowd watched as one bird tried to lift a heavy branch as part of its efforts to add to the nest. The bird couldn't do it. But the other bird grabbed the other end and together they flew the branch to the nest.

"We have a challenge," began Wise One. "This is our opportunity to take care of each other and our homes." So the whole village of Hy gathered to help with the plan to save their village. They identified a large boulder, and everyone looked for a way to help make their task a success. The men and women pushed the boulder with long poles. The elderly cooked meals. And the children carried food and water to the boulder team.

Meanwhile, each member of the Lo boulder-pushing team was assigned a pole. When one worker would falter, other Lo villagers would laugh and make critical remarks.

Yet when a Hy villager faltered, another would come over, place a hand on her shoulder, and explain a helpful technique or take her place for a time.

The Lo team's task was unsteady. During a round of derisive laughter, one pole cracked and another slipped. The Lo worker who was responsible for the accident was taking a break away from the others in a place where he thought the team leader couldn't see him. The boulder broke free and crashed through the Lo village.

After four days of sleeping in shifts and giving all their effort, the Hy villagers placed the boulder at the top of the volcano and successfully diverted the lava flow.

There once were two villages below a volcano.

The Hy village is still there.

From this legend we learn to nurture relationships, which is part of organizing for hope.

> *Many hands, hearts and minds generally contribute to anyone's notable achievement.*
>
> **WALT DISNEY**

A couple organizes for hope by catering to each person's individual strengths. Now let's see some of the principles or secrets of wealth building.

Earlier in this chapter, I emphasized:

To organize for hope means to make plans that can lead to positive breakthroughs.

How Ross Perot became a billionaire in eight years ...

Secret 1: Be courageous. Ross Perot had the courage to start his own company, EDS (Electronic Data Systems), and take on IBM—where he had been fired. To sell EDS' services, Ross and other former IBM salespeople approached the same clients they would have contacted when they worked for IBM. Ross began with only $1,000 in savings. The second gutsy thing he did was to give guarantees. EDS would estimate upfront how much it would cost to handle all of the client's data processing needs. Ross assured them that his services would be cheaper than if the client did it themselves internally. EDS would not deviate from their estimate to the client. This was courageous because companies avoid making ironclad estimates since projects often get extended and unknown problems rise up.

Secret 2: Be persistent. It took Ross 78 attempts (from his list of 110 companies) until he made his first deal. At that time, IBM formed a group of five people to start a whispering campaign against EDS. In another gutsy move, Ross hired one of the whispering campaign guys right out from under IBM.

Secret 3: Focus on reusable technology. EDS' data processing programs were usable (with minimal modifications) from state to state, especially when Medicare and Medicaid were beginning in numerous organizations. Ross' use of technology relates to: "Technology is always going to be a source for wealth" (said Mark Victor Hansen, co-creator of the *Chicken Soup for the Soul* series).

Secret 4: Motivate salespeople by giving them stock options. Ross' team of salespeople had a definite stake in the success of the company! As the company does better, the stock options rise in value. For example, Microsoft stock options rose in value, and many founding employees of Microsoft became millionaires.

5. Secret 5: Make a public offering. At the time, technology companies were offering stocks at 100 times current earnings. EDS' stock was at 14 cents per share, and it was offered at 118 times that amount—totaling $16.50 a share. After the public offering quickly sold out, Ross pocketed $5 million. His remaining shares totaled $154 million—a great return after only six years since being a disgruntled IBM salesman. Ross was 38 years old. Just two years later his shares were worth about $1.4 billion.

That's how Ross Perot became a billionaire in eight years. Ross Perot was certainly skillful as a salesman which helped him land contracts for his company EDS.

> *Identify your highest skill and devote your time to performing it. Delegate all other skills.*
>
> RONALD BROWN

In line with learning Ross Perot's secrets, *the Prospering Couple does better when dividing tasks according to each individual's natural strengths.* For example, the partner more adept with mathematics might do the taxes while the other separates the receipts into files by category. In this way the work is divided between the partners.

Also, tasks often get completed faster when the couple works together. The energy of 1+1 equals 11—as emphasized by Mark Victor Hansen, co-creator of the *Chicken Soup for the Soul* series.

To really organize for hope, the Prospering Couple needs to become skilled and take action with savings and budgets. By using his best skills, Ross Perot was organizing for hope. He began with around $1,000 in savings from his wife and in eight years became a billionaire.

Prospering Couples are Adept with Savings & Budgets

Secret 1: Take the pain out

Some people feel great deprivation when putting aside money. Perhaps they grew up in a household in which the income was small. One way to take out the pain is to create a savings account that uses an automatic deduction feature. That is, you choose a figure, like $30.00, and have that amount automatically deducted from your checking account on a monthly basis. Some of my clients set aside 10% of every income-related check. People often adjust very well to a smaller budget. After a few months they are often surprised to see how much their savings account has grown.

Secret 2: Reinforce your partner's sense of being adult

Often, the partner who tends to save money feels like she or he is "being the adult in the relationship." That is, this partner feels like the "bad guy" when putting the brakes on the other person's spending. *Here is the solution: have separate accounts, and each partner will feel in charge of her or his own budget.* This method helps a couple avoid arguments. Many years ago bestselling author Jim Rohn set up a "No Questions Asked" account for his wife. At the time, Jim earned the income while his wife worked as a full-time mother and homemaker. His wife felt better because she did not have to ask Jim for money, and she did not have to justify each expenditure. In addition to maintaining separate accounts, some couples set up a household expenses account into which they both make contributions.

Secret 3: Consider differences in money styles

One partner may have a tendency toward saving, while the other has a tendency toward spending. Sometimes it is valuable to have a therapy or coaching session to get a third person's perspective to help identify each partner's money-styles. Partners can learn that the combination of a money-saving style with a money-spending style can create both a good financial future and some joyful times each month. For example, because Allen likes fine dining, he and his partner put aside funds for going to a terrific restaurant once every month.

Secret 4: Separate couple issues from individual issues

When one partner's personal issue around money is causing much unrest, then individual therapy may be the best course of action. Some couples have a team of support: one therapist for the relationship and separate therapists for individual counseling that focuses on personal growth. Couples with financial challenges can seek therapy at places offering a sliding scale. Also, some psychology graduate programs offer therapy from graduate students (supervised by a licensed psychologist). At some institutions the hourly fee is only $10.00.

Secret 5: Use the Abundance Coffee Cups method

Use this method to see exactly where your money is going. Set up six coffee cups (or more) that represent your different accounts. Here are categories my clients have used:

- Long-term savings for a big ticket purchase (a new car, a vacation)
- Roth IRA (individual retirement account) savings for one partner
- Roth IRA savings for the other partner
- One night away per month
- Fun for the month (seeing a movie or eating at a restaurant)
- Flow of Abundance account

The Flow of Abundance account is like tithing (putting aside a percentage of your income for the venue where you get spiritual nourishment—a church, for example).

You can begin your Flow of Abundance account by putting loose change in the coffee cup designated for that purpose. People feel better when they devote even 1% of their income to something beyond themselves. My clients have donated to their church, battered women's shelters, animal care facilities and other worthy causes.

The purpose of the Abundance Coffee Cups Method is this: When any of the amounts exceed the capacity of a particular cup, put the cash into a savings account at the bank of your choice—and keep the checkbook in the cup.

One interviewer said: "People with IRAs and other big savings responsibilities will not use a coffee cup. This idea will only work with small change used for money towards restaurants, movies, etc."

I replied: "You put the checkbook of the separate account in the particular cup. The point is to develop a habit of dividing your income in a way that you can see daily and weekly progress."

Secret 6: Have some fun each month as a couple

This process promotes harmony in the relationship. Being sure to have some fun makes the

We remember that the Non-Entrepreneurial Partner tends to be more present-moment focused and may not have the long-term perspective of the Entrepreneurial Partner.

Also, by budgeting your finances for things that are purely for fun, partners take care of the inner child. The inner child is that part of each of us that retains the childlike desires to have fun and be nurtured. Also, the inner child is the source of personal energy—so it is vital to take care of your inner child.

Secret #7: Learn to budget each other's priorities

One couple I worked with set up two separate long-term savings accounts. He wanted a replacement car, and she wanted a vacation. They put aside money for each desire.

The principle for this chapter is: *Make hope part of the structure of your daily life.*

When you use the Abundance Coffee Cups, you can see small, tangible progress. This inspires the hopes that:

- We're learning to manage money well
- We're going to keep doing better

A New Way to Ease into Discipline to Improve Your Life

Developing new habits takes discipline.

Discipline is simply sticking to those commitments you make for yourself, which are made out of a love for your vision.

SUZANNE FALTER-BARNS

Suzanne Falter-Barns also wrote: "Get a coach or a support buddy to help you with [discipline and things you don't like doing]. Call or e-mail when you're balking at your commitment. If you get the answering machine, tell it that you'll be sitting down to work now, and will call back when the work is complete. Then make the happy call at the end of your work session."

My addition to this idea is something I mentioned earlier: *Ease into Momentum.* The idea is to take out the pain. And find something easy you can do to get started.

I call this the *Easy Part Start.* For example, when you place your spare change into your Abundance Coffee Cups, you're doing something easy that adds up to great results.

Seeing progress (even on a small scale with the Abundance Coffee Cups), inspires hope. You feel the hope that: "we're not going to stay at this level of finances. Things are getting better!"

Remember to organize for hope and set up your Abundance Coffee Cups (accounts).

Individual's Action Step

Write three things you can do toward obtaining your dream—so you can experience some hope and progress in your daily life. Set up your own Abundance Coffee Cups.

Couple's Action Step

Write down three cumbersome tasks that previously have been completed by one partner. Identify with your partner which one of you has the most strength in that area. Then figure out how you can balance out the situation. For example (as mentioned earlier), the "mathematical partner" does the taxes while the other separates the receipts into appropriate file folders.

Principle

Make hope part of the structure of your daily life.

Leverage Question

What can you do each day that creates progress and supports your feelings of hope about the terrific future you are creating?

Use Momentum

President John F. Kennedy started the process of momentum when he provided a vision and leadership with his proclamation: "I believe this nation should commit itself, before this decade is out, to land a man on the Moon and return him safely to Earth." At the time, there was no fully formed space program. Leadership entailed setting the goal before figuring out how to get it done.

"This nation has tossed its cap over the wall of space, and we have no choice but to follow it," said President Kennedy. He meant that we have no other choice but to continue the momentum of what we had begun. Similarly, Walt Disney's brother and partner Roy O. Disney said, "Decision-making is easy if your values are clear."

At various times the Prospering Couple will embark on new chapters in life. During these times the Prospering Couple will, like the early space program, be charting new territory—especially when seeking to get out of a financial rut. What counts is to keep the momentum going. Here is a story to illustrate this point ...

Legend of the Momentous Branch

A widow with two small children went to the Wise One of the village. She sadly explained that she did not have the time to fulfill her dream to build a house for her children to grow up in. Wise One said, "Come with me."

After a bit of walking, Wise One pointed to a tree. "That is your door frame."

The woman protested. "That's too big for me. I'll never move it!" With lightning flashes of a sword, Wise One cut the tree into twenty logs.

Wise One said, "Cut your large tasks into small tasks."

"How do I move these logs?" the woman asked.

Wise One replied by pushing one branch with a foot. The branch struck one log and then another. Soon all twenty logs were rolling down hill toward the widow's piece of land.

"Momentum," said Wise One, smiling. Later the woman practiced momentum by gathering building supplies while she was out shopping for groceries.

Days later Wise One led the widow on a walk into the woods. "Where are we going?" the woman asked.

"Education," Wise One replied.

In a clearing students were gathered around a master builder who said, "These techniques will help you to build quickly and with quality."

In three weeks the woman and her children moved into the first room of their new house. In one year their house was big enough to become an inn.

Soon after Wise One mysteriously appeared to the widow and said, "Now you know the keys to do more in less time. Education. Momentum. Slice a large task into small parts."

From this legend we learn to create momentum, gain the education we need, and use the power of slicing a large task into small parts.

To really support momentum, use both Effort Goals and Results Goals.

Effort Goal: This is a goal that you have control over. Something for which you can choose to devote your energy and effort. For example, a salesperson or business owner can choose the number of phone calls she makes to generate income.

Result Goal: This is a goal that involves an outcome. However, please note that we cannot control outcomes that are dependent on factors beyond our control like the weather, someone else's mood or how a particular company is doing in the marketplace. A salesperson says she wants to increase her quarterly sales by 20% (Result Goal). When she sets up her Effort Goal of increasing her phone calls by 30%, she can make progress. But she only increases her sales by 10%. She can still feel good about achieving her Effort Goal of increasing phone calls by 30%.

When you separate Effort Goals from Result Goals you can create steady progress and keep up your morale.

We notice that to get a particular Result Goal, like more sales, we can influence the outcome by putting energy into our Effort Goals. To get more done, here is a principle that I share with audiences: *Keep score and achieve more.*

For example, while writing a book, I note how many words I write in each session (which is how I "keep score"). I turn the process into a game. This ties in with my other favorite principle *Make it a game you can win.*

Devoting Time to Relaxation Improves Your Momentum

To keep up momentum, use an Activity-Recovery Pattern. In this pattern you devote yourself to doing activities that make up your Effort Goals—then take a break.

For example, Stephanie noticed that calling her friend in the morning slows down her momentum. She decides to write a report in the morning and call her friend as a reward after the work is done.

> *The time to relax is when you don't have time for it.*
> SYDNEY J. HARRIS

Researchers have discovered that one can reduce their "functional age" by years. Functional age is measured by an average person's physical abilities at a particular age. In one study, researchers had subjects spend just 20 minutes a day meditating (or quiet time for prayer). After three years the participants' functional age had been reduced by 12 years!

Make sure to focus on how you can enhance your momentum. Remember that your momentum is enhanced as you devote time to relaxing and recharging.

Individual's Action Step

Identify three things that slow down your momentum. List three things you can do that will stop the hindrances and help regain your momentum.

Couple's Action Step

Together, identify obstacles that have a tendency to slow down your momentum as a couple striving to move forward. Then come up with two alternatives for each obstacle. Figure out ways that each partner can provide support for the other. For example, Mark and Jenny notice that Mark procrastinates when it's his turn to do the laundry. They decide to do the laundry together on Saturday mornings in a leisurely way.

Principle

Keep score and achieve more.

Leverage Questions

How can you measure your progress with Effort Goals and Results Goals? How can you keep score and achieve more?

Practice Compassion

> *If you want other people to be happy, practice compassion. If you want to be happy, practice compassion.*
>
> **DALAI LAMA**

The *American Heritage Dictionary* defines compassion as: "Deep awareness of the suffering of another [person] coupled with the wish to relieve it."

We all go through tough times. The following is a story of one woman's journey through a valley of pain to the other side …

Legend of the Smoking Coal

A woman loved a man, yet, as the years passed, they grew apart. After their parting, the woman spent months feeling depressed. She went to see the Wise One of the village.

After hearing her story, Wise One said nothing but took her to a play. It was about a man and a woman drifting apart. The woman cried.

Later, the woman sat with the Wise One near a cooking fire. The woman was lost in her sad memories. Wise One threw a smoking coal at the woman. Seeing something come at her, she instinctively caught the coal.

"Ye-ow!" she cried and dropped the coal. She was startled right out of her sad thoughts.

She wanted to stuff the coal down Wise One's throat.

"Good!" Wise One began, "Now, you are here. Pain is okay. It is the step to growing. If you feel depressed, something must change—your situation or your attitude."

The Wise One leapt to a standing position and stepped away. The woman followed. Not knowing what Wise One would do next—and taking no chances—she paid attention to everything. She noticed the sparkling stream and the brilliant flowers along its path. Before she knew it she was smiling. She had let the flowers, trees and stream work their magic on her.

Her smile helped when she met a woman practicing archery in a clearing.

The archer taught the now-smiling woman the art of the bow and arrow. As time passed the new friends shared their dreams and heartaches with each other.

The woman became quite skillful at the sport. She went to archery contests and one day met a special man at an event.

They fell in love. This love endured. The woman had applied what she had learned from her experiences and earlier relationship.

Wise One mysteriously appeared, and said, "Pain is okay. You lived and learned. Now you love more fully."

From this legend we learn to listen to the lessons that are presented. Wise One said, "Pain is okay. It is the step to growing. If you feel depressed, something must change—your situation or your attitude." Over the years, some of my clients have chosen to seek medical help and find that in cases of severe depression, a combination of talk-therapy and medication is most helpful. The point is: the person seeks help, and thereby changes his or her situation.

Have compassion for yourself, and seek help when appropriate. Compassion is expressed through small, kind actions.

> *Be the living expression of God's kindness: kindness in your face, kindness in your eyes, kindness in your smile.*
>
> MOTHER TERESA

Express compassion for your partner. How do you know what your partner needs and treasures? Ask your partner!

> *There is more hunger for love and appreciation in this world than for bread.*
>
> MOTHER TERESA

We need to appreciate our partners as a gift and miracle in our lives. We felt that way at the beginning of our relationship. As I mentioned in a previous chapter:

Refresh your view of the miracles in your life.

It helps to really look at and listen to your partner.

> *I'm convinced that we're all dying of loneliness because no one looks at us.*
>
> LEO BUSCAGLIA

Listening is compassion in action. A powerful part of listening is the process of identifying Unnamed Fears. Unnamed Fears are part of the various levels of the free-floating anxiety people feel. Free-floating anxiety, as noted by psychology researchers, is: "a haunting, helpless feeling of apprehension."

The good news is that many people report feeling better just by expressing their Unnamed Fears. The process is like saying: "I named you. I've got your address. And now I'm going to take you down!"

> *To see your drama clearly is to be liberated from it.*
>
> KEN KEYES, JR.

We feel better, and we can act effectively, when we identify the Unnamed Fears.

Unnamed Fears form an invisible wall between love partners. We're going to tear down this wall. At this point, it is valuable for each partner to write down four troublesome situations and what may be going on.

In your personal journal, use this pattern:

Example Situation: Arguing about money

Unnamed Fear (that might be related): I'm afraid that I'll lose my job and that we'll lose our house.

Action to alleviate the Fear: I can update my résumé. I can take a night class to keep my skills up to date.

Our next step is to focus on loving thoughts to replace fear. Many years ago, I gathered my things while leaving work one evening from my job at a major corporation. A co-worker, who had chosen to work overtime, confronted me and said, "Some of us have endurance." His tone of voice implied, "I'm better than you." I had a momentary feeling of irritation. I also felt fear based on the thought, "If this person doesn't like me, he might make me look bad to my boss. And I am new here." But I remembered that I could choose to let go of fearful thoughts. So I responded, "I appreciate that you're working hard." With that I left to enjoy the evening with family. I felt lighter because I did *not* participate in the negative feelings. Also, I acknowledged his efforts by complimenting him. Love is feeling one's spirit and responding to events in a positive manner.

Truly, our spirit is bigger than our temporary feelings of hurt. Expressing compassion for yourself includes acknowledging your fear and then making a plan to take care of yourself to make things better.

Use this phrase:

> "Before now, I was afraid of _____. Now, I'm doing _____ to make progress."

It is vital to learn empowering patterns of thought. This is an essential part of *10 Seconds to Wealth*. You want to be at your best in the crucial moment.

> *Our achievements of today are but the sum total of our thoughts of yesterday. You are today where the thoughts of yesterday have brought you and you will be tomorrow where the thoughts of today take you.*
>
> BLAISE PASCAL

Listening to your partner takes energy. You must build up your personal energy to give your partner quality listening time. We build up our personal energy by nurturing ourselves and doing things to express compassion for ourselves. We cannot wait for someone else to take care of us.

> *Compassion for myself is the most powerful healer of them all.*
>
> DR. THEODORE ISAAC RUBIN

Also, be sure to practice compassion in your relationship. When possible, it is valuable to hire part-time help, like someone to help with housecleaning, bookkeeping or other projects. When money is short, consider doing a trade with a friend. For example, Sara's friend Monique is a bookkeeper. Monique helps with Sara's taxes and Sara baby-sits Monique's two children.

> *Nothing is impossible for the man who doesn't have to do it himself.*
>
> A. H. WEILER

Practicing compassion is the center of healthy, loving relationships.

> *To love a person is to learn the song that is in their heart, and to sing it to them when they have forgotten.*
>
> THOMAS CHANDLER

> *Trouble is part of your life, and if you don't share it, you don't give the person who loves you a chance to love your enough.*
>
> DINAH SHORE

Compassion is crucial to your approach to talking about money.

Some relationships, like cars, can be way out of tune. For these couples, talking about money may require a session in a therapist's office.

When your relationship is in a good place, use the following methods.

Secrets for Talking Effectively about Money

Secret 1: Respect timing. For many couples, talking about money after 9 p.m. is a bad idea. Make an appointment for another time.

Secret 2: Ask, "What could make talking about money a safe experience for you?" At times, one partner might say, "We need to save this for our Friday session with our couple's therapist." It is important to honor our partner's needs to feel safe. Some couples set up a "business meeting" on a particular day each month. During this meeting they discuss goals, accomplishments, and growth areas.

Secret 3: Place ideas on the "buffet table." Don't seek an immediate resolution. Many men feel discomfort if they cannot fix something quickly. These men need to take a deep breath and realize they are accomplishing something—that is, they are expressing love by focusing on simply listening.

Secret 4: Use a journal to avoid blurting out details. Some individuals find they feel so uncomfortable discussing money that they blurt out disturbing details. In defense, they say, "If I don't say it now, I'll forget." The solution is for these individuals to carry a small notebook (a journal) and write down the disturbing details for a mutually agreed time for talking about money.

Secret 5: Be respectful of your partner's Money Achilles' Heel. The myth says that Achilles was only vulnerable on his heel. His mother had held on to him by his heel when she dipped him in special water to make him invulnerable—leaving a spot that was missed by the protective water. One day an arrow hit Achilles' only vulnerable spot and killed him. In real life, many people have a particular weakness related to money. For example, my client Jose has a weakness involving money and food. As a child he skipped lunch to afford model plane kits. His partner needs to realize that the question "Do you want to go to XY Restaurant?" will get a "no" response. An effective question would be: "Would you be supportive of celebrating my promotion with me? I would like to go to XY restaurant. It would be fun for me if we share the experience together. Okay?" Jose feels better about saying "yes" to this type of question.

Secret 6: Ask, "What's most important to you about …?" Topics can include: a) a particular purchase, b) saving money for major purchases, c) saving for retirement, and d) living a happy life. Philosopher and author Joseph Campbell said, "I don't believe people are looking for the meaning of life as much as they are looking for the experience of being alive." Being alive means different things to different people. We need to ask questions and listen to our partner to learn what's most important to him or her.

Secret 7: Say, "Tell me about something you fear about money." Some people fear running out of money and becoming homeless. I know a number of people who avoid high school class reunions because they feel embarrassed and believe that they have done poorly with a career path and earning money.

Secret 8: Ask, "What do you need to …?" Topics can include: a) feel happy, b) feel safe, c) feel loved, d) feel respected, e) feel nurtured, f) feel heard, and g) feel that I really cherish you. Asking this question will help you get to the root of your partner's urgent needs. This is important because our hidden needs account for much of our extreme behaviors. Partners start working well to fulfill needs when they learn to communicate on a heart-to-heart level.

Secret 9: Ask, "Before we were a couple did you …?" Topics can include: "Did you save money?" and "Did you feel skillful with money?" Some problems couples face are not couple-problems. They are actually life-long personal issues that our partner needs to work on personally. This question helps us understand our partner's life-long patterns.

Secret 10: Ask, "What do you feel we need to learn about money?" This is an empowering question because it supports the feeling that you two are in the process together. This is an important exercise for learning to discuss finances in a positive manner.

Sometimes, it takes a while for one partner to be able to trust that conversations about money will be safe.

Trust comes from keeping a series of commitments.

DEANNA BERG

From this moment forward, we make a commitment to doing our best to be respectful toward our partner with touchy topics like money.

Remember to practice compassion. When you do, things will get better.

Individual's Action Step

List three of your habitual and fearful thoughts. List three empowering thoughts you can use to replace them.

Couple's Action Step

Each partner lists three fearful thoughts related to your relationship and abundance. Together, list empowering thoughts for replacing the fearful ones.

Principle

Practice compassion, and listen attentively.

Leverage Question

How can you remind yourself to listen attentively? (Perhaps, use posted notes on the bathroom mirror, in your car, or in your day planner.)

Let Go of What's Not Working

Bestselling author Erica Jong wrote: "I have not ceased being fearful, but I have ceased to let fear control me." The point is that she let go of what was not working: paralysis due to fear.

Prospering Couples gently identify a number of things that do not work. They then take steps to move beyond the things holding them back. In this chapter we will cover specific steps that help both the Entrepreneurial Partner and the Non-Entrepreneurial partner support each other and enhance their relationship.

First, let's look at the foundation of building a bright future.

To create a life of abundance, step forward and drop the useless baggage as you go.

Useless baggage can be a result of behavior patterns that once garnered praise—perhaps during childhood. For example, in her book *Nice Girls Don't Get Rich,* Lois P. Frankel expresses the premise that effective women drop the behavior patterns of "nice little girls"—that were instilled by parents and guardians. Effective women learn to be assertive and take care of finances. In this example, we can view the nice girls' behavior patterns as useless baggage.

Things to let go:

- Going into debt merely for consumer toys.
- Resentment over past mistakes.
- As a reflex, reaching for something that costs money to serve as an emotional bandage.

The tough part is this: It's easy for our partner to see our blind spots and to nag us about the weak spots in our personality. And this works both ways. It helps to remember what bestselling author Anne McCaffrey said: "Make no judgments where you have no compassion."

The Prospering Couple does well to take Anne McCaffrey's idea to heart.

It does not work when one partner tries to make the other partner his or her clone. No two people are exactly alike. People have differences, and that is good! I emphasize with my audiences: "We're like jigsaw puzzle pieces. We fit together."

Here is a story about letting go and what happens next …

Legend of the Supporting Branches

A young woman was a successful doctor in the village. She was known as a compassionate and sensitive healer. People felt better when she simply entered a room.

Then, day by day, she built a wall around her heart. Her patients just kept coming and coming—all were needy. The doctor found herself eating lunch on the run and working more and more hours. Finally, she began walking in a bit of a daze.

One day on her lunch break, she walked briskly to get some medical supplies from a nearby village. She was so tired and distracted she did not watch her step. She slipped and tumbled over the edge of a cliff!

Her hands frantically reached out. Just barely she caught onto the tiny ridges on the face of the sheer cliff. Her feet dangled over space five hundred feet below.

"Help!" she called.

Just then, the Wise One of the village mysteriously appeared.

"Help me," yelled the woman.

"Let go," Wise One replied.

"Let go?" the woman thought. "I'll be torn to shreds on the rocks below."

Wise One again said firmly, "Let go."

The woman was tempted because she knew Wise One's strange advice tended to work.

Yet the woman held on. Soon her hands gave out, and she fell.

But three branches jutting out from the cliff caught her.

"There is a path to your left," said Wise One.

The woman climbed over the branches and walked up the path to where Wise One stood.

Wise One began, "You were caught by supporting branches. I planted those. Perhaps you need to plant supporting branches elsewhere in your life."

The woman began visiting Wise One and learned about how to plant her own supporting branches:

- She went to a neighboring village and introduced herself to the doctor there. They became friends and shared their challenges and feelings.
- She exercised, doing flowing martial arts movements with Wise One.
- She changed her approach to her work.

Weeks later, the woman walked with a smile and came upon the cliff where she nearly lost everything—but instead gained her balance.

Wise One mysteriously appeared and said, "Plant your supporting branches and tend your garden."

From this legend we learn to let go of some routines, to modify other routines, and to include new helpful behaviors for nurturing ourselves.

Unfortunately, your partner might use work to fulfill too much of his or her emotional needs …

> *They intoxicate themselves with work so they won't see how they really are.*
>
> ALDOUS HUXLEY

To the person who puts most of his or her energy into work, I ask: What is going on? In many cases the person is afraid of being powerless. This person may feel somewhat powerless in her relationship or elsewhere. So it's tempting to stay at work where one feels effective.

Truly, we cannot make our partner's mood improve. However, we have some influence. The following steps will help the workaholic partner do better in guarding and enhancing his or her personal relationship.

Powerful steps for the Entrepreneurial Partner:

Schedule regular time with your partner. Schedule time just like you would set up important business meetings. Don't be like the man who arrives at success just in time to lose his marriage.

Schedule balance in your life. To maintain your personal equilibrium, schedule time for exercise, enough rest and great nutrition. The challenge for entrepreneurs is that a hectic schedule often leads to crashing when they get home. That is, they return home with no energy to share with their love-partner. Activities that foster balance provide energy.

Use a time management system to schedule the important parts of your life. Avoid focusing only on urgent tasks. Our love relationship may not demand our attention like a ringing telephone. But we need to devote time and attention toward nurturing ourselves and our relationship.

Listen first. Before automatically pouring your new ideas or business concerns on your partner, pause and ask your partner about his or her day.

Powerful steps for the Non-Entrepreneurial Partner:

Schedule your activities for when your loved one is busy. Marty uses a laptop computer to read his e-mail so he can sit near his wife as she studies for a college class.

Nurture your friendships. We all need to feel connected to other people. When we enjoy the support and love of friends, it's not necessary to depend only on our love-partner for support and companionship.

Get yourself on your loved one's schedule. Sit down with your partner and together pull out your day planners. Schedule activities that will enhance your closeness.

Schedule balance in your life. Devote time and energy to friends and family—and reserve quiet time and meditation for yourself.

Schedule activities for flying solo. My idea is this: *Flying solo is not being lonely.* Flying solo includes hobbies and self-nurturing activities, like painting a picture, taking a class, reading, going to art galleries, attending enriching seminars, and much more.

Take an interest in your partner's business activities. Be someone in whom your partner can confide. Ask questions and do some reading about your partner's business. Your partner's work is part of his or her personality. Demonstrate your care by listening and being informed. Stay positive and wait for your partner to ask for feedback. Avoid gushing advice.

The Prospering Couple practices forgiveness and learns to let go of resentment. We need to support each other as we take baby-steps forward—growing and learning.

Life is an adventure in forgiveness.

NORMAN COUSINS

Sometimes it is hard to forgive when we get used to wearing a Martyr's Badge.

Let go of the Martyr's Badge

The Martyr's Badge is a way of trumpeting how we make sacrifices for other people. It is a way of saying: "Look how much pain I endure. This is why I am a good person." It is a way to be a hero in your own eyes.

These comments have a Martyr's Badge tint to them:

- I'm so busy!
- I have too much to do.
- I always put everyone's needs before my own.
- Nobody helps me.
- I have no time for myself.

Each partner must take responsibility for taking care of her or himself.

Here are some wise comments to remind us to make space and time to take care of ourselves:

> *There is more to life than increasing its speed.*
>
> GANDHI

> *Four of five people are more in need of rest than exercise.*
>
> DR. LOGAN CLENDENING

> *A man is rich in proportion to the number of things he can afford to leave alone.*
>
> HENRY DAVID THOREAU

> *Unhappiness is best described as the difference between our talents and our expectations.*
>
> EDWARD DE BONO

> *I don't know the key to success, but the key to failure is trying to please everybody.*
>
> BILL COSBY

The way to avoid trying to please everybody is to learn to appropriately say No. *When you say No to some things, you are saying Yes! to others.*

Remember to let go of what's not working. If you're feeling burned out, then take it as a red alert! Get help. See a counselor or coach. Confide in a friend. Find a way to develop balance in your personal life.

Individual's Action Step

Do you have a tendency to be entrepreneurial (vision-oriented, risk-taker) or non-entrepreneurial (in the moment)? How can you be gracious to people who do not share that orientation?

Couple's Action Step

Turn to each other and say something like, "Please forgive me for not cherishing you and your natural brilliance. I see that you do the laundry and take care of the kids on Tuesday during my class, which really help me (or your relationship)."

Principle

Let go of what's not working.

Leverage Question

What's not working in your life? How can you replace the non-effective behaviors?

Energize to Serve

> *I don't know what your destiny will be, but one thing I know: the only ones among you who will be really happy are those who will have sought and found how to serve.*
>
> ALBERT SCHWEITZER

"Love is, above all, the gift of oneself," said Jean Anouilh. And Prospering Couples learn to give themselves to service.

The effective process is to find a method of wealth building that you like doing and that serves other people.

> *Work is love made visible.*
>
> KAHIL GIBRAN

> *It is faith in something and enthusiasm for something that makes life worth living.*
>
> OLIVER WENDELL HOLMES

Here is a story about a woman who literally fell into her line of work...

Legend of the Rut

A woman began her work at the market with lots of enthusiasm for her new enterprise. But after months, it became a grind: hawk your wares, wrap your wares, polish your wares ... and try not to fall asleep during the slow times.

Bored, tired and frustrated, the woman went to the Wise One of the village. She explained her situation as Wise One practiced ballet-like martial arts movements.

Wise One leapt up, grabbed a coil of rope from a high hook and threw it to the woman.

The next day she sat at her booth and idly played with the rope. She tied it into a lasso and swung the rope in small circles. This was fun! She practiced larger and larger loops and, before long, she was lassoing straw hats.

One day the ground roared and fissures tore open. Many booths of the market sunk deep into the ground—including the woman's booth and the woman!

It was dark and wet in the earth. She swung her coil of rope and lassoed a tree branch, pulling herself free just as the fissure clamped shut. She quickly ran to her neighbors who were also in trapped in the fissures. Using her rope she pulled them out of the ground.

Thereafter, large crowds came from miles around to watch the new heroine as she performed her rope tricks. Many people bought straw hats and other wares and, of course, coils of rope. The woman became wealthy, and she kept sunshine in her smile and her soul.

Wise One mysterious appeared and said, "You used technique to pull yourself from the rut in the ground—and the rut in your life."

From this legend we learn to energize to serve by responding to opportunities as they appear. In the above story, the woman used what she had (the rope) to save herself and her neighbors.

> *You are not here merely to make a living. You are here in order to enable the world to live more amply, with great vision, with a finer spirit of hope and achievement. You are here to enrich the world, and you impoverish yourself if you forget the errand.*
>
> PRESIDENT WOODROW WILSON

One interviewer asked me: "Why is serving good? How does it benefit a relationship—toward prosperity?"

When the Prospering Couple makes service part of the fabric of their life, they discover that the universe and Higher Power start helping them in their endeavors.

> *I have learned, that if one advances confidently in the direction of his dreams, and endeavors to live the life he has imagined, he will meet with a success unexpected in common hours.*
>
> HENRY DAVID THOREAU

The Prospering Couple learns to use their natural brilliance to serve; and the Couple feels better. They feel a part of the goodness and blessings of life. Other people seek to help them. And in this way, the Prospering Couple experiences the wonders of *energize to serve*. They feel more energy because they are proud of themselves.

Eleanor Roosevelt said, "Happiness is not a goal; it is a by-product."

Similarly, the Prospering Couple learns to develop a plan of service and income-earning that focuses on this question:

How can you serve on a massive scale and enjoy, as a by-product, financial freedom?

One interviewer said, "Few people serve on a massive scale."

"To serve on a massive scale is really about something I call Customer Delight. Customer Delight occurs when the person gains something extra and surprising. A thank you postcard can be extra and surprising. A follow-up call can be surprising. Sending an e-mail with a link to something about the customer's hobby can be extra and surprising," I replied.

The Prospering Couple knows that it becomes fun when you serve customers in ways that they become delighted. Once again, this is how the Prospering Couple benefits from *energize to serve*.

Many Prospering Couples also make a plan aligned with building a home business that serves people on a massive scale. The idea is to do activities that function like a series of graduated steps. The Prospering Couple seeks to serve a larger and larger group of people. For example, a personal coach can begin by serving twenty clients. Then she can:

- Give a speech at a local association
- Record the speech
- Make CDs from the recording
- Write and publish a book

- Develop a system that other coaches can use to serve clients across the world [this is part of the franchising process].

I have clients who make money while they sleep as customers from around the world buy my clients' products through the Internet.

In an earlier section, I shared these ideas:

We start enjoying life to the fullest when we have learned to let go of hesitation around the word profit. Dictionary.com defines profit as "An advantageous gain or return; benefit." When you put service and Higher Power first, you can create profit in a holistic manner.

Remember to find a way to serve—and enjoy the process, too.

Individual's Action Step

List three ways that you can increase how you serve and how these ways can create your profit.

Couple's Action Step

Talk about how you can help each other to express your personal natural brilliance and to serve others simultaneously. List three activities that each of you loves to do and feels would not be "standard drudgery work."

Principle

Express your natural brilliance and serve others in ways that are profitable to all involved.

Leverage Question

How can you serve on a massive scale and enjoy, as a dividend, financial freedom?

Conclusion of Chapter Five

The acrostic C.O.U.P.L.E. is used to help you examine the principles and Leverage Questions that will inspire you to achieve and support a grand flow of abundance in your life.

> C – Create (not compete)
> O – Organize for Hope
> U – Use Momentum
> P – Practice Compassion
> L – Let Go of What's Not Working
> E – Energize to Serve

I presented the Seven Secrets, that is, the six methods of C.O.U.P.L.E. plus "the process of talking effectively about money."

Also, especially in the section *Create (Not Compete)*, I shared with you how to increase romance with the *25 Ways You Can Help Me Feel Loved* list.

You have the power to choose your beliefs and choose how you live on a daily basis. You can choose to focus on scarcity or abundance. You can remind yourself with "I am grateful for … "

Before I go to sleep each night I write in my Daily Journal of Victories and Blessings (which I've mentioned earlier). A victory relates to an action I took—like exercising. A blessing is a gift—like talking on the telephone with an extended family member. I go to sleep feeling grateful for the blessings and adventures I enjoyed each day.

I am grateful for the opportunity to be supportive of you and how you welcome more opportunities for abundance.

Let's continue with the next section …

6

Create Confidence

In Chapter Five, you learned to increase both romance and wealth in your relationship.

In Chapter Six, you will learn about creating confidence. You will learn how to support your partner in developing confidence while increasing your own personal confidence. To take full advantage of the *10 Seconds to Wealth*, you need to be in the moment and express natural confidence.

Merriam-Webster.com defines *confidence* as "a feeling of consciousness of one's powers ... faith or belief that one will act in a right, proper, or effective way ... the quality or state of being certain."

The Prospering Couple learns the empowering possibilities of confidence. Also, the Couple learns that one's definition and understanding of confidence can help or hinder increasing prosperity.

Unfortunately, many people say: "I'll try that when I feel confident enough to do it." From my studies of (and conversations with) highly effective people, I realize that they move forward even when feeling fearful!

Our empowering definition of confidence is based on my process W.A.K.E.

> W – Want It From Your True Self
> A – Adapt
> K – Keep Learning
> E – Encourage Help

These are the four elements of real confidence. I use W.A.K.E. to remind us to wake up to the reality of true confidence. Trust yourself to have these four elements. And don't wait for the absence of fear to strive for what you want. No high-achievers I have ever talked with said that they waited for the butterflies in their stomach to subside before taking a challenging action. Dictionary.com defines courage as "The state or quality of mind or spirit that enables one to face danger, fear, or vicissitudes with self-possession, confidence, and resolution; bravery."

Here are empowering phrases about courage:

> *It takes courage to push yourself to places that you have never been before ... to test your limits ... to break through barriers. And the day came when the risk it took to remain tight inside the bud was more painful than the risk it took to blossom.*
>
> ANAIS NIN

Believe in yourself! Have faith in your abilities! Without a humble but reasonable confidence in your own powers you cannot be successful or happy.

NORMAN VINCENT PEALE

Optimism is the faith that leads to achievement. Nothing can be done without hope and confidence.

HELEN KELLER

Courage is the price that Life exacts for granting peace.

AMELIA EARHART

Life shrinks or expands in proportion to one's courage.

ANAIS NIN

We must have courage to bet on our ideas, to take the calculated risk, and to act. Everyday living requires courage if life is to be effective and bring happiness.

MAXWELL MALTZ

Fortune favors the brave.

VIRGIL

Confidence does not preclude fear.

> *To use fear as the friend it is, we must retrain and reprogram ourselves ... We must persistently and convincingly tell ourselves that the fear is here—with its gift of energy and heightened awareness—so we can do our best and learn the most in the new situation.*
>
> PETER MCWILLIAMS

Fear is not the problem. It's a means to an end. So the question is: What do you do with the fear?

Confidence is not the absence of fear. Fear challenges you to do what it takes to achieve your goals.

> *Remember that fear always lurks behind perfectionism. Confronting your fears and allowing yourself the right to be human can, paradoxically, make you a far happier and more productive person.*
>
> DR. DAVID M. BURNS

The Prospering Couple expresses faith in each other.

"Trust implies faith and confidence," wrote author Mark Goulston, M.D. This observation points to the importance of confidence for the Prospering Couple. We need to express support for our partner—that she or he will find the way to make things work.

> *Faith is to believe what you do not see; the reward of this faith is to see what you believe.*
>
> SAINT AUGUSTINE

From this quote you learn to hold a vision, because when you devote effort you can help bring about that vision.

> *Now faith is the substance of things hoped for, the evidence of things not seen.*
>
> THE BIBLE, HEBREWS 11:1

What does faith in your partner sound like? Here are examples:

- "I believe you."
- "So what's your plan?"
- "I know you'll figure it out."
- "I'm sure an idea will come to you."

People want to feel closeness and feel competent. When you say "So what's your plan?" you imply that your partner is truly competent.

Now, here is a story about courage ...

Legend of the Rope of Courage

A young woman and a young man loved each other very much, and they were the thinnest couple in the village. One day the young man made a brilliant but sarcastic remark against the village bully—which was a dumb thing to do.

In the heat of rage, the bully went after the young man with a sword.

Weaponless and outmatched, the young man fled. Hoping to save her lover, the young woman ran ahead of them. She went up to the Wise One of the village.

"Save my loved one!" she cried.

In response, Wise One stopped doing martial arts moves and threw the woman a coil of rope. The woman caught it. She didn't know what to do with it, but she had no time to ask and continued running.

She came to the village square where a bell was high above the ground on a scaffold. She knew that her lover, with the sword-swinging bully behind him, must run through the square. She got an idea that made her shake with terror. She would set a circle of the rope on the ground and then climb up the scaffold—but she was terrified of heights!

She loved the young man, so she did what she had to. After filling her pockets with stones, she climbed the scaffold with the greatest of care.

On her way up she thought, "He better appreciate this. I expect to be taken out to dinner at least once a week."

The young man ran through the square and under the scaffold. As the bully ran over the circle, the woman held tight to her end of the rope and jumped down. The rope sprang out of the sand and encircled the bully's feet. The rope then slid around a horizontal pole that acted like a pulley.

The woman passed the bully going up as she went down on the opposite length of the rope.

On his way up—upside-down—the bully dropped the sword.

Wise One mysteriously appeared and said to the woman, "You are courageous."

"I was terrified," she replied, swaying back and forth and still hanging onto the rope.

Wise One said, "Courage is being afraid and doing it anyway."

From this legend we learn that courage is not the absence of fear. We learn to take action and avoid waiting for ideal conditions. We do our best when we use what we know and the resources we have available at that moment.

Want it From Your True Self

This step is first because it is your source of power. You need to want an outcome, but it cannot be from wanting to please someone else. You need to connect with your True Self and to want the outcome from your True Self. That means your desire is from an authentic place in yourself—not just from a different place that comes from fear or the hope of gaining approval from someone.

In an earlier section, I introduced the term True Self.

Your True Self is that part of you that is strong, focused and filled with natural brilliance and courage.

On the other hand, the False Self, often referred to as the Ego, is made of fear. When you are stuck in your Ego you feel small, vulnerable and fragile. A number of people, when stuck in their Ego, feel irritable and angry. Anger is fear twisted.

An old phrase is: "Real pain comes from living a life not your own."

Saxophone master Kenny G was asked why he got a degree in accounting. He replied, "Some things you do for your mother." We notice that he did not devote his entire life to accounting. Kenny G pursued his real calling—music.

Similarly, Senator Barbara Boxer indicated her true calling when she said, "I really like what I'm doing now. People say I'm giving them energy and hope."

It is not the critic who counts; not the man who points out how the strong man stumbles, or where the doer of deeds could have done them better.

The credit belongs to the man who is actually in the arena, whose face is marred by dust and sweat and blood, who strives valiantly; who errs and comes short again and again; because there is not effort without error and shortcomings; but who does actually strive to do the deed; who knows the great enthusiasm, the great devotion, who spends himself in a worthy cause, who at the best knows in the end the triumph of high achievement and who at the worst, if he fails, at least he fails while daring greatly.

So that his place shall never be with those cold and timid souls who know neither victory nor defeat.

PRESIDENT THEODORE ROOSEVELT

Here is a story about discovering the True Self ...

Legend of Destiny and a Seashell

A young woman was a successful doctor in the village. But the day came when she didn't feel like dragging herself out of bed in the morning. Days became a dreary routine. One person had a cold, another had a broken thumb.

She was depressed and listless, and she snapped at her patients, husband and children.

She went to the Wise One of the village. It was a hot, humid day, making the woman's face drip with perspiration.

"Wise One," she began, "I have no energy. And recently I've been getting sick."

Wise One said nothing, but walked around a clear pool of water below a shimmering waterfall. The woman continued, "I thought I knew what I wanted to do with my life. How do I get my enthusiasm back?"

Wise One said nothing.

Being hot and sticky, the woman snapped, "Well, how?!"

Wise One gracefully pushed the woman into the pool of water. When she broke the surface of the water, she was going to break Wise One. But she discovered that she felt refreshed. Soon after she got out of the pool. The cool water quickly evaporated from her body, which become hot and sticky once more.

"Destiny is like a pool of refreshing water. You dive in and are refreshed. Then it evaporates. You must dive in again and again at different times and in different ways," said Wise One.

Over the next weeks, the woman tried new ventures. She tried selling rugs in the market. She tried fishing.

One day at the beach she stopped, lifted a shell and listened to it. She heard the sound of waves and remembered her childhood and her father pointing out the sound to her. She then remembered the stories her father told.

She jumped to her feet. The stories! That week between seeing patients, she began to write stories. Some stories were about miracle healings she had seen. Some stories were for children.

Now the woman woke up with a smile. She looked forward to each day. The moments of writing brightened her whole life. Yet there were days when certain passages would baffle her, and it felt like it would be impossible to make them work. But she struggled with them, and eventually she succeeded.

During those times of struggle, her healing work would feel special again. In this way, she enjoyed her double-destiny.

Wise One mysteriously appeared and said, "Destiny is what you truly want to do. Work at it and you earn your destiny."

From this legend we learn that destiny is what you truly want to do. And this relates to your True Self.

We unleash hidden personal energy when we pursue what is in our True Self. We align with our design. We are grateful toward Higher Power for the gifts of our natural brilliance. We are on the road to real happiness.

Again, I emphasize to be at your best in the *10 Seconds to Wealth*, it helps to be able to switch the direction of your thoughts quickly. My clients often choose to memorize certain phrases. Here are powerful thoughts on happiness:

Happiness is when what you think, what you say, and what you do are in harmony.

GANDHI

Happiness is that state of consciousness which proceeds from the achievement of one's values.

AYN RAND

Happiness is the key to success. If you love what you are doing, you will be successful.

ALBERT SCHWEITZER

Happiness is within. It has nothing to do with how much applause you get or how many people praise you. Happiness comes when you believe that you have done something truly meaningful.

MARTIN YAN, CREATOR OF THE TV SHOW "YAN CAN COOK"

One interviewer asked me: "How do you find out what your True Self really wants?"

"It's actually a life-long journey. It is about connecting with your natural brilliance. Your True Self is that part of you that is naturally creative and courageous. Some of us have become numb to what brings us true delight. It may take some structured effort to reconnect with your True Self. What did you love to do as a child? What idea about fun or fulfillment is at the edge of your thoughts? Do you want to try a cooking class? Are you drawn to some form of art? What times have you felt that you were at the right place, doing the right thing? The powerful thing to do is to start writing in your journal and answering questions like the ones I just mentioned," I replied.

Writing or talking about your feelings will help you identify your True Self. Talk with a friend or with a therapist about what you truly want (and answer questions that you find in the upcoming Individual's Action Step). Have your journal handy so you can write down your ideas

When you tune into what you truly want, you tap into a source of strong personal energy. Now, Dr. Elayne Savage shares insights about stretching, trying new actions and reaping the rewards.

Self-Acceptance, Self-Respect, and Self-Appreciation

Elayne Savage, Ph.D.

I'm so proud of my accomplishment. I just assembled four IKEA storage units. By myself.

And I didn't listen to the nay-sayers:

"You won't be able to do it without help."

"No way. It's too difficult."

"The directions are so confusing. Only drawings, no words."

"You'll get frustrated and give up before it's done."

My response was to stubbornly insist *I can do this!*

For a change I didn't buy into those old messages that in the past would have paralyzed me:

"Who do you think you are?"

"What makes you think you can do this?"

I just knew I could do the assembly. How? I was remembering another time when everyone warned me I wouldn't be able to do something.

I was eleven years old. Uncle Max gave me a headlamp for my bicycle. I was so excited when I opened the package, expecting to find a headlight. Then I saw many parts lying there, looking nothing like the picture on the box.

My dad offered to assemble it for me. Days turned into weeks. I kept asking "When?" He kept saying, "Soon."

Soon never happened. Each month that went by was another disappointment. I gave up on my dad.

I was determined to get that headlight mounted on my handlebars. I decided to put it together myself. Yes, I struggled with it. Yes, I made mistakes.

Eventually I got that headlamp up and working. My childhood success with that headlamp let me take on the IKEA challenge. I was able to tap into that childhood success and to trust it.

What's a Mistake or Three?

I did make some mistakes. More than once I had to disassemble my work and reassemble it. By the time I got to the second unit, I learned from my mistakes. I'm grateful I was able to tap into a long ago memory of an ability to put things together. I'm grateful to call up the ability to trust myself enough to attempt this project. I'm grateful that I could allow myself to make mistakes and not judge myself harshly. I'm grateful that I can let myself be proud of my accomplishment.

I'm grateful for the chance to experience self-acceptance, self-respect, and self-appreciation.

Lessons From the Yellow Submarine

Another way of transforming abilities is to practice borrowing from one compartment within yourself and move it to another.

Can you visualize a hallway with rooms on either side? Do you remember the scene in *The Yellow Submarine* cartoon movie? Remember how the Beatles characters were running back and forth across the hall from room to room?

Imagine that a room contains skills you developed in childhood and adolescence.

Think of this room as a storage area, with every possible type of storage container.

Can you imagine yourself rummaging through these early strengths that have been tucked away? Can you imagine selecting one or two? You can take your time as you let the process of choosing, sorting, and selecting unfold.

Then gather up this new energy you have found. Carry it across the hall to another room, another compartment, another part of yourself. Take it to a place where you have the space to appreciate your skills in a new way.

Consider ways you can recognize skills that exist in one area of your life and transfer them to another area. In this new space you have created, you might find this new energy begins to transform into something even more precious and useful.

Transforming Self-Rejection into Self-Acceptance

However, for some of us, recognizing and appreciating our abilities is not always easy. Some of us somehow missed out on the essential building blocks of childhood — things like self-esteem, self-assurance, or social skills.

Sometimes it seems that we only have stumbling blocks instead of building blocks.

I can also recall some experiences even earlier than the headlamp adventure. I can recall having real-life building blocks as a young child: my erector set. Perhaps some of you had building blocks as well. Maybe wooden alphabet blocks or Lincoln Logs or Legos.

Did you have a favorite? What was it? Can you picture the pieces now?

Visualize taking them down from the shelf and spreading them around you on a table or the floor.

Can you imagine what they felt like in your hands?

How did you put them together?

What was your step-by-step process of building?

What can you learn from recalling your building process?

Can you transfer these skills over to how you approach tasks and problems today? Instead of undermining, you can practice bolstering, reinforcing, fortifying, buttressing, bracing, or shoring up your resources.

For me, the most wondrous transformation of all is the process of transforming self-rejection into self-acceptance. Successfully putting together those IKEA storage units was an important step for me along the road of self-acceptance, self-respect, and self-appreciation.

> Elayne Savage, Ph.D., The Queen of Rejection,* is a communication coach and expert on taking things personally and the fear of rejection. A professional member of the National Speakers Association, she is a workshop leader, trainer, and consultant. Her relationship books, *Breathing*

Room –Creating Space to Be a Couple and *Don't Take It Personally! The Art of Dealing with Rejection* have been published in 9 languages.

510-540-6230

elayne@QueenofRejection.com

www.QueenofRejection.com

Dr. Elayne reminds us to build on our past successes. It's interesting to note that many children have a wonderful sense of persistence. Sometimes, parents finally exclaim, "All right. All right. You can have *one* cookie!"

Tap into your true self. Find out what your really want. What is the "cookie" that you want now?

Remember to focus on what you want from deep within your heart.

Individual's Action Step

Write down what you truly want. Then write down how you will feel differently when you get what you truly want. Will you feel creative? Safe? Uplifted? Proud of yourself for helping others? In tune with your heart?

Couple's Action Step

Each partner writes a list of what he or she truly wants deep down inside. Then, when appropriate, share with each other the personal list and brainstorm two ways that each partner can support the other to achieve what is truly desired in life.

Principle

Take action to support what your True Self really wants, and fulfillment blossoms in your life.

Leverage Question

How can you take action this week to move in the direction of what your True Self really wants?

Adapt

> *Take the first step in faith. You don't have to see the whole staircase, just take the first step.*
> MARTIN LUTHER KING, JR.

You can be confident in yourself when you are certain that you are flexible and can adapt to whatever comes up. In the above quote from Martin Luther King, Jr., we're encouraged to move forward even when we don't know all the steps.

> *A person should set his goals as early as he can and devote all his energy and talent to getting there. With enough effort, he may achieve it. Or he may find something that is even more rewarding. But in the end, no matter what the outcome, he will know he has been alive.*
> WALT DISNEY

Set up a Low Mood First-Aid Kit

To successfully adapt to situations, you need to learn how to get back on track after being hit by disappointment and pain. I guide my clients to set up a Low Mood First-Aid Kit.

The Low Mood First-Aid Kit is a list of things you can do, when alone, to nurture yourself. These activities or comforting objects can help you eventually flow through and out of a low mood.

My clients have written these items for their kit:

- Photo of my children
- My pets
- Chocolate
- A CD of my favorite singer
- A hot bath while enjoying an aromatherapy candle
- My Tai Chi class
- Doing Yoga while watching a Yoga DVD program

Music doth withdraw our minds from earthly cogitations, lifteth up our spirits into heaven, maketh them light and celestial.

SAINT JOHN CHRYSOSTOM

Many of my clients find that well-chosen music refreshes their minds and bodies.

Having a Low Mood First Aid-Kit helps us recover and remain flexible.

Here is a story to illustrate the process of staying flexible …

Legend of the Flexible One

A woman felt vaguely uneasy. Something felt off about her life, but she didn't know where to start to find answers on her own. So she went to the Wise One of the village.

"Stretch with me," said Wise One.

Every day for a year the woman stretched and did martial arts with Wise One. She delighted in her progress. She felt physically flexible, and she noticed that as she felt better, her confidence also improved.

Then one day an earthquake dislodged a tree, which fell on the legs of a little girl. The woman ran to help. Just as she was nearing the pinned girl an aftershock sent a thin tree falling toward the little girl's head. The woman's arms were not long enough. She could not reach in front of the girl in time. She stretched her leg out and kicked away the tree just in time.

Wise One came running and lifted the tree off the girl's legs. The girl was merely bruised.

Wise One smiled and said to the woman, "You were ready. Your arms would not do—so you used your legs. You were flexible—both in body and mind. To succeed, genius is not necessary. Flexibility and persistence prevail."

From this legend we learn the value of taking action and preparing to be flexible for tough situations.

In the legend, part of the woman's Low Mood First-Aid Kit was exercising with Wise One. Her exercise and stretching helped the woman expand her ability to adapt to new situations.

Here is a prime example of how people develop their skills so they can adapt to new situations. The Toastmasters organization helps people overcome the fear of speaking in public. At Toastmasters.org, the benefits of being a member are expressed:

> *Toastmasters offers a proven way to improve your communication skills. By participating in a fun and supportive Toastmasters group, you'll become a better speaker and leader and gain confidence to succeed in whatever path you've chosen in life.*
>
> - *Deliver great presentations*
> - *Easily lead teams and conduct meetings*
> - *Give and receive constructive evaluations*
> - *Be a better listener*

With warm appreciation, I support the value that Toastmasters groups provide for their members. And it has been an honor for me to be a guest speaker at various Toastmasters clubs across the United States.

My point here is: take action, get new skills, increase your "toolkit" and become ready to adapt well to new situations. With such skills, your confidence soars.

Remember that when you know you will adapt and remain flexible, you have the essential part of confidence.

Individual's Action Step

Identify two ways you can nurture yourself when the going gets tough. Write a list to comprise your Low Mood First-Aid Kit.

Couple's Action Step

Make a personal list of three things that get you down. Together, talk with your partner about your list and how each of you can do two supportive actions to booster your partner's energy.

Principle

Prepare for low mood times with compensating actions (in a Low Mood First-Aid Kit).

Leverage Question

How can you adapt and try different methods to deal with a situation you are now facing?

Keep Learning

You can be confident in yourself when you are certain that you will keep learning. Confidence is not just something magical that applies from project to project. Each project or situation is unique and presents unknown elements. To do well, we need to learn all we can while doing a new project or dealing with a new situation.

An important part of learning is discovering how to take care of yourself so that you have the stamina to persist.

> *Where there is peace and meditation, there is neither anxiety nor doubt.*
>
> SAINT FRANCIS OF ASSISI

A daily session of twenty minutes of quiet time (prayer or meditation) helps many people recharge so they can keep going forward. People who have a daily quiet time find that they feel calm more often during their day. This paves the way for learning. We can pay attention to the results of new situations, take classes, and listen carefully. We can challenge our mind with new music or visits to art galleries. One author said that he found any day to be successful in which he learned something.

Here is a story about how small steps create what we want.

Legend of Weaving a Rope

A woman who wished to lose weight went to the Wise One of the village. She said, "I go on a diet and two weeks later I gain back more than I lost."

Handing some strands of thread to the woman, Wise One said, "Note this individual thread. It is easy to break." The woman mimicked the Wise One and broke the thread.

Wise One next took several strands and wove them into a rope.

"Note, when woven into a rope, it is difficult to break. Come with me," Wise One directed. Wise One led the woman on a half-mile journey. She returned to Wise One in the following days for more walks, which grew longer each day. After two months the now trim woman took walks for her own pleasure.

Wise One mysteriously appeared, holding a length of rope and a kite. Wise One sent the kite skyward and gave the woman the rope.

Wise One said, "When you began walking, it was like a fragile thread. Each walk you took added another strand to the 'rope.' So you have mastered your walking-habit, and now your rope leads to the sky."

From this legend we learn the value of taking daily steps toward our dream. As the woman learned in the above story, our daily steps soon become a habit. The woman developed the habit of walking. Other people develop the habit of reading each day. Reading can be a great source of continual learning.

> *The man who does not read good books has no advantage over the man who cannot read them.*
>
> MARK TWAIN

Choose to develop empowering habits.

> *Habit is stronger than reason.*
>
> GEORGE SANTAYANA

> *Sow an act ... reap a habit; Sow a habit ... reap a character; Sow a character ... reap a destiny.*
>
> GEORGE DANA BOARDMAN

An important part of *keep learning* is to discover what you truly love to do.

> *You have to find something that you love enough to be able to take risks, jump over the hurdles and break through the brick walls that are always going to be placed in front of you. If you don't have that kind of feeling for what it is you are doing, you'll stop at the first giant hurdle.*
>
> GEORGE LUCAS

Your true confidence is enhanced when you are certain that you will do what it takes to learn from each situation.

Life gives us feedback. Some feedback we like: "Good job. Here's a raise."

Other feedback we don't like: "Sorry, too few people want to buy your product." Some people call that failure.

It's not a failure when you learn something!

Learn from the feedback. When it's good you learn what is working and what you need to continue doing. When feedback is bad, you learn that you must try something new and different.

The Prospering Couple realizes that success is learning something new.

How do you learn something? You ask powerful questions.

People prone to giving up ask disempowering questions like: "Why does this always happen to me?"

On the other hand, my clients focus on this Principle

The answer is in the question. Ask better questions. What am I learning here? How can we make this better?

Remember that as you keep learning and persisting, you are actually growing as a person and as a spiritual being. People don't give up so easily when they're flexible and enjoy learning new things.

Individual's Action Step

What new things can you do each day that will become a learning experience? Make a list.

Couple's Action Step

List three things that inspire your curiosity. Talk with your partner about how you two might enjoy looking into something on each person's list. Talk about learning new things together.

Principle

We develop confidence in ourselves when we take action, learn and persist.

Leverage Question

How can you support yourself to learn and persist in your efforts?

Encourage Help

Authors Robert Kiyosaki and Loral Langemeier say, "Wealth is a team sport."

Many successful people have an effective team that includes an accountant, attorney, executive assistant and others.

The truth is that one does not need to be the smartest person around. One only needs access to input from effective people. This is why great writers have great editors. Industrialist and philanthropist, Andrew Carnegie suggested his own epitaph to be: "Here lies a man who was able to surround himself with men far cleverer than himself."

You can be confident in yourself when you are certain that you will go out and get the help you need.

> *A tree is known by its fruit; a man by his deeds. A good deed is never lost; he who sows courtesy reaps friendship, and he who plants kindness gathers love.*
>
> SAINT BASIL

So how do we develop supportive friendships? We extend our hands. I frequently ask, "How can I be supportive of what you're doing?" The idea is to support others in a way that begins a circle of supportive friends and colleagues.

Many people you meet will respond to your kindness by helping you in return. As one of my book editors says, "That's what networking is all about." I have known her for twenty-seventeen years, and she worked on this book in your hands! That's a blessing of years of friendship.

Some people hesitate to offer help because they fear the request will be too big or time consuming. For example, Shaya asked my client Anna to advertise her new book to Anna's list of e-newsletter subscribers. Anna became instantly afraid because she knew that she could lose subscribers (and her own sales) by sending out too many advertisements.

I coached Anna to have a ready answer for this situation: "Shaya, you're my dear friend and I know how important this is to you. Let me see how I might be able to help you. Let me get back to you tomorrow or the next day." This gave Anna time to make a good decision. She gave herself *think-space*.

Anna came up with a solution. She called Shaya and said, "Shaya, here's what I can do. I can put your book with my products at the autograph table during my next speech. Right now I'm concerned that my e-newsletter subscribers are touchy about getting too many ads. But I would like to support your book sales by putting it up front at my autograph table. How's that sound?"

Shaya was gracious and thanked Anna for her help.

Since that time, Anna continues to ask friends, "How can I be supportive of what you're doing?"

This has been an example of building and maintaining a supportive friendship.

The Prospering Couple seeks competent, valuable advice from experts.

When seeking help from a top person in a field, approach the person in a helpful way.

For example, one actress sent me hyperlinks about film financing sources. This was good thinking on her part. Feature film producers and directors like me are frequently looking for funding opportunities. This actress developed a friendship with me, and I have cast her in four projects so far.

Another example: When I first started in the speaking industry, I hired a top speaker as my coach. As a result I immediately began making money. I also avoided years of just spinning my wheels. She showed me how to target the right audience and focus on making products.

Confidence is not something that magically applies to each new project. Each new project or situation will present you with new challenges and unknown elements. As I mentioned in a previous section: Going out and getting the necessary knowledge and support you need from the appropriate people can raise your confidence.

Remember to build relationships and encourage help.

Individual's Action Step

List five ways in which you would really triumph if you received help. Look up someone who has the answers you need. Find a way to get in touch with that person and schedule an informal interview. Note that many people are happy to give some free advice and share their knowledge. It's brightens the advisor's day! Be sure to send a thank you note to inform the advisor how you took action with the advice and how things turned out.

Couple's Action Step

Ask your partner about three possible ways you can help him or her. Use your day planners and schedule time to help each other.

Principle

Wealth is a team sport.

Leverage Question

How can you support others in a way that begins a circle of supportive friends and colleagues?

Conclusion to Chapter Six

In Chapter Six, we covered a powerful definition of confidence with the process W.A.K.E.

> W – Want It From Your True Self
> A – Adapt
> K – Keep Learning
> E – Encourage Help

These are the four elements of real confidence. I use the process W.A.K.E. to remind us to wake up to the reality of true confidence. Trust yourself to have these four elements. Learn to feel assured that you will do what you need to do—and that you will learn what you need to learn as you go along. An old phrase holds that we learn by doing. Understand that no high achiever waits for the absence of fear. The high achiever and the Prospering Couple focus on flexibility and preparation. To my audiences, I emphasize: *Courage is easier when I'm prepared.*

> *Spectacular achievement is always preceded*
> *by unspectacular preparation.*
> ROBERT H. SCHULLER

By studying the effective methods of high achievers (and this book), you prepare yourself for opportunities.

High achievers spot rich opportunities swiftly, make big decisions quickly and move into action immediately. Follow these principles and you can make your dreams come true.

ROBERT H. SCHULLER

7

Take Action as a Team for Real Abundance

In Chapter Five, we learned to bring more romance and wealth into our relationship.

In Chapter Six, we learned what real confidence is and how to develop it in ourselves and each other.

Now, in Chapter Seven, you will learn to work as a loving team to open the gate to a flow of massive abundance. When you work as a loving team you both naturally enter a heightened state that makes it easier to do well during the *10 Seconds to Wealth*.

We will use the process T.E.A.M.

- T – Take Over the Weak Spots
- E – Encourage Entrepreneurship and Support
- A – Adapt to Personal Styles
- M – Make Good Luck

Let's continue ...

Take Over the Weak Spots

> *If we learn not humility, we learn nothing.*
>
> **JOHN JEWEL**

These are the important questions: Are you coachable? Will you humbly learn from each situation and discover your weak spots? Will you learn from your partner?

> *Above all the grace and the gifts that Christ gives to his beloved is that of overcoming self.*
>
> **SAINT FRANCIS OF ASSISI**

The self we are overcoming is the False Self or Ego. This is the part of you that is made of fear and feels vulnerable. On the other hand, we look to connect with our True Self—that part of you with natural brilliance and courage, which are gifts from Higher Power.

For example, my client Amanda writes in a journal to connect with her True Self. I invited her write about "I am proud of myself for ... " She uncovered that she is happy with her compassion and how she takes action to support her friends, family and co-workers. This gave her the strength to look at her personal areas to improve.

> *I claim to be a simple individual liable to err like any other fellow mortal. I own, however, that I have humility enough to confess my errors and to retrace my steps.*
>
> GANDHI

We need to be vigilant about our weak spots. To be vigilant is to stay aware of your personal areas that need improvement.

Here's a personal example: As a film editor, I tend to be a fast-paced cutter, which means that I put together sequences in which individual images have short durations. I need to compensate for this tendency because the most effective feature films have varying rhythms.

Know your tendencies *and compensate for them.* As a solution, I have a slow-paced editor look over the first draft of my edited scenes and offer suggestions to me.

Sometimes it is better to ask for help. In today's fast-paced world, we don't have time to become terrific at all skills. We need to celebrate our natural brilliance and become great at expressing our natural brilliance.

Then, the second part of creating success is to identify and pay attention to your personal weak spots. But also remember your areas of natural brilliance. With this strategy you and your partner can work together to accentuate each of your strengths and compensate for the weaknesses.

The Prospering Couple has partners who compensate for each other's weak areas.

There is a reason why two people become a couple—a blessed team. It is amazing how two people fit together like jigsaw puzzle pieces. I have a natural tendency to celebrate a vision; while my sweetheart focuses on the present moment. My weak spot can be overworking. So she helps by making sure I get outside and enjoy a walk in a park. Together, we are unstoppable.

One couple I know, Gerald and Rebecca, has a special arrangement. Rebecca has dyslexia, so Gerald reads the fine print on all documents. And Rebecca, who is a natural at all things mechanical, takes care of household-related repairs.

> *Count your blessings. Once you realize how valuable you are and how much you have going for you, the smiles will return, the sun will break out, the music will play, and you will finally be able to move forward the life that God intended for you with grace, strength, courage, and confidence.*
>
> OG MANDINO

Here is a story about discovering the gifts we have deep inside …

Legend of Building a Temple

There came a time when a temple was needed to house the scrolls containing the legends of the village. The village members wondered who would be chosen by the Wise One to build the temple. Would it be the most successful builder in the village?

Around this time a young woman came to Wise One. She wanted to like herself more; to believe in herself. Wise One said nothing but handed

Part III, Chapter 7   *Take Action as a Team for Real Abundance*   •   **255**

the young woman a scroll. The young woman unraveled it and read: "To the builder of this temple … "

The young woman quickly rolled up the scroll and turned to hand it back to Wise One. But Wise One had vanished.

The young woman panicked. It was certain that the whole village would somehow hear she was chosen. What if she couldn't do it? She'd have to move to another village. And her parents would have to endure the shame.

But what if she did succeed in building the temple? She would prove to herself and the world that she could do anything. She had a chance. Wise One had chosen her.

She wanted to learn to believe in herself. "But I don't even know how to cut a plank of wood," she moaned.

Wise One mysteriously appeared and led the woman on a brisk walk. They arrived at a sparkling pond. Wise One pointed, guiding the young woman to look into the pond. She saw a shadow of the shape of her head and shoulders. As the water settled, she viewed herself holding up her hand, but with nothing in it.

Wise One unsettled the water with a wave of a hand. Now the young woman could see that she was holding a saw. She looked at her hand. There was still nothing in it. She looked for Wise One, but her mentor had gone.

Setting a look of determination on her face, the young woman went in search of a saw and schooling. She also noticed that the scroll in her pocket said the temple must be complete in one year.

The young woman went to the most successful builder and asked to team up with him to build the temple. Upset that he had not been chosen for the project, the builder refused. The young woman went to ten more builders in search of one to learn from. One kind builder agreed to guide her. She gave herself a realistic goal of building a small temple.

Every day the young woman studied building techniques, and everyday she worked on the temple. She asked people to join her. Many did.

One day a storm came and knocked down the young woman's first two walls. She cried.

The young woman went to the pond and saw herself crying in the mirror of water. When the water settled she saw herself with the finished temple behind her. The water reflected her smile.

Wise One mysteriously appeared and said, "You see yourself finishing. I demonstrated my faith in you, and now you have faith in yourself."

The young woman finished the temple. Her story became the final legend of the village.

From this story we learn the importance of enhancing our faith in ourselves. The legend is a metaphorical story about visualizing. An old phrase is: Things are made twice. First in our minds then in the outside world.

It is crucial to have faith in yourself. We need faith to energize us to take action in areas that are our natural weak spots … so we ask for help … and so we devote effort to make things better.

> *Courage and grace are a formidable mixture.*
> MARLENE DIETRICH

Remember to be vigilant about your weak spots. You don't need to solve each weak area. You can get help.

Some of us are great with doing home improvement projects. Others can't pound a nail without missing the nail and finding their thumb—ouch!

Some people easily balance their checkbooks. Others need to form a search party for their receipts.

Here is an important point: Identify people who can provide support for your weak spots.

- Ask for help from your partner. Realize, however, that no one person can be the sole support of another person.
- Use the buddy-system with a friend. My client Terrie supported her friend by being her companion at the dentist's office. In return, Terrie's friend sat near her and cheered Terrie on as she made her first cold calls to prospective customers.
- Seek advice from professionals.
- Listen to educational audio programs and read books like this one to give you support when you need it—like when it's 11 p.m., and everyone important to you is asleep.

And consider this: If you don't have a skill, hire it! Or trade efforts with a friend when cash flow is low.

Helping each other is one way to feel grace and enjoy our blessings. In the film *Cocoon: The Return*, one wife told her husband how glad she was to help him by massaging his aching back—after they had returned to earth. (Apparently there was no back pain on the benevolent aliens' planet.) Part of the gift of a loving relationship is to ease each other's pain.

Individual's Action Step

List three of your personal weak spots. List four resources that can help with your weak spots. (Would it help to hire a personal organizer for a couple hours?)

Couple's Action Step

List three personal weak spots. Talk with your partner about how you can help each other—and perhaps, hire someone to help. List four possibilities that can help you compensate for a weak spot. Place one possibility on the calendar and begin taking action steps in the right direction.

Principle

Fill in your partner's gaps.

Leverage Questions

Ask your partner: What tasks make you feel uncomfortable? What do you tend to procrastinate on? How can I work with you to fill in the gap?

Encourage Entrepreneurship and Support

Some people seem to be born entrepreneurs. They are risk-okay as opposed to risk-adverse. Early in his career, Walt Disney suffered when his top character Oswald, the Lucky

Rabbit and some team members had been taken over by a ruthless distributor. This was a disaster. But Walt Disney then felt determined to move through disappointment, fear and financial upheaval in order to improve things.

Walt's wife Lillian (the Non-Entrepreneurial Partner), described her view of the situation: "He gambled everything we had—which wasn't much, but seemed a lot to us—on the Oswald series. All he could say, over and over, was that he'd never work for anyone again as long as he lived: He'd be his own boss. I didn't share his long-range viewpoint. I was in a state of shock, scared to death."

Walt Disney had so much faith in his own judgment and intuition that he persevered even when his wife could not see his vision for a bright future.

> *It is good to have a failure while you're young because it teaches you so much ... it makes you aware that such a thing can happen to anybody, and once you've lived through the worst, you're never quite as vulnerable afterward ... I hope to stay young enough in spirit to never fear failure.*
>
> WALT DISNEY

Often, couples discover that their partner is their opposite in terms of tolerance for risk. The idea is to avoid trying to make your partner similar to you.

Value both entrepreneurship and support

One interviewer said, "Most people are not entrepreneurs." Her point was that many people do not have their own business.

However, we can focus on a definition of entrepreneurship that includes having a future-focus, a vision for a better life, a tolerance for pain in the present, and being okay with risk taking.

So when we talk about the Entrepreneurial Partner we are addressing the one who puts her or his career very high on a priority list. This is the partner who tends to work many hours.

The interviewer continued, "It's hard for me to see the idea of an entrepreneur inside a corporation."

I replied: "Let's look at what entrepreneurs do. When you're an entrepreneur:

- You set a vision.
- You go your own way.
- You take responsibility for results.
- You are assertive.
- You lead people.
- You lead yourself.

Some form of these entrepreneurial actions can be done within an organization. And it's true that this takes good people skills and some finesse."

Prospering Couples learn to appreciate each other's differences.

> *Marriage is the alliance of two people, one of whom never remembers birthdays and the other who never forgets.*
>
> **OGDEN NASH**

One possible solution is to buy the forgetful partner a Personal Digital Assistant that beeps one week before someone's birthday. The idea is find a workable solution to help the absent-minded partner.

My client Rick posts a sign on his bathroom mirror to remind him of his couple's therapy appointment. His wife Nancy doesn't like the sign, although she knows it helps her husband fulfill his commitment. Nancy must balance out her aesthetic preference with her priority to support their relationship.

Here is a story that talks about how to develop balance ...

Legend of the Tightrope

A young man was a successful doctor in the village. People knew he was conscientious and caring. His days were filled with more than enough patients. But he needed a vacation, he needed sleep, he needed something.

The young man went to the Wise One of the village. He explained his situation. Wise One pointed to a tightrope that was suspended over a shallow pond.

"You want me to walk across that?" the young doctor asked.

"Walk the rope if you wish the fulfillment of your challenge."

The young man crawled on the edge of the platform. He started across, fell, and dangled in mid air. Using his legs and hands, he began crawling across the rope upside-down to the other side.

Then his hands gave out. He landed with a resounding SPLASH!

Yet, because he was desperate, the doctor came back and tried again. The stress of his life was tearing him apart. He wanted to learn Wise One's lesson.

Some days Wise One instructed the young man to return to the tightrope at an earlier time. This meant the young doctor had to finish work earlier that day.

Some days Wise One led the young man through exercises.

Many days Wise One had the young man sleep a little longer than usual.

Together, Wise One and the young man ate healthy food.

One night Wise One led the young doctor to a special building. "What do I do here?" the young man asked as they approached the building.

"Dance," replied Wise One.

The young man did as he was instructed. He danced and had a joyous time. To his surprise, he soon met a special young woman at the event.

Each day the young doctor went further in his journey across the tightrope—until one day he walked gracefully across. The young man's new friend applauded. And the young man realized that he felt good!

Wise One mysteriously appeared and said, "The tightrope is life. Some people crawl. Some people dance across. It's a matter of balance."

From this legend we learn to develop balance in ourselves. One thing that partners can do for each other is to support activities that provide balance for their partner. For example, my client Serena says, "I'm going to take a Yoga class." Her husband Joe replies, "Sounds good. I'll take the kids for Chinese food that evening and have your dinner waiting for you when you get home."

Express support with the Moment of Appreciation

A Moment of Appreciation is a brief time—even just two minutes—when one partner gets to enjoy a triumph by describing it to the other partner. My client Jeremy asks his wife Althea, "I'd like a Moment of Appreciation in about 15 minutes, okay?"

She agrees. Fifteen minutes later Jeremy shows her three sketches for the cover of his upcoming book. It is a moment of celebration. She says, "That's looking good. Good job."

> *The deepest principle in human nature is the craving to be appreciated.*
>
> WILLIAM JAMES

In this chapter we are emphasizing the value of support. We feel supported when our partner expresses appreciation. It is also support when the Non-Entrepreneurial Partner realizes that leadership can be a gift from my Entrepreneurial Partner.

> *Leadership is getting someone to do what they don't want to do, to achieve what they want to achieve.*
>
> TOM LANDRY

For example, author Stephan Schiffman and his wife set goals together—which created leadership for their family. They determined how many workshops Stephan must sell in order for them to afford a new dining room set. They worked together as a team. They supported each other and strived toward a goal.

One interviewer asked me: "What if neither partner is an Entrepreneurial Partner?"

I answered: "We're talking about tendencies toward entrepreneurial thoughts and behavior. I have seen that usually:

- One partner is more tolerant of risk.
- One partner is more future-oriented.
- One partner wants to try more things to gain money.

On the other hand, the Non-Entrepreneurial Partner tends to be more present-moment focused."

The point is to support your partner *and avoid trying to make her or him similar to you.* Value your partner for his or her natural tendency to be entrepreneurial or supportive.

Express the Positive Intention in Your Conversation

One time I felt abandoned by my sweetheart. She was off in the other room relaxing and watching television. Upon seeing her later, instead of expressing my irritation, I said, "I missed you." That was the positive intention. And when we came together to hug and kiss, I stopped feeling abandoned. And she helped me by looking over some character designs for an animated feature film I was working on. She later told me, "I think you did a good job. It made me feel like I needed to spend more time with you."

Remember that the Prospering Couple values both entrepreneurship and support.

Part III, Chapter 7   *Take Action as a Team for Real Abundance*   • **265**

Individual's Action Step

Where do you need to express leadership in your own life? What have you procrastinated on? Write down what you can do to take an easy step forward.

Couple's Action Step

List two things that often get you into an argument. Identify two ways you could rephrase your comment so that the positive intention is expressed first. Then talk this over with your partner. Ask questions like: "When I'm feeling lonely, will it help if I say 'I missed you' instead of just 'Where were you?'"

Principle

Inspire comfort in conversation. Express the positive intention first.

Leverage Question

How can you convert a situation that causes upsetting reactions into a situation that produces positive responses?

Adapt to Personal Styles

The art of life is to flow with things as they appear. We need to flow with the personal styles of our partner. Personal styles are patterns we find in the other person. In this section we will talk about:

- Personality style
- Thinking style
- Pain-interaction style

When you learn to flow with your partner's personal styles you open the door to harmony, romance and wealth in your relationship.

Here is a story that emphasizes the importance of flowing with life ...

Legend of the Flow

A spin kick smashed into a young man's face. It lifted him off his feet and crashed him to the ground. The bully looked down and sneered, "Next time, you bring money or I won't be so kind."

The young man went to the Wise One of the village to learn martial arts. Although he was an eager student, the young man complained to himself each time Wise One had him redo a set of forms because his movement was off. Wise One saw the discomfort on the young man's face.

So Wise One took him to a stream and pointed to a rock standing in the middle of the moving water. Wise One said to the young man, "You are the rock complaining that the water is tearing against you."

Then Wise One threw a twig into the stream. Wise One used a long stick to turn the twig toward the bank and said, "Steer yourself to the port you choose."

Wise One continued, "In practice, accept the process that leads to quality. In life, learn to flow."

The young man remade his attitude. From that moment onward, when he grew tired of the hardships of practice, he would chant in his mind, "Accept the process. Accept the process."

And Wise One saw the young man continue to improve.

One day the young man stood in a line at the market to buy food for his family. To his horror, and feeling the pain of guilt in his stomach, the young man realized that he would be late for his lesson with Wise One. Remembering "Flow," the young man hailed a passing friend to take a message to Wise One. Still thinking of Flow, the young man did leg stretching exercises while waiting in line.

Then, suddenly, the bully's foot landed on the young man's back. The young man flowed forward with the blow, did a somersault, and landed squarely on his feet. The bully did a flying kick toward the young man who flowed out of the way as the bully hit a wall and knocked himself unconscious.

Wise One mysteriously appeared and said, "The art of life is Flow. You flow with the punch, out of the way, and in another way."

From this legend we learn the value of flowing with things as they appear in life.

Prospering Couples Flow with the Other's Personality Style

Based on the work of a number of researchers, I share the ideas about personality styles with easy-to-remember animal images.

> **The Lion**—A person who is the leader, hard charging and bottom-line oriented.
> **The Beaver**—A person who is analytic and like an engineer. He or she can be slow to make decisions; seeking first to have all the facts, graphs and tables. This person fears making a mistake or looking unintelligent.
> **The Peacock**—A person who loves to socialize and show off. He or she can be poor on follow-up.
> **The Dog**—A person who demonstrates loyalty and who loves routine and comfort. This person cares most about the impact that changes have on people. The Dog is slow to change and often dislikes change.

Janet has the Dog-style personality. After 44 years of marriage, her husband Mario (Beaver-style) will still get disappointed when he brings home new artwork and receives no supporting enthusiasm from Janet. I explained to him that Janet will like his purchase as soon as she gets used it (in Dog-style fashion).

In fact, time and again, Mario would later say, "How about we give this item to our son's friend?" It was never a surprise when Janet protested. She had become used to the item and was now attached to it.

Understanding personality styles can help you avoid a lot of ruffled feathers and hurt feelings.

Another common style mix in a relationship involves the Lion and the Beaver. The Lion often dislikes listening to the Beaver because the Beaver adds a lot of details into a conversation. And the Beaver finds that the Lion makes decisions too quickly and without enough research.

The Dog dislikes the Lion because the Lion appears heartless and only concerned with the bottom-line.

As life would have it, many of us are in a relationship with someone who has the opposite personality style. Here are good practices:

1. When talking to a Lion, the Beaver can express the conclusion first, and then ask, "How much supporting detail do you want?"

2. When talking with a Peacock, the Lion can say, "So you'll have the report ready at 2 p.m. on Tuesday? I'll call you then." (Two days before the actual deadline.)

3. When talking to a Dog, the Lion can say, "This is similar to what you're already doing. And, this is how the team members will be okay in this situation."

Prospering Couples Flow with the Other's Thinking Style

Two major thinking styles sometimes come into conflict with the other:

1. **Convergent thinkers** are comfortable with detailed schedules and routine. These are methodical people.

2. **Divergent thinkers** can't stand detailed schedules and often have messy desks. These are creative people who feel trapped by routine. Their minds jump around from topic to topic. It is helpful for the divergent thinker to place on the desk a container of files. Then, the divergent thinker can write ideas on sheets of paper and place them into the files, by category. With his or her mind clear, the divergent thinker can keep focused on the task at hand.

With great relief, a woman in the audience of one of my speeches said, "I don't have A.D.D.—I'm a divergent thinker!"

Often a convergent thinker marries a divergent thinker. The Prospering Couple flows with two different people with opposite thinking styles. We realize that we fit together like jigsaw puzzle pieces. We realize a convergent-thinking partner can go to the divergent-thinking partner and ask: "What do you think can go wrong with this project? And how can I prepare myself to avoid such mistakes?" The divergent thinker will surprise her partner with flashes of insight. The partner who listens benefits a lot!

Prospering Couples Flow with the Other's Pain-Interaction Style

The pain-interaction styles include:

The Move-Toward Goal Style: The Entrepreneurial Partner easily endures pain and discomfort because

> she or he is living partly in the future—when the dream will become a reality. This partner is moving toward the better future.
>
> **The Move-Away Goal Style:** The Non-Entrepreneurial Partner often is more focused on the present moment and runs away from discomfort and pain.

On a Sunday afternoon, the Entrepreneurial Partner might say, "Let's get the taxes done!" (She's living in the future when the tax refund check arrives.) On the other hand, the Non-Entrepreneurial wants to relax on Sunday and often cannot see a bright future. The Non-Entrepreneurial Partner cannot see past their current troubles. (Macaroni and cheese for dinner four nights this week.)

To help the situation, the Entrepreneurial Partner will make sure there is something to look forward to each week—which will comfort the Non-Entrepreneurial Partner and help him or her endure the start-up phase of wealth building.

It's important to note how the two personality types aid each other in these times. The Entrepreneurial Partner will benefit by listening to her or his Non-Entrepreneurial Partner. And the Non-Entrepreneurial Partner can help the Entrepreneurial Partner avoid getting out of balance and burning out.

Remember to honor each other's personal styles. Celebrate how your differences fit together.

Individual's Action Step

Identify your own personal styles of:

- Lion, Beaver, Peacock, or Dog
- Convergent or Divergent Thinking
- Pain-interaction style

Find ways that you can flow with your partner's styles.

Couple's Action Step

Discuss your individual personality styles. Find safe ways to discuss tough issues.

Principle

Honor each other's personal styles. Celebrate how your differences fit together.

Leverage Question

How do you honor your partner's personal styles?

Make Good Luck

"Good luck!" our friends often tell us when we're trying some new venture. Dictionary.com defines luck as: "Good fortune or prosperity; success."

To create good luck we focus on:

- Integrity
- Courage
- Action
- Connection (networking)

- Service

I've found that luck is quite predictable. If you want more luck, take more chances. Be more active. Show up more often ... Successful people are always looking for opportunities to help others. Unsuccessful people are always asking, 'What's in it for me?'

BRIAN TRACY

Oprah Winfrey has had good fortune, which has come from hard work.

Luck is a matter of preparation meeting opportunity.

OPRAH WINFREY

Oprah also noted: "At the roll call of your life, at the end of your life, what really matters is who did you love and who did you offer love to."

Here is a story about how things turn out well with sufficient preparation ...

Legend of Appearances

"If you do not improve you will lose this job," said the woman's employer. The woman staggered homeward, tears filling her eyes. The Wise One of the village mysteriously appeared and said, "Come with me."

Wise One led the woman to a crystal blue lake. The woman leaned over to dive in. The water looked so refreshing. Wise One put a restraining hand on her shoulder. "Pass your hand through the water," Wise One suggested.

"Ouch!" said the woman as her hand struck a sharp rock just below the surface of the water. Just then a tiger bounded toward Wise One.

Wise One stood on tip-toes, arms overhead, and roared. The tiger hesitated and turned. It leaned down for the drink it had come for and struck its nose on the sharp rock below the surface of the water.

Realizing what happened, the woman said, "You appeared big." Wise One said, "Yes. And you are a good worker. Yet your work area gives the appearance that you are disorganized."

The next morning the woman arrived early at work. She set a new schedule for herself. She now arrived before her boss and left after him. And she kept her work area clear.

Her boss was so impressed he gave her a promotion.

Wise One mysteriously appeared and said, "Now you know the power of appearances."

From this legend we learn to make good luck and improve our lives by ensuring that we appear as competent as we really are.

Make luck by opening the door to grace.

Grace is unmerited favor from Higher Power. Some spiritual paths hold that to gain grace one must participate in certain rituals. Meanwhile, other spiritual paths say that Higher Power never abandons us. This idea is echoed in this quote:

> *Grace is available for each of us every day—our spiritual daily bread—but we've got to remember to ask for it with a grateful heart and not worry about whether there will be enough for tomorrow.*
>
> SARAH BAN BREATHNACH

Grace is often a matter of being open to Higher Power's blessings. An old Quaker prayer is: "While you pray, move your feet." This means pray and take appropriate action, too.

> *The world needs dreamers and the world needs doers. But above all, the world needs dreamers who do.*
>
> SARAH BAN BREATHNACH

Use Your Integrity and Courage in Tough Situations

One way to open the door to grace is to learn to avoid overreacting in difficult situations. We learn to Pause. Stop your reaction. Respond. For example, my client Patrick felt frustrated when his vendor failed to respond to voicemail messages. Patrick started to write a sarcastic e-mail message that began with "Can I ever trust you to reply to your voicemail?" Then he remembered to pause and stop his reaction. He responded by deleting that particular question from his message.

Later, when talking face-to-face with the vendor, Patrick expressed his concerns. He said quietly, "Receiving no response to my voicemail does not work for me. It looks like I'll need to get another vendor who can respond faster and honor my deadlines."

Patrick expressed his personal integrity (that includes a feeling of wholeness) by telling the truth to the vendor. Patrick also demonstrated courage by confronting the situation directly. And he demonstrated compassion by using a kind tone of voice while talking in-person with the vendor.

On the other hand, chastising someone through an e-mail message can create a situation of misinterpretation and anger. When possible, it is better to express what is not working for you in-person or via telephone.

Networking will Increase Your Good Luck

I coach my clients in the skills of making good first impressions and networking at industry events. Here are some methods:

1) Ask gentle questions. You create rapport when you listen carefully.

2) Ask: "What are you looking forward to?"

3) At the closing of your conversation say something like: "It's been great talking with you. It would be good to stay in contact. Do you have a business card?" If the person does not have a business card, take out your own card to write on the back. Then say, "Oh, I'll make one up for you. What's your e-mail address?" (Many people find it easiest to begin new business relationships through e-mail.) If the person has a business card, say something like: "Let's trade." This whole process helps you avoid appearing aggressive.

Look for opportunities to give a presentation at an association or two. You'll make many contacts. Also, you will be presented as an expert—as an exceptional person. What a great way to initiate new contacts. Consider joining Toastmasters—the group for helping one gain public speaking skills.

Networking is a terrific path to gain more lucky opportunities. Be sure to look for ways to help your new acquaintances. Using e-mail, you could send a link to a website related to their area of interest. You can ask: "How can I be supportive of what you're doing?"

Prospering Couples Consider Pulling Together a Team

> *Of all the things I've done, the most vital is coordinating those who work with me and aiming their efforts at a certain goal.*
>
> WALT DISNEY

Remember that good luck is about taking action from a stance of integrity and courage. In this chapter, we discussed practical methods, like networking, for increasing prosperity.

Realize that practical methods work best in the context of a positive spiritual approach. Earlier, I mentioned the Dalai Lama's comment: "If you want others to be happy, practice compassion. If you want to be happy, practice compassion."

In a nutshell, one of the best ways to make your networking a success is to listen attentively to a new person. You demonstrate true compassion when you listen well. And you will make good luck!

Individual's Action Step

Identify ways in which your daily life is not supporting your integrity, courage and connection with others. Identify three things you can do this week to incorporate integrity, courage and connection.

Couple's Action Step

Discuss with your partner something that is bothering you. Where do you need good luck? Is there some way that you can bring compassion to the situation? Can you be kind to someone—or even be compassionate toward yourself? Discuss how your partner might be able to support your efforts.

Principle

Make good luck through integrity, courage and connection.

Leverage Questions

What can be a breakthrough to a better life for you? What would be good luck for you? How can you increase your good luck by enhancing integrity, courage and connection in your daily life?

Conclusion of Chapter Seven

In Part III, we learned to really work together as a loving team.

We have learned to use the methods of T.E.A.M.:

- T – Take Over the Weak Spots
- E – Encourage Entrepreneurship and Support
- A – Adapt to Personal Styles
- M – Make Good Luck

We have learned to honor each other's personal styles and natural brilliance. We have learned to avoid trying to make over our partner as a clone of ourselves. And we realize that we are different people that grow stronger when we cooperate with each other.

Part IV

8

Secret Influence to Get You Out of Trouble

Restore a Relationship after a Screw Up

This section is in your hands because I got in trouble—big, serious trouble. My elderly father was angry with me and he had cut off communication. It was then I realized that my father, who was 71 years old, had limited time left on this planet. I could not wait for him to change.

I had seen someone die in front of me and had known several people who died, so I felt an urgency to keep my relationships in a healthy and positive condition. The healing of the relationship with my father was in my hands.

The technique I used to resolve the situation with my father I will reveal later (in "Flex Your Options"), but it was one of the new and different methods to restore relationships that you will learn from this book.

Other books on persuasion and influence often focus on the context of sales and, even, politics, but there is a time when influence is absolutely crucial to restore a relationship, friendship or interaction with a prospective customer! You may even need to restore your relationship with your boss or you may be fired.

This book will help you when you:

- Need to be forgiven
- Made a blunder with a prospective customer
- Need to make up for a mistake with a current customer
- Have lost the trust of a dear friend
- Realize your relationship is faltering and you did not even do anything wrong
- Need to work effectively with creditors so you can get out of debt and back on your feet

This material will even help a spouse to repair and restore a marriage.

An interviewer once asked me about this claim, saying, "That's a big thing to look at."

I replied, "We're talking about restoring trust. We're also looking at how to listen to another person so that he or she can express all the pain and know deep down that you care."

We will use the I.N.F.L.U.E.N.C.E. process:

       I – Inquire

       N – Nurture

F – Flex your options
L – Listen
U – Understand
E – Energize
N – Negotiate
C – Create (not compete)
E – Embrace

I will refer to the person you want to influence as the offended person. The whole idea is you made a mistake or blunder that has caused damage in the relationship. And now, the offended person associates even talking to you with pain. You want to restore the relationship and help the person trust you again.

In this section, you will learn how to practice the Secret Influence Process, which includes how to:

- Strengthen yourself
- Remain in a calm state of being
- Communicate your concern and kindness
- Take action with the F.A.R. (forgiveness, amends, regret) methods

In the upcoming sections, you'll learn to apply all four elements, and then you'll be able to act effectively in the *10 Seconds to Wealth*. Remember that you need advanced relationship skills so that you create and protect relationships that are your source of opportunities that bring financial abundance and fulfillment. Let's begin …

Inquire

How can you take action towards restoring a relationship? First, you need some vital information. That is, you have to inquire about the offended person's requirements. Along that line, I did some research about forgiveness and healing relationships. In their book *The Five Languages of Apology,* Dr. Gary Chapman and Dr. Jennifer Thomas identify these five languages:

1. Expressing regret: "I am sorry."
2. Accepting responsibility: "I was wrong."
3. Making restitution: "What can I do to make it right?"
4. Genuinely repenting: "I'll try not to do that again."
5. Requesting forgiveness: "Will you please forgive me?"

The point is that people have different preferences as to what makes a "real apology." For example, when I have discussed this topic with college students in my Comparative Religion class, many of them felt strongly that it is not an apology unless the person says, "I was wrong."

Upon personal reflection, I realized that when a family member apologizes to me, I also have a certain preference. It is related to "genuinely repenting." However, I noticed that the phrase "I'll try not to do that again," leaves me feeling uneasy. My preference is to hear, "Here is my plan so I can avoid doing that again."

Discover the Offended's Preferred Language of Apology

At some point, if possible, ask, "Would you please talk about a time when someone apologized in a way that worked for you?"

An interviewer asked me about this, "What if the person is extremely angry? Would he really answer such a question?"

I replied, "It's true. There are times when the offended person will walk away and not even answer; or the offended person will hang up on you if you try to talk with him or her on the telephone. Timing is crucial. Sometimes, it helps to ask this question with a neutral third person present. Maybe a mutual friend."

Trudy saw her friends Calendra and Penny taking a coffee break. Steeling herself, Trudy walked up and said, "Hi, Calendra, Penny." Penny flinched; she was the offended person.

Trudy continued, "This will just take two minutes. Penny, I was wondering (because I want to get back into your good graces) if you might tell me about what makes a real apology to you?"

Penny pointedly turned to Calendra and said, "If you want, you could tell Trudy that a good apology requires that the person say, 'I was wrong.'"

Trudy replied, looking at Penny, "Penny, I know now that I was wrong. And I—"

Penny abruptly got up and walked away. But Trudy felt that she had made a start. She had publicly stated her intention to apologize, and made a good first attempt.

At one point, I was working with a colleague, "George." I did my best to bring up a topic in a gentle way. But he took offense.

I said something like, "You don't need to do a workshop on this title. We could open the possibility of another team member doing the workshop." Frankly, I was stunned with the venom in his response. Apparently, he thought I was being unfair by not setting it up that only he had the first pick of the topics.

At that point, I realized that his intense emotions metaphorically stuffed his ears, so he couldn't hear me. Eventually, I said, "How can I make amends?"

George's response surprised me. He replied, "I don't know how. But thanks for asking." And, here's the good part. His icy demeanor melted and our interactions were positive once again.

This is the power of inquiring.

Principle

Inquire about what the offended person thinks is a good apology.

Power Questions

Are you comfortable asking the question "Would you please talk about a time when someone apologized in a way that worked for you?" Or would another form of question feel better to you? Write down three possibilities.

Nurture

To return to someone's good graces, you need to be strong. You need patience and energy. In essence, you must nurture yourself.

> *Better keep yourself clean and bright; you are the window through which you must see the world.*
>
> GEORGE BERNARD SHAW

Let's face it. You may have made a mistake, but it hurts you that the person is not forgiving you. In fact, you may find yourself to be angry. Say something in anger and you have poured lighter fluid on the flame of the offended person's blazing upset.

We're talking about you becoming strong so that you can influence the person to become calm and eventually let positive feelings rekindle. Throughout this book, an important point is that you influence another person by developing kind, compassionate energy in yourself.

Secret Influence is this: you nurture yourself *so that your positive state of being guides the offended person to soften a hard stance.*

So with our discussion of nurturing, we're actually talking about nurturing yourself during this crisis time.

> *Realize that true happiness lies within you. Waste no time and effort searching for peace and contentment and joy in the world outside. Remember that there is no happiness in having or in getting, but only in giving. Reach out. Share. Smile. Hug. Happiness is a perfume you cannot pour on others without getting a few drops on yourself.*
>
> OG MANDINO

You become powerful as you realize, as Og suggests, that true happiness lies within you. Happiness is not merely "feeling good." It is a deep knowing of your capabilities. Make yourself capable of withstanding a storm with poise and calm. In my book *Nothing Can Stop You This Year,* I share the nurturing power of the Low Mood First Aid Kit.

My clients have noted these parts of their personal Low Mood First Aid Kit:

- Inspirational book or audio CD
- CD player with favorite music CDs (or iPod)
- Photo of his or her children
- Photo of himself or herself with romantic partner in a joyful mood at a relaxing place
- Reminders to take a walk outside, soak in a hot bath or call loving friends

It is crucial to have certain activities that you can do on your own to elevate your mood.*

Method 1: Let a Negative Thought Float Away

My client, Amanda, has a recurring thought that can drain her energy in seconds: "My mother doesn't respect me or my choices. She thinks I'm an idiot." After working with me, Amanda has developed a process in which she just allows that thought to flow away. She treats her thoughts like leaves floating

---

* If you or someone you know has persistent, severe low mood experiences, medical help may be needed. For many people, a combination of medicine and talk-therapy has proved effective for working with symptoms of clinical depression.

down a stream of water. In fact, she looks for another thought immediately—something uplifting like: "I love the comments of my students. They tell me how I helped them improve their artwork and that I have given them hope to pursue their artistic careers." I call this process the *Floating Leaves Method.*

This process of letting a negative thought float away and then choosing to focus on a positive, uplifting thought can help you live more moments in an empowered way. You'll feel better more of the time!

Method 2: Use Write Down–Rip Up to Handle Anger

Anger can drain us of vital energy that we need to pursue our big dreams. Years ago, when I worked in a particular corporation, a manager said something to me that was so rude, offensive and inappropriate that my internal reaction was intense anger. Fortunately, I had heard about writing down my thoughts to get them out of my system. I added an important twist: I ripped up the page and put it in my pocket. If that manager had found my comments, I would have been shown the door!

By ripping up the page, I also ensured that I did not re-read my comments. I got them out of my system, and the rest of my day was not permanently marred by one person's momentary crass behavior.

You now have a method to empower yourself when someone attempts to cut you down. Make the choice to use the Write Down–Rip Up process, and you will strengthen yourself.

Method 3: Use a Pattern-Interrupt to Shift to a Positive Mood

Often, words are not enough. We need to put our body into action, which will create a ripple effect in our thoughts and feelings.

For example, my client Max uses a lightly closed fist tapped twice on his right thigh to snap out of a negative thought pattern. When he feels tired at work, he taps his closed fist and tells himself: "I can do this. I can do this."

The process of using his body combined with empowering words functions as a Pattern-Interrupt for his previous behaviors. You can choose how to interrupt self-defeating behaviors.

- Identify a self-defeating behavior pattern. Write it in a personal journal.
- Write down two ways to use your body and an empowering idea. (Use a Pattern-Interrupt process to elevate your mood.)

Remember, low moods come and go, but we have choices for how we ride them out. We can take action to help shorten the duration of a low mood.

If you're not feeling good in this moment, you can use certain sentences to switch the direction of your thoughts. This is crucial because from thoughts come feelings. I call this process: Use a *switch-phrase*. It's like shifting a rail switch so that a train gets on a new track and into a new direction. The switch-phrase is crucial part of your being at your best during the *10 Seconds to Wealth*.

> *Quotations when engraved upon the memory give you good thoughts.*
>
> WINSTON CHURCHILL

For example, I have memorized a number of quotes from notable people. Just in an instant, I can recall Eleanor Roosevelt's comment: "Do what you feel in your heart is right—for you will be criticized anyway."

I can use the comment as a guide. And this comment can switch me into an empowering state of being.

Principle

Nurture yourself when you're in a crisis in which an offended person refuses to forgive you.

Power Question

Which Low Mood First Aid Kit method seized your attention? Pull out your day planner or calendar and schedule time to use that method. Take action.

Flex Your Options

Imagine that someone you love and care about has abruptly severed all communication. Feels bad, right?

That's what happened to me, and it led to my writing this section to be helpful to you.

As I mentioned earlier, my elderly father cut off communication with me. He would not come to the phone when I called, and he had my mother say, "He's busy." I was aware that, at 71 years old, my father had a limited amount of time remaining on this planet.

He felt he was absolutely right. He had no interest in hearing me or in changing. The healing of the relationship was completely in my hands alone.

He cut off my options. First, no phone calls. Next, he would leave the house if I visited my parents in the city where they live.

This section is about flexing your options. Clearly, I needed to find another option—another way to communicate with my father to express my appreciation of his previous kind and supportive actions.

Expressing Gratitude Can Restore a Relationship

So I found a different way to connect with my father. I sent him a happy-looking card, which depicted Kermit the Frog playing the banjo.

I wrote:

> *Dad,*
>
> *Happy today. Thank you for holding me to high standards. This has made my life better.*
>
> *Love, Tom*

This heartfelt comment from me helped my father feel better. Soon we were talking on the phone and meeting in person again.*

> *Have the courage to act instead of react.*
>
> OLIVER WENDELL HOLMES

If I had followed my father's unfortunate example, this situation could have turned into a grudge or a feud. The problem with delays when people are feeling bad is that people can become thoroughly entrenched in their own opinion and point of view. It becomes even more painful to loosen up from being so rigid.

Consider this old spiritual phrase: Would you rather be right or happy?

Apparently, when we look around at this world, numerous individuals prefer to be "right"—to the point of war and other horrible outcomes.

> *Nothing is softer or more flexible than water, yet nothing can resist it.*
>
> LAO-TZU

---

* My father and I had a heartfelt conversation, to include this story in this book.

So now, I invite you to flex your options. Pull out a sheet of paper or your personal journal and write down three names of important people in your life. Next to each name, write three ways you could express appreciation for that person (even an unreasonable supervisor, for example).

> *Give us grace and strength to forbear and to persevere. Give us courage and gaiety and the quiet mind.*
>
> ROBERT LOUIS STEVENSON

Stevenson's comment reminds us that we may need to pray to a Higher Power for help. That is a powerful option!

> *When I stand before God at the end of my life, I would hope that I would not have a single bit of talent left, and could say, "I used everything You gave me."*
>
> ERMA BOMBECK

So use your imagination and creativity to find ways to communicate appreciation—even when someone has temporarily caused you pain.

Your intention to bring healing to the relationship is primary.

> *Your best work is not the triumph of technique but the purity of purpose.*
>
> TOM MARCOUX

Make a Schedule to Take Action

When you really want something, in this case to restore a business or personal relationship, you need a schedule. Not just a goal. An old phrase is a goal without a deadline is just a wish. So you need a schedule.

You have lost the trust of the offended person. You need to rebuild that trust. It takes time—and consistent effort.

> *I write five pages a day. If you would read five pages a day, we'd stay right even.*
>
> ROBERT PARKER

I shared this quote for three reasons: to provide a bit of humor; to show the commitment to daily action; and to remind us about how a relationship works. We note a "doer" and a "receiver." In the case of the quote, we have a writer and a reader.

To restore your relationship, what do you need to do? It comes down to three actions.

Schedule These Three Actions and You Will Go F.A.R.

To make it easy to remember, I refer to the F.A.R. process:

- *Forgiveness*—ask for forgiveness.
- *Amends*—seek to make amends.
- *Regret*—express your regret.

My distinction is that you need to do these actions repeatedly until the person "gives in" and finally says, "Okay. Okay. I forgive you."

Jack forgot to pick up his girlfriend, Sarah, at the train station. She had previously warned him that she was sensitive about "being abandoned." She even told him the story that she had been left at a day-care center on the afternoon when her parents had a big blow-up that culminated in their divorce.

Sarah's grief and anger were so huge that they surprised her. Sarah delivered the "killing blow" by yelling at Jack: "You're just as thoughtless as my father!"

Jack remembered that he wanted to go F.A.R. in his relationship with Sarah so he set up his personal schedule:

- Once a week, ask for forgiveness
- Three times a week, express his regret
- Four times a week, take action to make amends

He not only scheduled these actions into his day planner, but also went even further. To amend his faulty behavior, he purchased a personal digital assistant that would provide him with an alarm to remind him to perform these actions. It took some time but eventually Sarah forgave Jack. She mentioned that his consistent effort helped.

I once read: "A goal is accountable when it's countable."

How to ask for forgiveness

You could say something like: "Our relationship is so important to me. I know I did wrong. It's tearing me up inside that we're not close. Would you please forgive me?"

A number of people need significant time to get to the place of forgiveness. They might even say, "I want to forgive you, but I ... but I can't now—not yet."

So you need to maintain your own patience and continue to consistently follow through with F.A.R.—ask for forgiveness; make amends; and express regret.

By the way, for me, if a family member hurts me, what counts to me is to hear his or her plan on how the mistake will not happen again. That is big part of making amends to me.

Just keep taking action and realize:

All difficult things have their origin in that which is easy, and great things in that which is small.

LAO-TZU

Your small steps add up to melting the offended person's heart.

Nature does not hurry, yet everything is accomplished.

LAO-TZU

Principle

You truly flex your options when you schedule the actions to restore the relationship.

Power Questions

How are you going to schedule the F.A.R. process? That is, what specific times will you: ask for forgiveness; make amends; and express your regret?

Listen

What is crucial for you to restore a relationship? Listening. Let's face it, the offended person wants to bend your ear over and over again, to ensure that you hear exactly what you did wrong and the hurt you caused.

It is up to you to make it easier for the person to tell how his or her heart is in agony.

> *When we are listened to, it creates us, makes us unfold and expand. Ideas actually begin to grow within us and come to life.*
>
> BRENDA UELAND

It helps if, at appropriate times, you say something like:

- I know I was wrong. I'm really upset that I hurt you. Do you want to tell me what trouble my mistake caused you?

- I can hear how hurt you've been feeling. Do you want to tell me more?

After the offended person has expressed his or her feelings for a time, it may seem that the person has run out of gas. However, to really facilitate healing it is often better for us to ask: "Is there anything else?" You'll be surprised at what comes up next. A friend told me how she listens, sometimes for two hours, to a roommate until the roommate "runs out of gas." Then her roommate is okay.

Dr. John Gray talks about how men make the mistake of trying to block their female romantic partner from "hitting bottom." When you listen to the offended person, you are allowing the person to hit bottom and take you with him or her!

At that point, it is like the offended person is yelling: "See! See what damage you caused! You should feel bad about this!"

> *Courage is found in unlikely places.*
>
> J.R.R. TOLKIEN

It takes courage and strength to listen to an offended person. But only through listening will you help the person feel heard and respected.

Use Reflective Replies

A powerful part of listening is expressing Reflective Replies. This is the process of providing a metaphorical mirror so that the person knows that you really heard him or her. Here are examples:

- That sounds like that was frustrating ...
- That sounds like it upset the whole thing. How could you go on from there?

Your first step to healing your relationship after you have made a big mistake is for you to devote significant time to listening.

Samantha was surprised when her business partner, Dave, rushed into the office and shouted, "You were supposed to carry the ball while I was in New York!" At that point, Samantha found it helpful to listen to Dave without offering defensive comments. After Dave cooled off, they worked together to come up with a new plan that better reflected their different talents and inclinations.

Listening is powerful.

Principle

When you're listening, you help the person drain off his or her feelings of being offended.

Power Question

How can you take care of yourself so that you are strong enough to listen to the offended person's anger and restrain yourself from making defensive replies?

Understand

When can understanding a situation help you heal a disrupted relationship? When you can reduce the intensity of your own feelings.

For example, imagine you're in a restaurant. The waiter slams your dish on the table in front of you and the way he plunks down your utensils gets on your nerves. It's easy to think, "What a jerk! He doesn't care about being kind and helpful. He should get another job!"

But now imagine that you know that three minutes ago he received a phone call confirming that his young son has leukemia. If you understood this, wouldn't that cool down your anger?

> *I hear and I forget. I see and I remember. I do and I understand.*
>
> CONFUCIUS

What do you do? You take a moment to imagine how your mistake may have caused big, painful feelings in the offended person. This use of your imagination can help you be more patient as the offended person expresses negative feelings.

> *You don't develop courage by being happy in your relationships every day. You develop it by surviving difficult times and challenging adversity.*
>
> EPICURUS

> *All the great things are simple, and many can be expressed in a single word: freedom, justice, honor, duty, mercy, hope.*
>
> WINSTON CHURCHILL

You must hold the hope for reconciliation for the relationship. The offended person does not have the strength or vision. You must hold the vision.

Because you made the mistake, it is your duty to the relationship to be patient. You need to let go of your preference that the offended person hurry up and forgive you already! To get to the point of forgiving you, the offended person must go through his or her own personal grief process.

In essence, you do your duty by taking action to express the three elements of F.A.R. Our earlier example included:

- Once a week, ask for *forgiveness*
- Three times a week, express *regret*
- Four times a week, take action to make *amends*

To make the best of the process *10 Seconds to Wealth*, you need to get clear in your own heart. What do you truly want? To restore the relationship? Then, you need to step forward with courage, kindness and persistence.

It took me four years of consistent effort to help one of my most treasured friendships heal after a bumpy time when a business project failed. Through my efforts and the responses of my friend, our friendship flowed onward. This friendship has lasted more than 27 years.

To Inspire Forgiveness, Give Forgiveness

I once heard a speaker say that the fastest way to experience something is to give another person the experience of it. You want forgiveness to be granted to you from the offended person, then you need to forgive the offended person. What? Yes, you need to forgive the offended person for not granting you forgiveness immediately. Isn't the offended person hurting you because he or she has not said, "That's okay. You're normally a kind and trustworthy person. This is unlike you. You're forgiven"?

> *You will never change things by fighting the existing reality. To change something, build a new model that makes the existing model obsolete.*
>
> R. BUCKMINSTER FULLER

You need to be the model of forgiveness. And in *Chapter Nine, To Influence, You Must Have Energy, Poise and Charisma*, we will cover techniques so that you get stronger.

Here, I want to emphasize that enhancing your understanding can assist you in making better decisions. You'll decide to give the other person a break. You'll restrain yourself from saying unkind words when you feel irritated. You'll make consistent efforts to demonstrate your concern and desire for the relationship to heal.

Principle

Enhance your understanding, and it is easier for you to be patient and to restrain from expressing negative reactions.

Power Questions

Can you imagine the hurt feelings your mistake caused for the offended person? Does this help you give the other person a break? Can you set aside your preference that the person forgive you quickly? And can you keep "doing your duty" and continue your F.A.R. efforts?

Energize

Have you heard someone or yourself say, "When I have the energy I'll try that"? The truth is that we often find energy when we take effective action. The energy arises as you experience doing the appropriate actions.

> *There is no way to happiness. Happiness is the way.*
> DR. WAYNE DYER

Have you noticed that if you smile, you feel better? Researchers have noted that merely putting a pen in a test-subject's mouth (which approximates a smile) actually helps people feel better!

So the question is, what are these good and appropriate actions?

In this chapter, we will identify what works in two situations:

- Enhancing your romantic relationship
- Enhancing a business relationship

Enhancing your romantic relationship

Are you ready for some profound information that can greatly increase the daily happiness that you and your romantic partner experience?

Here it is: Dr. Gary Chapman communicates profound strategies in his bestselling book *The Five Love Languages*.

Here are the five primary love languages:

1. Words of affirmation
2. Acts of service
3. Receiving gifts
4. Quality time
5. Physical touch

At the beginning of courtship, we drop everything and throw all kinds of loving actions into the mix. In that way, we're bound to, by accident, provide the loving kindness in the way our partner needs.

So how does this relate to getting out of trouble—that is, healing your relationship—if your partner feels offended?

We need to pay close attention to our partner to discover his or her primary love language.

The tough part is that after you have been a romantic couple for a while, then you return to your standard, busy, daily life. And that preoccupation with daily busyness causes our loved one to starve for love!

An interviewer asked me, "Why?"

I replied, "Just to survive in this fast-paced modern world, we often give all our energy away at the office. We leave the remaining crumbs for our partner."

Make Every Loving Gesture You Do Really Count!

We don't have extra time to be flailing about—guessing, failing, getting frustrated and angry.

When you learn your loved one's primary love language—and you speak it well—you will save a lot of time that was formerly lost to misunderstandings. We lose time and energy when we're torn up inside because of misunderstandings.

Now, I'll give you some examples of how my clients have expressed love via the five love languages:

Words of affirmation

You hold her hands and look her in the eyes and say, "Honey, I really appreciated how you listened to all my new business ideas. It means so much to me because I really treasure your insight. I know it took a lot of effort for you. I know you really love me."

In your personal journal, write down your own version of words of affirmation.

Acts of service

You ask your loved one, "What can I do that would help you feel really loved by me?"

Women like delightful surprises. Yes, my sweetheart tells me that all the time.

For example, Matthew washed the dishes so that his wife returned home to a cleaned kitchen.

In your personal journal, write down your own version of acts of service. By the way, ask your partner. Often what we think is a great service is something that is not even on our partner's radar screen. So "do unto your partner as she would prefer done unto her."

Receiving gifts

Throughout the year, listen carefully for what your loved one says he or she would love to see or own. If she says, "I just love flowers!" you have received your marching orders. If he says, "Oh, if only I had a Craftsman power tool, I could make my cabinet really sturdy," you have an idea for a helpful gift.

Also, think of providing gifts on days other than your partner's birthday, Valentine's Day or the Holiday season. I provide a gift and write, "Happy Today!"

In your personal journal, write down your own version of receiving gifts.

Quality time

About quality time, Dr. Gary Chapman writes, "Giving another person your undivided attention communicates, 'You are important to me.' Quality time means no distractions. The TV is off ... ."

For example, my client Harry had to learn that his wife had different feelings when he talked about his latest project. Although Harry felt he was talking from his heart, his wife heard something else: "Here we go again. Harry's talking about work." Even though Harry puts his heart into his work (his own business), his wife considers quality time to be talking together about something else. And quality time is about listening to your loved one.

In your personal journal, write down your own version of quality time.

Physical touch

Many hard-charging men only allow themselves to be nurtured and protected in their loved one's arms. Researchers report that many women find it difficult to be touched or to reach out with loving touches when they feel hurt. It becomes a burning bridge that cannot be crossed, until one of the partners reaches out with courage and extra effort. This is precisely the reason that learning each other's primary love language is crucial. Without the goodwill created by speaking your love partner's love language, there is no foundation or energy to reach out to each other.

To make life even more complicated, researchers show that often:

- Men don't feel loved without sexual intimacy
- Women don't feel capable of sexual intimacy without emotional intimacy/closeness happening *before* any possible sexual intimacy

Keep physical touch happening throughout your days, include holding hands and hugging.

Writing about hugging, Dr. David Schnarch, in his book *Passionate Marriage*, introduces a crucial, powerful technique that he calls *hugging until relaxed*. The idea is to embrace each other while standing on your own two feet—both literally and metaphorically. Dr. Schnarch writes,

> *"The basics require four sentences: Stand on your own two feet. Put your arms around your partner. Focus on yourself. Quiet yourself down—way down."*

This is a process that takes practice. I know this from personal experience. My mind moves fast and when I'm working I move fast. It is important for me to practice making a transition to a relaxed state of being.

In your personal journal, write down your own version of physical touch.

Enhance a Business Relationship

We have been talking about actions that create positive, life-enhancing energy—both your own energy and that of the other person.

Here is a big energy drain in a business relationship: notice how people make snap judgments and become offended when someone fails to express appropriate gratitude. Suddenly, all the positive energy that was building in the relationship has been drained away.

The problem is each individual has different requirements for what feels like a good expression of gratitude.

As mentioned earlier, Gary Chapman points out that each person has a personal "love language." If you speak the person's language, he or she will truly experience your gratitude. (This is something that I talk about in my book *Be Heard and Be Trusted: How You Can Use Secrets of the Greatest Communicators to Get What You Want.*)

The five love languages

1. Words of affirmation

2. Receiving gifts

3. Acts of service

4. Quality time

5. Physical touch

Our goal is to appropriately and effectively express gratitude and create positive feelings.

You want to express your gratitude in a way that the person can readily accept and feel.

Now, I'll provide examples of how you can appropriately express gratitude when working with a colleague or customer.

Words of affirmation

"Joe, thanks for all your efforts. You were really effective in finding solutions so that our two teams could work together. Thank you."

Receiving gifts

A small, appropriate gift that relates to the person's hobby can be helpful. It's great when we honor people. Many businesses honor long-time customers with coupons for discounted products or services.

Acts of service

Often, a customer will appreciate receiving an article that relates to the hobby of her son or daughter. In this way, you can enrich your business relationship with the customer. The idea of service is that you extend an extra effort for the other person's well-being.

Quality time

When meeting with a new customer, turn off your cell phone. When someone stops talking to us, and places accepting a cell phone call above us, it hurts. Don't let that happen with your new customer.

Physical touch

Each person needs to be careful about physically touching a customer. If the new customer had earlier extended his or her hand for a good handshake, then you can shake hands as part of expressing gratitude. However, some people, such as Donald Trump, do not like to shake hands. In that case, you can nod and smile.

~~~~~~~~~

In summary, we have talked about ways to create positive energy. In a personal relationship, express your love in the appropriate love language. In a business relationship, express gratitude in a way that the other person can readily accept and feel good about. And if you are working with people from different cultures, read a book* and attend workshops to learn the appropriate etiquette.

Principle

To create positive energy in a relationship, express your good intentions according to the "language" the other person readily takes in.

••••••••••••••••••••••••••••••

* My book *Be Heard and Be Trusted* covers a number of details about how to interact with people of different cultures.

Power Question

In talking with your loved one, would you feel comfortable asking, "Remember the last time you felt totally loved, what happened?" In a business relationship, listen carefully to the customer's comments. Notice if she says that another business really showed her that they appreciated her business. Notice what brings light to her eyes. Find a way to express your appreciation in an appropriate and similar manner.

Negotiate

What is one of the hardest questions to ask in the process of healing a personal or business relationship? I have noticed that people hesitate to ask, "How can I make amends?"

One reason clients have given me for why they hesitate is due to the fear that the offended person will ask for too much. In this section, I'll show you how to negotiate so that you can regain the trust of the offended person.

Negotiate for time to consider what you will agree to

The American Heritage Dictionary defines negotiate as "to arrange or settle by discussion and mutual agreement." Now, that definition avoids the distasteful baggage that a number of people put on the term negotiate.

Donald Trump is a person with fans and detractors, but many people do acknowledge his negotiating skills. He described his ten negotiating tips:

1. Know exactly what you want, and focus on that.
2. View any conflict as an opportunity. This will expand your mind as well as your horizons.
3. Know that your negotiating partner may well have exactly the same goals as you do. Do not underestimate them.
4. Patience is an enormous virtue and needs to be cultivated for successful negotiation on any level.
5. Realize that quiet persistence can go a long way. Being stubborn is often an attribute. The key is to know when to loosen up.
6. Remain optimistic at all times. Practice positive thinking.
7. Let your guard down, but only on purpose. Watch how your negotiating partners respond.
8. Be open to change—it's another word for innovation.
9. Trust your instincts, even after you've honed your skills. They're there for a reason.
10. Negotiation is an art. Treat it like one."

When you want to exert secret influence to get you out of trouble, you can use a number of the above tips. And now, I'll show you a powerful method: gaining *think-space*.

Avoid fear and gain *think-space*

You do not need to fear the offended person's response to your question, "How can I make amends?" The important detail is to be ready to respond appropriately to gain think-space. Think-space is my term for having both time and an expanse so that you can carefully consider a request. Sometimes, a person can become a people-pleaser and say yes too quickly.

Make sure to express your concern and desire to heal the relationship. You ask: "How can I make amends?" And after the offended person responds, you can say:

"I'm glad that you told me that. I'm interested in doing what will help us take care of the mistake I made and for us to feel closer again. Let me think about this overnight. I'm not sure how I can do what you're talking about. But I'm going to really look into it."

In a business transaction, you can replace "feel closer again" with something like:

"I'm interested in doing what will help us take care of the mistake so that you feel good about moving forward with our first plan."

What to do in your next conversation

When you have your next conversation after the offended person has stated her "demands," it is important to begin with what you can do. A reply can be like Steve's comment to his wife:

"Janet, I have thought carefully about what you said. First, I'm glad to tell you that I can take the kids on Tuesday and Thursday nights so that you are free to attend the classes you mentioned.

I can also do the laundry first thing on Saturday mornings. I'll still need to look into the Sunday thing. At this moment, I feel I'd better hold on to my Sunday afternoon bike ride. In fact, I think I made my mistake because I let myself get upside-down and too stressed out. So let me make a good start with Tuesdays and Thursdays. And we'll keep talking, okay?"

When Steve says this, he includes the following strategies:

He makes sure that Janet knows she is winning

"Janet, I have thought carefully about what you said. First, I'm glad to tell you that I can take the kids on Tuesday and Thursday nights so that you are free to attend the classes you mentioned. I can also do the laundry first thing on Saturday mornings."

He does not over-promise

"I'll still need to look into the Sunday thing. At this moment, I feel I'd better hold onto my Sunday afternoon bike ride. In fact, I think I made my mistake because I let myself get upside-down and too stressed out."

He ends with the positive news

"So let me make a good start with Tuesdays and Thursdays."

He demonstrates that he wants to care for her needs

"And we'll keep talking, okay?"

> *To me, there is no greater act of courage than being the one who kisses first.*
>
> JANEANE GAROFALO

By agreeing to take action and by holding his ground about the Sunday bike rides, Steve is demonstrating love and courage.

> *The softest things in the world overcome the hardest things in the world.*
>
> LAO-TZU

In this quote Lao-tzu is referring to water, which over the years can create something as impressive as the Grand Canyon. Similarly, once you ask, "How can I make amends?" and you start negotiating solutions, you can overcome a hardened heart.

Principle

Ask how you can make amends, gain think-space and realistically negotiate how you can take positive action in a helpful direction.

Power Question

How can you ask for think-space? Consider something like: "I've listened carefully. I'm going to need to see how I can make this happen. How about we talk about it tomorrow afternoon?"

Create (Not Compete)

What do you do when someone is offended and you did nothing wrong?

We discover that the first thing we need to do is put our ego in check.

> *When I was young, I observed that nine out of ten things I did were failures. So I did ten times more work.*
>
> GEORGE BERNARD SHAW

We might say that it is "work" to restrain ourselves from expressing our impatience. Often, an offended person seems to forget every kind word or action that we have done for years! Pain is powerful. It can fill the offended person's world until they cannot see past it.

So we're left with doing "ten times more work." Often, since we have caused the damage, we must undo what we have created. And, there are times when the other person has misinterpreted something and we need to continue to be kind to the offended person until he or she can view things with more insight.

> *When you are content to be simply yourself and don't compare or compete, everybody will respect you.*
>
> LAO-TZU

So we must not "compete" or compare ourselves and our previous patience with the offended person's current "unreasonableness."

What we must do is create opportunities to show kindness to the offended person. As I mentioned in the prior chapter, we ask, "How can I make amends?" and then we get busy.

> *Kindness in words creates confidence. Kindness in thinking creates profoundness. Kindness in giving creates love.*
>
> LAO-TZU

A number of spiritual authors emphasize, "Would you rather be right or happy?"

So now that we have made a mistake, we must remind ourselves: "What I really want is healing for this relationship."

Keep on the lookout for ways to show that you care. Send a little gift. If you are rebuffed, try again in two weeks. If necessary, make a kind gesture once a month.

We never know what will happen next. Perhaps sometime in the future, the offended person suffers a big disappointment or even a loss of a loved one. Who is there to provide comfort? You are.

Someone made a comment to me that had a lasting impact: "When my mother died, my friends disappeared."

Many people will disappear because they don't know how to handle the situation.

But you, who are acting like a hero to restore the relationship, can call and gently ask, "Is there something I can help with?"

Principle

If you feel the offended person is not as kind or forgiving as you are, shift your thoughts. Focus on how you can create opportunities to demonstrate your concern and kindness toward the person.

Power Questions

Are you feeling slighted by the offended person's forgetfulness of how you have been trustworthy in the past? Shift your thoughts to how you can create opportunities to be kind and helpful. What are the offended person's concerns? Can you provide a helpful article sent via mail (yes, snail mail with a hand-written note)? Can you send a soothing card or, perhaps, a CD of soothing music?

Embrace

> *Be like water making its way through cracks ... You put water into a bottle and it becomes the bottle. You put it in a teapot; it becomes the teapot. Now, water can flow or it can crash. Be water, my friend.*
>
> BRUCE LEE

In order to get into the good graces of someone you offended, you need to be like water. And you need to embrace the process. When you ask someone, Will you forgive me? the offended person has the right to reply, "No. Not yet." You also need to embrace your own feelings about this. You might be feeling terrible, and have thoughts like: "How dare he not give me a break this time! After all the times I have forgiven him!"

> *To love means loving the unlovable. To forgive means pardoning the unpardonable. Faith means believing the unbelievable. Hope means hoping when everything seems hopeless.*
>
> G. K. CHESTERTON

You're going to need to embrace yourself. You need to nurture yourself. If your partner has withdrawn from you, then you are now grieving and in pain. You must gain support from other sources. Perhaps seeing a counselor will provide you with the essential support you need during this crisis time.

> *One man with courage makes a majority.*
> ANDREW JACKSON

When I talk about embrace, I am emphasizing that you need to embrace your new role. You are now the healer of the relationship. You are the only one whom you can count on to do what is necessary to guide the relationship forward—after taking enough time to acknowledge the hurt you created.

You become the "one person who makes a majority." You will provide the spiritual leadership for the relationship.

I know this is true because I have had to take on this role. For example, at one point I did something that I felt was right for my family, but it caused great inconvenience to a friend. So I had to keep calling that friend once a month for two years to seek to restore the relationship. This friend was being guided by his family members to "write me off." I knew in my heart that if I did not keep up the effort, that friend would just disappear. Now, both my friend and I are glad about my persistence.

A spiritual idea holds that, in a relationship, the person who is more "sane" at the time needs to take care of the relationship. It may seem to be a stretch to say that the offended person is not completely sane. But have you heard about people being "blinded by anger"? The truth is that someone who is blinded by anger or pain does not have access to his or her full senses. The offended person cannot remember all of the times that you have proven trustworthy. So not only must you remain consistent in showing your concern and kindness, but you must do even more.

So embrace your new role, gain the support you need and persist like the hero you are now becoming.

Principle

Embrace your new role in providing spiritual leadership to the relationship—and be sure to nurture yourself along the way.

Power Questions:

What have you lost now that the offended person has shut you out? Can you go to family members, friends and/or a counselor to gain the support you need to remain strong, kind and persistent?

Conclusion to Chapter Eight

In Chapter Eight, we have explored the I.N.F.L.U.E.N.C.E. process:

> I - Inquire
>
> N - Nurture
>
> F - Flex your options
>
> L - Listen
>
> U - Understand
>
> E - Energize
>
> N - Negotiate
>
> C - Create (not compete)

E – Embrace

We realize that the secret influence to get you out of trouble is mainly about becoming stronger and being in a calm state for yourself.

Your Secret Influence is how your calm state of being can transfer to the offended person and soften a hardened attitude.

You must provide spiritual leadership to yourself and to the offended person so that healing can take place.

Your secret influence includes specific methods of asking questions to help the person express her pain and then to show how you have truly heard her.

In the section on "embrace," we looked at possible sources of support. This process is so crucial that in *Chapter Nine, To Influence, You Must Have Energy, Poise and Charisma*, we will cover essential methods so you can enhance your own healing. Let's move forward …

9

Influence Through Energy, Poise, & Charisma

How to Heal When Life's Too Much

In Chapter Eight, you learned specific methods of asking questions so that you can demonstrate your sincerity with the offended person.

In Chapter Nine, you will learn the heart of the Secret Influence Process. You must become stronger and maintain a calm state of being. Then your kind and calm state of being can ultimately transfer to the offended person. She or he will become free to let go of the pain and then join with you in moving the relationship forward. This ability to remain calm helps you be at your best during the *10 Seconds to Wealth*.

As I mentioned earlier, the Secret Influence Process includes the following:

- Strengthen yourself
- Remain in a calm state of being
- Communicate your concern and kindness
- Take action with the F.A.R. methods (forgiveness, amends, regret)

Chapter Nine focuses on:

- Strengthening yourself; and
- Remaining in a calm state of being.

> *Being deeply loved by someone gives you strength; loving someone deeply gives you courage.*
>
> LAO-TZU

When you have offended a loved one, you have just lost a major source of strength. With your loved one holding you at arm's length, you have suffered a loss. You are now grieving. So now you need to learn How to Heal When Life's Too Much.

The idea of *How to Heal When Life's Too Much* began when I slept every night at the Sequoia Hospital to be with my sweetheart who was at death's door. And while commuting to see her in the hospital, I was rear-ended by a commercial truck. My injury sent me to Stanford Medical Center.

At that point, one idea filled my mind: How to Heal When Life's Too Much. At that time, with my sweetheart in the hospital and with me in another hospital, I truly felt overwhelmed.

Some days later, my train derailed as it arrived in San Francisco. I joked with friends, "I'm not getting on a plane this month!"

In order to strengthen yourself, you need to engage in the process of healing on a moment-to-moment basis.

We use the H.E.A.L. process:

> H – Humor
>
> E – Energize
>
> A – Act
>
> L – Listen

Let's move forward …

Humor

Sometimes, we hear, "Well, just humor him. Let him say what he needs to say." We profoundly affect our lives when we listen to our physical and emotion pains. We humor them; that is, we accept them. We say, "Okay, illness I hear you. Hmmm, I imagine you're telling me to slow down."

As I mentioned, I found myself at Stanford Medical Center after being rear-ended by a commercial truck. My attention was seized at the beginning of physical rehabilitation. As the physical therapist manipulated my injured neck area, I felt great sadness and discomfort. I felt quite vulnerable. I could have resisted this. Instead, I paused to experience the situation and told her, "I'm feeling kind of … vulnerable. Like I was a 20-year-old who woke up in a 90-year-old body."

In this way, I "humored" the messages of my body and my life. I listened. I did slow down, and I asked my sweetheart's family to help cover more shifts at the hospital. I listened to my body by viewing the physical therapy and personal exercise sessions as my time to focus on my needs and my body.

> *People who keep stiff upper lips find that it's damn hard to smile.*
>
> JUDITH GUEST

Humor and laughter are also lifesavers. Norman Cousins, best-selling author of *Anatomy of an Illness,* was diagnosed with an incurable, life-threatening illness. He found that 15 minutes of laughter gave him two hours of pain-free sleep. His program, which led to his full recovery, included watching films of Laurel and Hardy, Abbott and Costello and the Marx Brothers.

Similarly, it helps if you create comfort and joy for yourself. Enjoy opportunities to laugh through interacting with friends and viewing films.

> *We don't laugh because we're happy; we're happy because we laugh.*
>
> WILLIAM JAMES

One of my clients found that he brightened his life by making time at the end of his work day to watch a half-hour television show called *Whose Line Is It Anyway?* He set his digital video recorder to record episodes. This was an essential ritual just as valuable as regular exercise sessions. Some people have called laughter "inner jogging."

Emergency medical personnel know the value of "gallows humor" or dark humor to relieve tension. My point is that if any humor occurs, just welcome it and let it flow. Each day is a lifetime, and we welcome the good moments and we handle the bad ones.

> *Why should we think upon things that are lovely?*
> *Because thinking determines life.*
>
> WILLIAM JAMES

Principle

Learn to create more acceptance and humor in your daily life.

Power Question

How can you experience humor on a daily basis?

Energize

How can we can energize ourselves? First, pause and notice if you have you given up on a personal dream. You can reconnect with your dream. Many times, your spirit leads your body. Imagine a time when you faced doing the dishes, and then a family member suggested seeing a movie at the theater. Suddenly, energy coursed through your veins. And you did the dishes in record time!

Similarly, my clients have devoted just 15 minutes to a hobby and found that their whole day was brightened. Additionally, good nutrition and exercise help you expand your personal energy.

A primary source of energy is found in the process of *replace fear with love*. For example, when my sweetheart was in the operating room, I turned my tears and fears into a song of positive prayer—which I played and sang for her after she regained consciousness following the surgery.

When you're serious about recovering your energy you learn powerful coping behaviors.

When the tragedies of September 11, 2001 occurred, many people feared that additional terrorist strikes would occur in more U.S. cities. Immediately, my team and I responded by providing information and presentations to help people cope with the immense stress.

At that point, I pulled together research and spoke to audiences about the C.O.P.E. process. I include that process here because personal and natural disasters occur at various times.

Using the C.O.P.E. process guards your energy. Remember, you need positive, calm energy to exert secret influence. (Again, the following tips were those I presented in the period following the September 11th tragedies.)

> C – create time-pockets
>
> O – open to what is unchangeable
>
> P – prepare your options
>
> E – expect and focus on the good

Create—Create time-pockets

Take time to create a little peace for yourself. Don't leave CNN on constantly; maybe check in every two hours (if you're checking on a disaster). Keeping CNN on constantly keeps you in an adrenaline state. When the adrenal glands function too much, you can be vulnerable to health problems. During recent wars, people left CNN on all the time and suffered greatly. Take time to exercise. Make time to read spiritual books. Devote time to talking with family members with the TV off. We need to express our feelings. See a counselor if you feel in distress. Gather in support groups. Make some times when you distract your mind. Seeing a movie can be just the release some people need. Maintain as much of your daily routine as possible.

Open—Open to what is unchangeable

You are a spirit having a human experience. Whatever spiritual practices appeal to you, devote time to them now. Some people feel too stressed to engage in meditation at this time. But the answer is to still to turn off the TV or radio, and take some quiet time for yourself. Write in a journal. Attend a spiritual workshop or devote time in nature. Read spiritual books to gain a larger perspective.

Prepare—Prepare your options

To handle fear, make a list of options. Call an out-of-state friend/family member and set up a place so that family members can call and leave/pick up messages. Talk with friends, get more perspectives and more ideas.

Expect—Expect and focus on the good

We need to release our fear and stress during a tough time. We need to direct our own thoughts in positive directions. This is called Expectation Management. Focus on these thoughts and expectations:

- There is room for hope.
- In this moment, I am all right.
- I can handle this.
- I can learn what I need to do.
- We'll get through this together.
- Things will settle down eventually.

Learn to Replace Worry

Many people connect being a good person with worrying about other people. It is important to consider that a replacement for worry is being concerned, taking action (preparing) and letting go. Researchers note that unrelieved stress can cause health problems. It is crucial that everyone becomes conscious of having a coping strategy.

To use the C.O.P.E methods is to form a pattern of supportive habits for your healing.

> *Habit is stronger than reason.*
> GEORGE SANTAYANA

> *All things are difficult before they are easy.*
> THOMAS FULLER

Thomas Fuller's quote reminds us that when we start doing new actions they can feel awkward and hard to do. Eventually, we can find that the new healthy habits feel natural. It takes time and practice.

> *I hear and I forget. I see and I remember. I do and I understand.*
> CONFUCIUS

Be sure to support your personal energy; develop habits that give you times of refreshment and renewal. Then, you'll have the energy and patience to sincerely listen to the offended person.

Principle

To heal, create more personal energy.

Power Questions

How can you support your personal energy? What are people or situations that drain your energy (energy-drainers)? How can you eliminate or reduce exposure time to energy-drainers?

Act

Do you ever feel so tired that you long for a time with no fear and no worries? The solution is to function well even when fear is present.

To practice the secret influence to get you out of trouble is to take action to strengthen yourself. Not only do you have the usual bumpy road, but now you're dealing with the added pressure of the offended person's wrath. So we'll now focus on empowering actions you can implement.

> *I have not ceased being fearful, but I have ceased letting fear control me.*
>
> ERICA JONG

The idea is to avoid letting the fear of rejection paralyze you from attempting to contact the offended person. Take appropriate action.

> *Wisdom, compassion, and courage are the three universally recognized moral qualities of [people].*
>
> CONFUCIUS

So what kind of actions do you take to rebuild your relationship with the offended person? You have your actions aligned with wisdom, compassion and courage.

> *Do the thing you fear and the death of fear is certain.*
>
> RALPH WALDO EMERSON

> *Feel the fear and do it anyway.*
>
> SUSAN JEFFERS

Identify what you really want and take a step toward it. So if you want the offended person to remember how thoughtful you are, be sure to send a card or gift on important days, such as birthdays and anniversaries. And create an important occasion, such as celebrating some accomplishment that the offended person did months or years ago. You can show how you remember the person's successful efforts. Your card can read, "Happy Two-Year Anniversary for Getting Your First Manuscript Written!"

An interviewer asked, "Is this process of celebrating someone's accomplishment appropriate for business?"

"Yes!" I replied. For example, some years ago, author Dottie Walters told me about how she sent a clipping of an article and congratulated a prospective customer for his recent promotion.

The newly promoted man said to Dottie, "You were the only one who noticed." So we must remember that developing a business relationship involves paying attention and acknowledging people's accomplishments.

Also, take action to nurture and care for yourself. Answer this question: *How can I take better care of myself now?* Then, note your answer and take a step towards nurturing yourself. Find the support you need. Many clients complain to therapists, "My mother doesn't ... [or] my sister doesn't ... " Therapists respond, "What? Were you expecting her to do something different? Were you expecting her to change? Who else can give you the support you need?"

A major act towards healing is to say no graciously and effectively. Learning to say no paves the way so you can say yes to something else. Often it helps to say, "Oh, I'll have to say, 'No, thank you,' at this time. My plate is full. How about I help you brainstorm about someone who can help you with that?"

Another healing action is to use music for relaxation or inspiration. As I type this, I am listening to the music soundtrack of the Indiana Jones movie *Raiders of the Lost Ark*. The love theme is playing, and I feel at peace. Soon, I will feel the surge of energy provided by the heroic theme. Remember, your subconscious mind is listening at every moment. When I hear the heroic theme of Indiana Jones, I feel heroic, strong and capable.

Principle

Press on despite fear and take appropriate action to demonstrate your care and concern for the offended person.

Power Questions

How can you show your care and concern for the offended person? Can you send a postcard or gift to celebrate the bright moments of the person's life?

Listen

Who do you wish would really listen to you? Probably one of the first people you thought of was the offended person (if you're reading this book during a difficult time).

Sometimes, when a crucial person is not listening to us, our solution is to listen to ourselves and the lessons of life. Listening is vital to understand life's lessons for us. An old phrase holds, "Life's lessons are repeated in different forms until we learn them." Listen to your body. Does it crave rest? Give it what it needs. Become an expert on healing yourself. If you have some affliction, do some research on the Internet. But remember that statistics can be misused. If a traditional doctor says, "Only two percent of people recover from this," consider that you may be able to nurture yourself and join that two percent.

Realize that, spiritually speaking, we really don't know what a particular illness means in our life—or in the lives of others. That's why I emphasize a concept I call healthy humility.

Healthy humility means to realize that our perceptions may be limited in the moment and that Higher Power may have a greater good in mind.

When my sweetheart was at death's door in the hospital, she experienced an incredible outpouring of love from friends and family members. She soon recovered from major surgery. Certainly, losing an organ was not her preference. But she said, "I didn't know that my friends care so much about me."

We can learn so much by flowing with life as it comes. During the times when I was forced to slow down due to an illness, I have discovered opportunities to grow in empathy with others who face physical challenges.

Life's Lessons & Experiencing Spiritual Awakening

A special form of listening is the process I refer to as the Divine Aha! When you are reeling from the pain of having someone you love unable to forgive you, it becomes essential for you to listen more—to yourself, the other person and life.

In some moments of life, our soul awakens. We call this the Divine Aha! as in "Aha! Now I get it." Here are useful methods for these moments:

- Be okay with pain that lights your way to the Divine Aha!
- Talk about what you're learning
- Write about what you're learning
- Be gentle with yourself

Accept Pain that Lights Your Way to the Divine Aha!

Sometimes, pain is what grabs our attention. I want to support you to exercise the real freedom that you have. You have the freedom to find your part in any situation that bothers you. Responsibility is really the ability to respond. Responding is choosing rather than reacting (as if by reflex).

To illustrate how pain can light our way to a Divine Aha!, I'll share an example from the world of speaking. When I speak to audiences, I give my loving energy. Many people have written to me about the value, compassion and laughter they've received and enjoyed. But the Divine Aha! arrived in my life when a certain unfavorable critique shook me up.

I had been invited to give a presentation about making books and audio programs. However, the particular critical review showed that the reviewer was not letting my new ideas mix in with his current perceptions. He also included negative comments from two colleagues.

But if I would just pause, I could learn something from this painful review. On the surface, I had been called to teach people how to take action so they could add products to their income-generating activities. But the truth is that many of these audience members were in pain. I realized this when I remembered their comments were about the fear of making mistakes with their first products.

A number of audience members needed me to metaphorically hold their hand. They needed me to acknowledge fears and concerns. If I merely provided a quick answer like, "The easy way to do this is … " then I was not acknowledging their current situation.

The pain of reading this particular critique led me to look for new ways to interact with audience members. I learned that during a presentation, it's helpful to slow down, perhaps, sit in a chair for a moment or two, and talk quietly with the audience. When addressing an audience that seems edgy, I can say:

"Let's pause for a moment. That last idea seems to have been unusual. It may bring up some questions, or resistance, or even some fears. And I can relate to that. I started off as a painfully shy boy, playing the piano for seniors in a retirement home. I was deeply afraid. My leg was shaking so badly, I was afraid that it would fall off the sustain pedal and make a big thud sound. So now, we're talking about trying a couple of new actions.

And we're here together. Let's talk about it. Who has the first question?"

To illustrate the discomfort of trying new things, I can introduce a physical process of having people fold their hands. People tend to favor putting one thumb over the other. They find that switching positions and placing the other thumb on top to be uncomfortable. The idea is that the audience members experience the discomfort of something new, and they can apply it to making space for the discomfort of new ideas.

An old phrase holds: "We often learn more from failure than success." So if you offend someone by an inadvertent mistake, you have the opportunity to learn from the situation.

Let's look at the possibility of being okay with pain lighting the way to the Divine Aha! In my example about learning new ways to address an audience, I experienced a new realization as part of my Divine Aha!

"Some of my ideas may be new and uncomfortable to certain audience members. It's like switching to rap music in the middle of a Mozart concert. I've lived with these ideas. It's important for me to slow down at times. Then I can gently offer the audience time to stir the new idea into 'their soup.'"

In a way, that one painful, intense critique did me a favor. Ever since then, I have found it valuable to slow down, sit down for some moments and quietly connect with my audiences. So some of my best learning has been in response to tough times.

Talk About What You're Learning

During interviews with people who have made their dreams come true, I discovered that they were teachable and coachable.

Researchers mention that many people are most teachable after their first heart attack. But the good news is that many of us can open up to learning life's lessons with less pain and danger. When I felt shaken by that unfavorable critique, I talked with my dear friends. I took responsibility and said, "What I'm learning is …" I also contacted a personal coach to get another perspective.

Write About What You're Learning

This chapter began as notes in my personal journal. We need to make space to learn life's lessons. Your life is important. It's worth you writing about it. I often write about things that I want to cherish as my life lessons.

For example, I once heard a speaker tell about a speech he gave when he was 20 years old. In his audience, a woman said, "Young man, I'm 72 years old. Why should I listen to you?" He replied, "I heard that we teach what we need to learn. Tonight, I'm going to talk about love and forgiveness. I guess I need to learn about them." The woman replied, "Young man, you have my attention."

This story reminds me to be genuine and let go of the idea of trying to be perfect.

Be Gentle with Yourself

The night that I was reeling from the painful comments in the particular critical review, I wrote notes while wrapped in a favorite blanket and entranced by soothing music from the motion picture soundtrack *Somewhere in Time*. These were ways of being good to myself. And I repeated the process in writing this chapter to communicate with you—from my heart to your heart.

As my clients and audiences learn communication skills, I gently share this idea:

"To communicate is like tossing Nerf balls, and some people catch them—and some do not. The idea is to get better at tossing the Nerf balls more closely and gently to others. You can do everything right, and still someone may not feel like catching the Nerf ball."

You'll feel better as you tell yourself: "I learn from everything." This is part of healthy humility. In a particular moment, we have perceptions. And good questions can help us reach the next level as we go deeper than our surface perceptions.

When you seek to heal a relationship with the offended person, you can explore these questions:

- What is my part in this situation?
- What can I learn here?
- How can I approach the person in a gentle way that he or she would prefer?
- Is it possible that I did my best and the other person was just closed off to connecting with me?

It is helpful to write in your personal journal, what you are learning—especially as the lessons come in with some pain attached.

There is no coming to consciousness without pain.

CARL JUNG

Forgiveness and Your Happiness

How You Can Work Well with the Offended Person

In his book *You Can Be Happy No Matter What*, Dr. Richard Carlson writes: "Don't attach conditions on your happiness."

This applies to you staying in a calm state of being and being able to transfer your positive energy to the offended person. In a nutshell, we're talking about using a definition of forgiveness that supports your happiness. If you're a happy person (generally), you'll have more patience and strength to keep making overtures toward the offended person.

One of Richard Carlson's main points is that we can let go of a particular thought and, perhaps, avoid related negative thoughts that can create a bad mood. He also notes that a bad mood can obscure creative solutions. Instead, it's helpful to make choices to support our well-being.

For example, I was driving with a friend who has clinical depression. Sometimes, it is a heavy load to interact with this person. My friend said with a typical energy-draining whine, "I'm tired. My feet hurt." I had the thought, "I wish that, in this relationship, I was not the only person carrying hope—and creating positive energy." Now, at that moment, I was on the edge of an emotional cliff. I could have added, "Marcus, here, doesn't do a thing to help me feel better … "

Instead, in that moment, I chose to stop the possible negative spiral of additional painful thoughts. I chose to focus on the positive things in that particular moment: a blue sky, and we were fortunate to have a car. I then thought about how we're fortunate to be able to see and hear. And with that, I turned on the car's radio for a possible energizing song to hear.

In just seconds, I thought of something else, which kept me in a positive mood.

I chose to not attach a condition on my happiness. My friend does not need to change so I can be happy or "proven right." I don't need to be proven right so I can be happy. I chose to let go of trying to present my case for actively seeking positive thoughts. If my friend wants to hear what I think about the subject, he can ask me—or read one of my books.

> *A man is rich in proportion to the number of things he can afford to let alone.*
>
> HENRY DAVID THOREAU

At this point, let's look at "rich" in terms of peace, calm and poise.

Can you imagine how much more effective you would be in building a peaceful resolution with the offended person if you were—in yourself—peaceful, calm and poised?

So I invite you to come up with a pattern to remind yourself that, in each moment, you have a choice. For example, my client Sara silently repeats this idea: "It's just a thought. Let it flow away." This is a good practice for things that are not in our control—like a loved one's current mood.

Also I have a phrase: *Catch yourself in a moment of happiness.* As I write these words, I'm in a moment of happiness.

> *All the happiness in the world comes from thinking of others; all the suffering in the world comes from thinking of only oneself.*
>
> SHANTI DEVA

I add, Think of others, act and get caught up in the adventure. What I mean is that while you are helping someone else, you get caught up in the exhilaration of the moment.

Remember to listen to your deepest heart.

How do you listen to your heart? You ask essential questions such as:

- Who are you?
- What do you want?

Give yourself quiet time, and notice how your answers change. At this moment, I feel I am a happy spiritual being connected with Higher Power and people.

And, I want to continue my adventure expressed as: "I help people experience enthusiasm, love and wisdom to fulfill big dreams." Other desires, including supporting my loved ones, more world travel, directing motion pictures and joyful prosperity, fall under my "I help people" umbrella. That is, as I help more people, more financial abundance comes into my life.

Every year, I do things I have never done before. And in this spirit, I invite you to write in your personal journal. Identify your answers to:

- Who are you?
- What do you want?

- What new things can you do (today, and this year) to enjoy life and plant seeds for realizing your dreams?*

~~~~~~~~~~~~~~~

As I have mentioned before, when you are seeking to restore a personal or business relationship, you need to nurture yourself.

During such a tough time, many people find comfort and renewal in exploring a spiritual connection. Actor Alan Arkin said, "Success is achieving what works for you inside." At one time, Alan was considered one of the top three actors in the world—but he felt great discomfort.*

Since discovering meditation and a personal spiritual path, he said, "I find our association with the universe and God to be extremely comforting."

F. Murray Abraham won great fame and an Oscar with his role as Salieri in the motion picture Amadeus. Later, he was in a car struck by another—and, sadly, two young men died. Rescuers had to cut the actor out of his car. He went into depression, asking, "Why had I been spared?"

"To act!" his friend said. F. Murray Abraham then decided, "Acting is my gift and my obligation to God."

> *There are no great acts. There are small acts done with great love.*
>
> MOTHER TERESA

•••••••••••••••••••••••••••••••••

* To help you make extraordinary progress, please consider my book *Nothing Can Stop You This Year!* Visit TomSuperCoach.com.

I invite you to find your gift. Also, find your comforts. (Yes, I'm listening to my favorite music as I write these words.)

Find ways to be okay with pain as it lights your path to your Divine Aha!

Many blessings on your journey.

Principle

Heal by listening to your body, your heart and your relationships.

Power Question

How can you remind yourself to listen? (Posted notes on the mirror, books on listening, etc.)

Conclusion of Chapter Nine

We have explored the H.E.A.L. process:

- H – Humor
- E – Energize
- A – Act
- L – Listen

Remember, that the Secret Influence Process begins with you strengthening yourself. When facing tough feelings and situations, we have tools for working with illness or unease in our lives.

We have been looking at how to heal when life's too much. We can help ourselves when we use Humor, then we Energize, Act and Listen.

When we feel life's too much, it is often that we're "too much." That is, we're too much in a hurry, or too distracted. Or we're allowing unhealthy thought patterns to run us. An old expression holds, "Some people think the same things they thought last week and last year. These people are not living ten years; they are living one year ten times."

The powerful way to heal when life's too much is to stay open and continue searching for new ways to grow and learn. Keep reading, listening to audio programs and attending workshops and spiritual gatherings.

Stop being "too much." Get out of your own way. Enlist the assistance of medical professionals, other healers, spiritual teachers, coaches, friends and family members. You can feel better.

Let's remember that in order to give to others (including the offended person) we need to keep ourselves in good shape mentally, physically and spiritually. Continually impact yourself with healing and nurturing materials.

> *Decision-making is easy if your values are clear.*
> ROY O. DISNEY (WALT DISNEY'S BROTHER AND PARTNER)

You have the power to choose your beliefs and choose how you live on a daily basis. You can choose to focus on scarcity or abundance. You can remind yourself with "I am grateful for … "

As I mentioned earlier, before I go to sleep each night, I write in my Daily Journal of Victories and Blessings. A victory relates to an action I took, such as exercising. A blessing is a gift, such as talking on the telephone with an extended family member. I go to sleep feeling grateful for the blessings and adventures of each day.

I am grateful for the opportunity to connect with you through this book. I wish you a journey of love, abundance and blessings.

In *Chapter Ten, Say YES to Yourself: Reduce Stress and Increase Ease,* you'll learn more ways to strengthen yourself and to positively influence the offended person toward healing your personal or business relationship.

Let's continue …

10

Say "Yes" to Yourself

Reduce Stress and Increase Ease

In Chapter Eight, you learned to ask gentle questions to help the offended person express his or her pain and start the healing process.

In Chapter Nine, you learned to strengthen yourself and enhance your own healing.

Now, in Chapter Ten, we will explore reducing stress and increasing ease. Our focus point is to *Say YES to Yourself*.

Why is this important?

Because the offended person is saying a big no to you. In essence the offended person is denying that you have any good intentions. It is as if one mistake wiped clear every kind word and every self-sacrificing effort you have ever done. If the offended person is your partner, friend or family member, this is truly painful.

This whole section on the Secret Influence Process is vital to your being at your best with the *10 Seconds to Wealth*. The person who get to a calm state of being can improve relationships, both personal and business.

As I mentioned earlier, the Secret Influence Process includes:

- Strengthen yourself
- Remain in a calm state of being
- Communicate your concern and kindness
- Take action with the F.A.R. methods (forgiveness, amends, regret)

When I give my presentation *Say YES to Yourself: Reduce Stress and Increase Ease* in a hospital or association meeting, I notice that the attendees welcome the opportunity to learn how to enhance their personal energy.

Imagine that you want to have the energy to:

- Shine at work and look good to your boss
- Persuade customers
- Be good to your loved ones when you return from a workday
- Withstand the emotional storms of the offended person

Wouldn't it be great to be able to flow with any change that comes up in the office? To stand strong and not be knocked flat. Instead, you can have the skills to respond to any stressful situation effectively; to have calm and poise; to demonstrate effective leadership. And, let's face it, to just feel better as you go through your day. That's what we're going to discuss here in Chapter Ten.

We will explore the S.A.Y.Y.E.S. process:

S - Step off the stage
A - Accept better care
Y - Yield to recovery
Y - Yearn for energy
E - Encourage your best
S - Support your team

When you learn these methods, you will also expand your feelings of confidence.

Let's stride forward to better days ...

Step off the Stage

Do you frequently feel that you have to be on your guard when in front of other people? How much time do you get for relaxing?

By "stage" I mean anywhere you're with people. Being on stage is anytime when you feel some amount of social pressure. The point is that you need to recharge as you go through your day.

Let's remember that the Secret Influence Process requires that you guard your energy so that you can patiently listen to the offended person.

> *We don't stop playing because we grow old; we grow
> old because we stop playing.*
>
> GEORGE BERNARD SHAW

The person who steps off the stage simply feels better. Part of feeling better is to have some time for relaxation and, yes, playing.

Researchers note that the most effective people use this pattern: activity then recovery.

What does this look like? It can be as simple as one hour working on a report—that's the Activity part. Then, you get up, step outside your office and walk around the block. That's the Recovery part.

Then back to work. My clients often find that a five minute walk—their form of recovery—energizes them to return to activities that require concentration.

People need to become what's known as a corporate athlete. A corporate athlete is an expert on using energy and replenishing energy. Corporate athletes pay attention, and learn their personal style of using energy and replenishing energy. And they make effective plans to use the Activity-Recovery pattern.

It takes a lot of energy to keep up your professional face. It's a façade. You need times during your workday when you can catch your breath, and step away from other people. This is what I mean by "step off the stage."

Just a little time will do. Years ago, I worked for a particular organization in downtown San Francisco. There was no spare room at this firm. During my lunch break, I would step on to the balcony with a chair, sit down and meditate. You can rest in a restroom stall—if necessary. You can go to your car and rest there. You can rest by walking on the steps between floors. Here is a question to ask yourself:

Power Question How can I step off the stage?

A Power Question is a trigger. Top professionals use positive triggers to shift how they respond to things that come up during their workday. Each of us can use a Power Question to get us thinking of better actions.

The easiest way to see this distinction is to think of the opposite. Here's an Energy-Draining Question: "Why does this always happen to me?" Ow. I can feel it. I'm leaking energy! Help!

Now let's look at the opposite, two Power Questions: "How can I turn this around? Who can help me?"

That's it! Now, I feel like myself! Strong, poised, confident. I feel that I have resources.

Awareness and action

In many years of coaching clients, guiding audiences and speaking to students at Stanford University and Academy of Art University, I learned that to increase success and fulfillment, we need two things: awareness and action.

When I share with you a S.A.Y.Y.E.S. method, we're increasing awareness. When we use the Power Question, we're using a positive trigger to get you going with effective action.

If you normally maintain a packed schedule, take five minutes between appointments to return a call to a friend. Laugh a little. Take your mind off things.

At other times, get away from others and give yourself the gift of silence. Take a brief walk. Sit in your car and listen to soothing music.

> *Music washes away from the soul the dust of everyday life.*
> BERTHOLD AUERBACH

Each one of these brief actions is a way to step off the stage. Like a brief, mini-vacation, it is your moment to get away from other people and energize yourself.

This mini-vacation is crucial. Why? Because part of the F.A.R. process is sincerely expressing regret. And it is tough to remain in the painful, regretful place.

So be sure to get some time away from the offended person so you can recharge your batteries. The truth is the offended person wants you to express regret and to feel sad and in pain.

A human being often needs a break! So get time away, and get off the stage.

Principle

Step off the stage (give yourself recovery time).

Power Question

How can you step off the stage? (Write a list of five things you can do at different points in your day.)

Accept Better Care

Imagine seeing your best friend working in the manner you do. Would you counsel him or her to take an appropriate break? It is likely that you would. Here is the important question to ask yourself repeatedly through the workday:

How can I take better care of myself right now?

> *Progress is impossible without change, and those who cannot change their minds cannot change anything.*
>
> GEORGE BERNARD SHAW

> *We need nutrition, exercise, sleep and health care. Treating ourselves as worthwhile [people] helps us feel worthwhile. [Give your] soul a better home.*
>
> TOUCHSTONES
> A Book of Daily Meditations for Men

To accept better care is a powerful process for healing. Many of us get so caught up in our work that we do not take care of ourselves.

Many people find comfort through spiritual practices. Here is a prayer that enriches many lives.

The Serenity Prayer

> *God grant me the serenity to accept the things I cannot change, courage to change the things I can, and wisdom to know the difference.*
>
> REINHOLD NIEBUHR

Pull out your personal journal and write down the Power Question *How can I take better care of myself right now?*

Then quickly, in 20 seconds, write down six ways you can take action to nurture yourself.

> *There is more to life than increasing its speed.*
> MAHATMA GANDHI

> *Your healthy functioning is where your wisdom lies, it is your peace of mind, your common sense, your satisfaction in life, and your feeling of wholeness.*
> RICHARD CARLSON

In other words, healthy functioning consists of the moments when you have felt good! Some of us are going through tough times and we may find it hard to remember when we felt good. Okay. Recall a moment of laughter. For example, when my sweetheart came through an operation that removed her spleen, she said, "Well, I'm lighter now." That was a moment of humor.

Healthy functioning is when a human being is living in the moment and in an authentic way. On the other hand, each of us has a thought system. This is a pattern of thinking that was set up in childhood. If your parents argued about money, then some part of you thinks, "Money is a source of arguments." That is *not* a solid, stuck-in-the-cement truth. Talk to enough people and you will hear different ideas, such as, "Money is a source for planning." Or my comment:

> *Money is a tool I use well for the benefit of all.*
> TOM MARCOUX

"You can't satisfy your thought system," wrote Richard Carlson. The point is that when you fall back into your thought system, you are likely to get stuck in other dark or sad thoughts.

> *It's impossible to feel gratitude for something when you are too busy trying to improve it.*
>
> RICHARD CARLSON

Imagine, taking a breath and enjoying the moment of sitting with a family member. Imagine just being grateful that you're both still here, on this planet. "Gratitude is the antidote to depression," Richard Carlson declared.

> *Light is more powerful than darkness. Healthy functioning is more powerful than unhappiness ... You don't find light by studying the dark.*
>
> RICHARD CARLSON

From this statement, we can realize that a balance is needed. Certainly, it sometimes helps to reflect on what may be an unhealthy pattern of behavior in your life. At one point, I noticed that I had chosen a series of partners who were emotionally shut down. At that point, I ended the unhealthy relationship I was in.

So an insight can give you some energy to take a new step forward.

On the other hand, studying every bad mistake and bad feeling can become overdone. As mentioned earlier, Richard wrote, You don't find light by studying the dark.

So let's balance things out by focusing on the light! This is a source of healing. What is light and wholesome in your life? Well, you can read! Or someone is reading this to you.

So let's take that step in healing: reach toward the light.

How do we do this? We make a choice in the moment.

For example, my client Stephen had an argument with his father on the phone one evening. It had been a 12-hour workday for Stephen, a CEO. He mentioned that he made a thousand decisions that day. His father, a retired blue-collar worker, scoffed at that idea. Like a knee-jerk reaction, Stephen felt angry. His tone of voice was intense, and he ended the conversation abruptly.

After the phone call, at midnight, Stephen recalled the conversation and felt remorse.

Stephen had a choice; one option was to obsess over his errors in the conversation. And if he continued on that path, Stephen could recall every irritable conversation he had ever had with his father. Or Stephen could choose the second option: to let the negative thought flow away—as if on a river.

It helped that Stephen chose to write briefly about the situation in his personal journal. He wrote:

"Next time, I'll remind myself that my happiness does not depend on being proven right. It doesn't depend on my father understanding my situation. He can't really. He's lived with a separate psychological reality. His blue-collar work was different than my corporate work."

Then, Stephen let his negative thoughts drift away. To help with this, he reached for his iPod and listened to some soothing music.

And in making this decision and choosing to let go of negative thoughts, Stephen was giving himself better care.

Let's remember that if you take care of yourself well, you will have more energy to devote to restoring your relationship with the offended person.

Principle

Focus on accepting better care.

Power Question

How can I take better care of myself right now?

Yield to Recovery

When do you appropriately yield in your life?

When we drive a car, we must often yield to oncoming traffic. And in life, we must yield to the truth that researchers discovered about optimal human functioning: humans do best when they use an Activity-Recovery Pattern. This means that the person is active and then rests for an appropriate period of time. Top tennis pros, in a two-hour match, are active for 20 minutes. They rest in between outbursts of energy. For an office worker, the person can write a report in the morning, then later "rest" by doing something less taxing—perhaps, some photocopying.

> *Taking responsibility to get away [for a break] is a good cure for self-pity and exhaustion.*
>
> TOUCHSTONES
> A Book of Daily Meditations for Men

Here is a helpful question: *How can I use the Activity-Recovery Pattern?*

The Calm-Tai Chi Movement

Special breathing and movement release tension from the body. During my presentations, the audience enjoys The Calm-Tai Chi Movement, which comes from the combination of my degree in psychology and training in Asian movement.

Stand with your feet apart as wide as your shoulders. Bend your knees slightly. Now, raise your arms in front of you, palms down and open. Once your arms are stretched out in front of you with your hands at shoulder height, gently pull your hands back toward your shoulders.

Then gently lower your hands until your hands are loosely hanging at your thigh level.

A number of Tai Chi DVDs are available in stores and online—so that you can see what I have just described.

My addition is for you to add what I call Affirm-Breathing. As you breathe in say an affirmation silently in your mind, such as: I am relaxing, or God relaxes me, or Higher Power holds me safe.

As your lower your hands, breathe out and again silently say your affirmation.

Quiet time (prayer, meditation, more)

A major proponent of meditation was asked, "How long do you meditate each day?"

"Three minutes," the spiritual teacher replied. He emphasized that a consistent three-minute daily habit was more beneficial than an unfulfilled intention to do a 20-minute meditation daily session.

Do three minutes help? Ask my sweetheart. She has seen how I become much more at ease when I take even a mere three minutes on a train to devote to quiet time and deep breathing.

Carry a timer in your briefcase or purse and discover the benefit of at least three minutes of quiet time. Please realize that connection with Higher Power can happen in an instant. So three minutes truly can bring you tangible peace.

Principle

Be sure to yield to recovery time.

Power Question

How can you use the Activity-Recovery Pattern?

Yearn for Energy

One day in my office, I felt so drained that I could barely sit up in my chair. My usual lively energy had vanished and I was afraid. This moment reminded me of a time when I was in a cave. The cave guide had us turn off all lights. Complete darkness. I could not see my hand, which was only three inches in front of my eyes. For a second, I felt almost a weight of darkness.

What can you do if you feel a heavy burden at work? The human mind has a terrific "switch" built in. Just like in a cave, you do not fight darkness with darkness. You light one candle. For the human mind, the candle is a question.

> *A prudent question is one-half of wisdom.*
> FRANCIS BACON

That tough day when I had significant work to do, I was feeling cast adrift and with no connection. In a quiet place in my rational mind, I knew that this report would somehow ultimately serve a number of people. But I needed that "switch." So I asked myself, "Where is the joy?"

Then I realized the joy was a few steps out in the future. My joy would occur when I would speak before an audience (using the ideas of the report). The fun would be sharing the ideas and creating humor in the moment.

That was where the joy was. At that point, I had a connection to the purpose for the report, and I felt energetic.

Power Question Where is the joy?

Gain Energy through Talk, Walk, Write

You can call a friend (or even speak into an audio recording device) and gain energy. Just talk about the project and then ask aloud, "Where is the joy?"

Then your mind starts looking for the answer. You could say, "Where is the joy? I don't know. I guess the joy is … " And your mind will ultimately fill in the blank. It helps to write down your answer, so later, you can review and support your energy.

Often we feel sluggish because our body actually craves to move. So how about combine "talk" and "walk." Take a walk and use your cell phone (or audio recording device).

Energy, Money, and Healing

Many of us lose so much energy to our habitual thoughts about money. We need to be careful about the jokes we share with friends, like, "There is more month at the end of the money."

Feeling upset does not help in our purpose of healing ourselves.

Money is a tool I use well for the benefit of all.
TOM MARCOUX

Money is such a crucial topic related to healing both ourselves and our relationships that I wrote and narrated the audio program *Wake Up Your Spirit to Prosperity.*

Here I want to emphasize: from our thoughts come feelings. So if you have a reflexive, negative thought about money, you can switch the direction of your thoughts. Just momentarily visualize a "cancel button." Then do the motion of pressing the button and say the word "Cancel!" Then immediately state silently an empowering replacement-thought. For example, you can remember:

Who is rich? He that rejoices in his portion.
BENJAMIN FRANKLIN

Imagine this. You are prosperous in this moment. How? It is likely that you ate breakfast. You can read this. And at this very moment, you are not on the phone arguing with a creditor. So in this moment, you are okay!

My client Serena responded to this idea with a big smile. "You're right! I am okay."

Anytime you want to feel an increase in energy, remind yourself to say: "I am grateful for _____." And fill in the blank.

> *The key to momentum is always having something to look forward to.*
>
> WYNN DAVIS

And this reminds me of the old phrase: "Happiness is something to do, someone to love and something to look forward to." Concentrate on these elements, and your energy will increase. Remember to ask, "Where is the joy?"

Principle

Find the joy as part of what you're doing.

Power Question

Where is the joy?

Encourage Your Best

What secret do many people miss at their workplace? As you walk into stores and restaurants, how often do you see listless people who look like they're just doing time—as if in a prison?

The secret they are missing is when you do your best, you feel good. You even find fun on many occasions.

> *Make not your thoughts your prisons.*
> **WILLIAM SHAKESPEARE**

The thought, "Ugh! I have to do this!" drains energy like holes in a water tower.

When I first began working at the age of 15, I found myself one summer working five days a week at Levi Strauss, weekends for A & W Restaurant and one evening a week for Underwriter's Laboratory. One thing that sustained me was having these thoughts:

> *Wherever I am, I will serve. And I'll make friends.*
> **TOM MARCOUX**

I realized that whatever job I was doing, I had the opportunity to do my best and feel good about the whole thing.

> *Just do what must be done. This may not be happiness, but it is greatness.*
> **GEORGE BERNARD SHAW**

No one ever got excited about doing barely enough to get by. And many people hold great fear about their jobs. The solution is to become known for being excellent in the skills highly valued in your particular workplace. Ask yourself, "What am I best known for?" Then, make sure that you do what will help you be known as a crucial team member.

The question "What am I best known for?" is a pillar of your personal brand. A personal brand does for an individual what a product brand does for a company. In essence, the personal brand is a clear and brief message of what you offer and what the listener can trust you to do.

In my book *Nothing Can Stop You This Year*, I relate a number of personal branding strategies. And, here let's focus on how helpful it is for you to hone your message about your work into these two areas:

- "This is what I offer."
- "You can trust me to listen carefully to your concerns, devise an appropriate process, and come through for you."

Top performers repeatedly talk about how they honed their skills with their natural talents. They express their natural brilliance. Researchers are now emphasizing that success goes to those people who choose to accentuate their strengths and delegate to others who have better skills or inherent talent in other areas.

In your personal journal, answer these questions:

- What are my strengths?
- How can I express my strengths vividly so people know what I offer is exceptional?
- How can I get help in areas that do not coincide with my strengths?

For example, I rely on a team of people who demonstrate talent in editing, accounting, illustrating, filming and more. This has set me free to continually hone my talents in speaking, writing, directing films, leading various teams and guiding people to communicate powerfully.

Focus on your strengths and express your natural brilliance.

Principle

Focus on expressing your personal brilliance.

Power Question

What are you best known for?

Support Your Team

Describe a team. What do the team members share? A feeling of connection. Often, a common dedication to one goal. At Pepsi, they had one goal, which they verbalized in two words: "Beat Coke."

Secret influence truly occurs when you look on the other person as part of your team. You work with him or her. You communicate in ways that make it easy for the person to take in your message.

> Do **not** do unto others as you expect they should do unto you. Their tastes may not be the same.
>
> GEORGE BERNARD SHAW

In order to experience support from your co-workers and supervisor, you need to first support them. This starts the flow of good will. They are all true individuals with different personality styles. In my book *Darkest Secrets of Persuasion and Seduction Masters: Protect Yourself and Turn the Power to Good*, I present a number of facets of personality styles. Here, we'll cover a brief overview. Personality styles can be described in this manner:

> **The Lion:** A director-type person who is a hard-charger with little patience. This person wants to hear the brief details and to know the impact on the bottom line.
>
> **The Dog:** A relater-type person who values a human connection over changing to make things better. This person likes routine.
>
> **The Beaver:** An analytic-type person who is a detail-obsessed, engineer-type person. Often, this person is slow to make a decision.
>
> **The Peacock:** A socializer-type person who loves talking about ideas with people, and who is quick at decision making and often poor on follow-up.

Here's an example. My client Theresa was presenting to a group of people and she took into account their personality styles.

Personality Style

Theresa's Methods

Beaver ("analytic" or "engineer" or "accountant")

Theresa used a list of methods that she formed into a process: P.R.E.S.E.N.T.

Dog ("relater")

Theresa asked audience members, "What are you hoping or expecting that I will be talking about today?" Then, she wrote down their topics and questions.

Lion ("director")

Theresa checked off the topics/questions as she went through them. The director-type person appreciates seeing progress shown by checking off the topics.

Peacock ("socializer")

Prior to her talk, Theresa walked around the room and met the audience members. She wrote down people's comments. She shared some comments in this manner: "I was talking with Tony, and he mentioned that the XYZ works best when … How about a round of applause for Tony?"

Here is another example. John has a "director" (Lion) style, and he compensates for it. In the middle of a conversation with Susan, a relater (Dog), John slows down and asks gentle questions. He listens first.

> *Know your tendencies and compensate for them.*
> TOM MARCOUX

John takes a different but helpful approach when working with Matt, an analyzer (Beaver), John invites Matt to prepare in a special way before their next weekly meeting. John says, "Matt, write some notes on three alternative solutions. Then endorse one and tell me your reasoning when we meet on Friday." In this manner, John supports Matt's analytic personality style. John also supports his own "director" personality style that calls for brevity.

Learn about the personality styles and tailor your message to the individual. Also, realize that the offended person is likely the opposite from you in personality traits. So tread softly. Communicate in a way that the offended person can easily take in your message.

Principle

Learn to flow and support personality styles—to enhance joy and harmony in relationships.

Power Question

How can personality styles help you do better?

Conclusion to Chapter Ten

In Chapter Ten, we have covered the S.A.Y.Y.E.S. process:

- S – Step off the stage
- A – Accept better care
- Y – Yield to recovery
- Y – Yearn for energy
- E – Encourage your best
- S – Support your team

Remember, the essence of secret influence is to nurture yourself, place yourself in a calm state of being and then encourage the transfer of your calm state of being to the offended person.

In *Chapter Eleven, Effectively Work with Creditors so You Can Get Out of Debt and Back on Your Feet,* we will explore how you can bring more peace to your daily life. From that foundation, you can have more energy to devote to healing your relationship with the offended person.

Let's move forward …

11

Work Effectively with Creditors

Get Out of Debt and Back on Your Feet

What causes major breakups of romantic couples? Money troubles. What creates anxiety for many people? Intimidating calls from creditors and collection agencies.

If you are upset in relation to money troubles, it is hard to have the energy to remain patient when dealing with the offended person.* So this section will help you improve tough

• •

* At the time of this writing, people are dealing with doctor/hospital bills, disabilities, long-term unemployment, family member addiction, and legal fees. Top financial advisors, including Suze Orman, suggest contacting resources including the National Foundation for Credit Counseling (nfcc.org). Some people find it necessary to seek local resources like a food bank or a shelter or sign up for reduced utility bills when income is low. Suze Orman discusses the true last resort of bankruptcy, and she recommends the overview at www.credit.com/slp/chapter8/Bankruptcy.jsp. On the Fair Debt Collection Practices Act (FDCPA), which limits the actions creditors

situations. I first shared this information in my book *Truth No One Will Tell You.*

When I looked up "debt quotes" with Google.com, I noticed an interesting label: "Debt quotes/Financial Responsibility."

Empower yourself by seeing responsibility as the ability to respond. In this section, we will arm you with methods so that you can respond. You'll learn how to talk with creditors in ways to set up reasonable repayment schedules.

As I mentioned earlier, the Secret Influence Process includes:

1. Strengthen yourself

2. Remain in a calm state of being

3. Communicate your concern and kindness

4. Take action with the F.A.R. methods (forgiveness, amends, regret)

Remember, when you nurture yourself you can go into a calm state of being. Secret influence occurs when you transfer that calm state of being to the offended person. At that point, eventually, the offended person will drop his or her blinders and, perhaps, recall your past kind and helpful actions.

An interviewer asked me, "How do you transfer positive energy to the offended person?"

I replied: "Through your eyes, body movements, smile and vocal tonality. We communicate constantly. The offended per-

----

can take, she recommends the discussion at www.credit.com/credit_information/credit_law/Understanding-Your-Debt-Collection-Rights.jsp#2 son picks up all the subtle cues. If you have positive energy inside, it naturally radiates out from you."

Sometimes a profound idea appears very simple:

> *If you want to be rich, solve problems.*
>
> ROBERT KIYOSAKI

If you solve important problems at work, you are likely to gain raises and promotions.

If you create a product and it solves problems, you are likely to gain a significant number of customers.

In fact, I was inspired to write this section because I recalled the idea *solve problems*. This led me to the question: What problem dominates people's thoughts? Money troubles. To be at your best during the *10 Seconds to Wealth,* you need to take action so you avoid being distracted by money troubles.

When it comes to debt, the target is to learn how to turn things around. We will use the T.U.R.N. process:

- T – Talk
- U – Understand
- R – Right-size
- N – Nurture

Let's step forward …

Talk

What's one of the most important things a person needs to do if he or she can't pay their bills?

Talk to the creditors. You heard that right.

> *You must call credit card collectors, tell them the truth and deal with your situation head-on.*
>
> SUZE ORMAN

In this section we will cover:

- How to ask for lower payments
- How to create a positive atmosphere during the call so that the person is more likely to cooperate
- How to ask to talk with a supervisor and how to flow with the conversation once the supervisor arrives

The Benefit of Making Arrangements with Creditors

Once you make arrangements to make small payments toward your debts, *you'll feel better* in some important ways.

> *Keeping what you have and creating what you deserve is not only about money. It is about the absence of fear, which is an even greater blessing than the absence of want; and fear tends to disappear when you tell the truth.*
>
> SUZE ORMAN

How to Ask for Lower Payments

First, *rehearse* with a friend so that you feel you're ready. Also have your notes in front of you. The clerk on the phone will not see that you have your notes and a "script" in front of you.

> *Courage is easier when I'm prepared.*
> TOM MARCOUX

Second, before you dial the phone number be sure to sit down and make sure you have calmed down. My client Marina found that she felt better after she chose an affirmation and repeated it before calling a creditor. Her choice was: "God holds me safe." An affirmation can work when it is personal and means something to your heart.

Once you dial and have a creditor's team member on the line, you can say something like: "Hello, I want to set up a payment arrangement ... "

Please know that even a small payment of even $5.00 is a demonstration of good faith. It is truly a good start. At this point, the person on the other side is feeling good—at least a little bit. The creditor has someone calling her and seeking to make the situation better. Good for you!

An interviewer asked, "Won't some creditors say, 'That's not enough,' and then say something intimidating and require at least $50.00?"

Yes. That can happen. However, if you start making payments, you'll see that creditors will usually cash the checks. Also, you are creating a good history of taking positive action.

You can say, "I can only send $5.00 at this time. I'm certainly looking to make this better. And I am aiming to make a good start now."

How to create a positive atmosphere during the call so that the person is more likely to cooperate

The idea is to turn the creditor into a friendly associate. You do this by expressing appreciation.

> *If properly appreciated, we feel better ... We become more open to listening and more motivated to cooperate ... You are more likely to reach a wise agreement than if each side feels unappreciated.*
>
> ROGER FISHER AND DANIEL SHAPIRO

So as soon as possible in your conversation with the creditor, say sincerely, "I appreciate how you're making this as pleasant as possible."

As a side note, years ago, I found that I often gained cooperation quickly (even when getting a vendor to correct his mistake) by starting my conversation with: "I'm hoping you'll have good news for me."

How to communicate with your supervisor

Sometimes the first person you talk with truly cannot help you. They are likely bound by policies that hold no flexibility. The person often starts merely repeating himself, and says that he cannot do what you're asking for. But the supervisor often has more leeway.

You can say, "Well, it looks like it's time to talk with your supervisor."

Sometimes, you need to maintain a firm voice and keep repeating your request. You may need to ask, "Are you saying I cannot talk with the supervisor?" Your conversation is being recorded, and it is likely that the clerk on the phone does not want to be caught telling something that is not true. So he may pass you to the supervisor at that point.

There are times when you need to say, "Oh, something is happening here. I'm going to have to hang up now." And then you end the call. The reason for this strategy is that when you call back, you may be fortunate to get a different clerk. In any case, be prepared to repeatedly, firmly and politely ask to speak with a supervisor. (I have found it helpful to even call another time and get a different supervisor.)

When you talk with the supervisor, gently ask for his or her name with: "Hello, I'm [your name]. And you are … ?" A few times during the conversation add appreciative comments while using the person's name. You can say, "Trina, I appreciate your helping me with this." You may need to ask the supervisor to repeat an explanation or detail, and you can say, "Oh. I appreciate you giving me that information. Would you please repeat the part about XYZ, I'm putting that into my notes."

When you say the above you are expressing appreciation and you are giving a quiet alert that you are taking notes.

~~~~~~

A place for truth-telling … with your friends and your family

A number of people get into significant credit card debt by charging vacations and consumer goods. To get out of debt, it will be necessary to change habits.

One time, my sweetheart and I wanted to take a vacation with friends. But then a project did not yield the funds that we had expected. So I had to call our friends and tell the truth:

my sweetheart and I could not attend because a project had not worked out as planned. Over the years, I have made it a practice to save up in advance before taking a vacation.

In fact, I know a couple who saved for five years so that they could go on a cruise.

> *Never spend your money before you have it.*
> THOMAS JEFFERSON

Good Debt v. Bad Debt

It is true that there are some expenses that are valuable enough for using "good debt." For many people, getting a college education leads to a higher paying, more satisfying job—so student loans would be "good debt." But going into debt to buy the latest consumer goods, such as a top-flight home entertainment system, may be not be a match for building a life with financial abundance.

Good debt could be an appropriate business loan. For example, one time I gained a loan for a project that later gave me credibility. This credibility led to my later gaining $223,760. To me that was good debt. Basically, the answer is this: *"Good debt involves creating a true asset."* A college education can be a true asset. My business project was a true asset. You get the picture.

As this is being written, many Americans have been hit by a foreclosure crisis in that they had agreed to variable rates related to their mortgages. So it essential that you get legal advice to make sure that a loan agreement will *not* have clauses that could result in harm for you. Be sure to get advice from someone who is on your side—that is, a person who does *not* have an agenda in conflict with your well-being. (For example, be aware that various mortgage vendors truly want to close the deal with you; that's how the vendors get paid.)

Make informed choices and you can improve your financial situation.

Principle

Rehearse before you talk to creditors.

Power Question

Which friends or family members can help you through good rehearsals before you talk to creditors?

Understand

Understand this: if the creditor gets any kind of payment from you, the creditor feels as if he or she is winning. Making a $5.00 payment is a good start. Financial advisors such as David Bach and Suze Orman emphasize that it is often advisable to pay the highest interest loan or credit card first.

In this section, we're talking about *secret influence to get you out of trouble*, and here I want to emphasize that you can influence a creditor to improve a situation. For example, financial advisors note that you can search out the lowest interest rate credit cards, and armed with this information you can return to your own credit card vendor and encourage them to lower your rate. The credit card vendor would rather retain you as customer than to lose you to another credit card company. It is important for you to study reputable sources of financial information so that you have the tools and information you need to improve your situation.

> *If you feed your mind as often as you feed your stomach, then you'll never have to worry about feeding your stomach or a roof over your head or clothes on your back.*
>
> ALBERT EINSTEIN

Often, we notice that many people who truly succeed had to work two jobs simultaneously—for years. For example, Albert Einstein worked as a clerk in a patent office while he pondered light, space and time. In 1905, while working in that patent office, Einstein had four papers published in the *Annalen der Physik*, the leading German physics journal. Physicists to this day look on these papers as significant achievements. And Albert Einstein did two things simultaneously: he worked to make a living and he pursued the area of his natural brilliance *to make a life.*

Principle

Understand that you'll need to do extraordinary things: study financial information and perhaps, work more than one job.

Power Questions

Where do your talents and skills actually reside? Could you invest in yourself by taking a class or getting coaching to help you turn a hobby into a side source of income? (Today's economy often requires people to develop multiple sources of income.)

Right-Size

What do many chronic debtors have in common? Their lives are out of balance; in other words, their lives are "wrong-sized." For our discussion, a definition of wrong-sized includes these elements noted by experts who assist people to recover from financial mistakes.

"Wrong-sized" means:

- A person's expenditures have exceeded his or her income
- A person uses the act of buying stuff to feel some pleasure and to numb some hidden pain
- The person is out of balance and uses stuff to distract him or her from her pain or sense of emptiness

> *If you borrow $10,000 on your credit cards and pay only the minimum payment with an interest rate of $19.98%, it will take you more than 37 years to get out of debt ... [and] you will have forked over nearly $19,000 in interest charges.*
>
> DAVID BACH

Early in my working life, I learned two things. Have two nice pairs of pants and avoid using a clothes dryer on your dress shirts. By not using a dryer on my dress shirts I avoided shrinkage of my shirts—and I avoided having to buy new shirts! At that time in my life, that was an example of taking action to "right-size" my life and purchases.

Reduce the amount of your purchases. Put in safety measures so that you do *not* overspend. Financial advisors talk about: a) only bringing cash to the grocery store; b) batching (grouping) your errands so that you save gas money; and c) writing down a spending plan. A number of people avoid the word "budget." Instead, they use the name "spending plan" as something that can empower you to make effective choices. My clients often use the title: Financial Abundance Plan.

Remember to include some enjoyable experiences. Otherwise, you may find an unhealthy pattern occurring. For example, someone who does not eat breakfast may find herself eating a huge dinner. Deprivation can cause binge behavior. This is the reason that I am emphasizing putting a plan in place so that you have some enjoyment (on a modest scale) each month.

To set a plan and follow through does take effort.

> *I will do what others will not do, so in the future I can do what others cannot do.*
>
> **RANDY GAGE**

> *Success is having good relationships, fulfilling employment, and being as healthy as you can be.*
>
> **LARRY WINGET**

Our definition of success and our beliefs about "the good life" impact our daily actions. If a person says, "I deserve this," every time he is near the display of DVDs in a store, it is likely that he will purchase another DVD (that will eventually sit on a shelf, gathering dust).

Let's go back to Larry Winget's definition of success: Success is having good relationships, fulfilling employment, and being as healthy as you can be.

We notice that this list does not include: a car as good or better than the Jones; the best-looking house in the neighborhood; 27 pairs of shoes ...

Oh-oh! Perhaps, I have gone too far. It's true that many of us tend to have a soft spot for something (like shoes). I admit it: my soft spot is books. Early in my work life, I was strategic in how I gained books. A debuting hardcover book is most expensive. If I would demonstrate patience, I could wait for the paperback book to appear one year later. Less cost. And today, you can purchase the paperback book as a serviceable used book through Amazon.com.

An interviewer asked, "So how do we avoid making impulse purchases?"

I replied, "It's a multi-layered process. You need a plan and then to work your plan."

To Avoid Impulse Purchases and Handle Your "Soft Spot"

- Carefully choose your definition of success.
- Have safety measures; for example, go shopping with a friend who tends to save money and is careful with purchases.

- Replace troublesome behavior with helpful behavior; for example, take a walk in a park instead of a shopping mall.
- Use a Self-Nurture Chart and make sure that you experience enjoyment (without spending money) on a daily basis.

My client Kevin came to me about concerns that he might make some spending mistakes while his wife was away visiting family. Kevin wisely understood that with his wife temporarily absent, he would be experiencing loneliness and some pain. From our conversation, Kevin created this Self-Nurture Chart.

Self-Nurture Chart™

Nurturing Action	Mon	Tues	Wed	Thu	Fri	Sat	Sun
Reading in hot bath	√			√			√
Hot bath listening to music and resting his eyes			√		√		
Comment in a journal to Becky (wife)		√				√	
Prayer for Becky to be safe and have a good trip	√			√			
Tai chi (outside?)	√		√			√	√
Yoga (outside?)					√		
3 minutes of silence			√				
Have a list of friends—and call one		√				√	
Watch episode of a funny TV show					√		
Ride bicycle outside			√				
Walk outside, even for 10 minutes	√					√	

Kevin did at least two of these actions on each day and found that he felt better and he avoided impulse-spending.

It's all about making choices that empower you.

You may decide to increase your value to the company where you work. Or you may decide to start a company of your own on the side. Author Michael Masterson writes:

> *"Every successful start-up business is one that has quickly and correctly answered [these] questions: 1) What is the most cost-effective way of attracting customers? And 2) What is the best way to keep those customers buying?"*

Michael Masterson emphasizes that each business needs to focus on "1) Lowering the cost of acquiring new customers and 2) Increasing the lifetime value of each existing customer."

Rather go to bed supperless than rise in debt.

BENJAMIN FRANKLIN

Now that is an extreme idea. How about we change the idea to something like: go without some lattés and fancy restaurant dinners. I have a bachelor friend who spends (not invests) thousands of dollars on eating out. Then, at one point he came across the idea: "$1,200 saved with compound interest of 8% would yield $12,000 in 30 years." At that point, he realized that he wasn't only losing $1,200 in that year, he was also losing $12,000, too!

And yet, I remember my own bachelor days in which I lived for a time on spinach, brown rice, some vegetables and tuna fish. I was saving my funds for my projects. That is, I was devoting money to building assets: projects that would gain me professional credibility.

We're talking about right-sizing your life and your expenses. And this is really about focusing on your true values and priorities.

> *Low overhead equals freedom.*
> — TELLER (OF THE TEAM PENN AND TELLER)

Principle

"Right-size" your life and purchases so that you can build a future of financial abundance.

Power Questions

What is your soft spot? (Shoes? DVDs? Books?) How can you make a spending budget so that you can occasionally reward yourself with your "soft spot," but have ways to restrain yourself from going overboard?

Nurture

Getting out of debt is hard work. You absolutely need to nurture yourself. You must keep your strength up.

But the big question is: what are you working for as you stretch yourself to get out of debt? *What is your big benefit?*

> *Financial Independence is [when] you have the resources to live a satisfying, comfortable life, accomplish your dreams and goals, and have more fun doing what you do.*
>
> BARBARA STANNY

Here is a secret: *You can feel financial independence now.* How? This quote gives us a good direction:

> *We do not remember days, we remember moments.*
>
> CESARE PAVESE

The idea is to focus on times when you felt good and had what you needed to enjoy the moment. Earlier, I shared this example, and it bears repeating here. Years ago I was in Disneyland with a friend. At the time, I did not have much money. But as I looked around the theme park I felt rich—as if the whole park was there for me. Certainly, Disneyland was there for the thousands of people present in the park. But I could stroll through the theme park with a big, joyful smile on my face.

On the other hand, my friend, who also was on a limited budget, had a completely different mindset. She was upset because she could *not* buy everything that she had a passing fancy for in the stores. She did not enjoy the abundance of just *being* in Disneyland!

My point is when I looked around Disneyland and smiled, I was, in that moment, feeling financial independence. I wasn't thinking about payments to the dentist, health insurance or anything else. I was in the moment. Again, let's remember the above quote: "*We do not remember days, we remember moments.*"

It is crucial that we nurture ourselves. This is especially true for those of us who have entrepreneurial pursuits. For example, there was a time I was feeling overwhelmed. I mentioned to my sweetheart, "I feel like a racehorse." She replied, *"Run in better races."*

What would "better races" be? I decided to pull back from certain activities that were not yielding the best results in both serving people and bringing in financial abundance. For example, there was a time that I chose to stop leading acting workshops. I found that my location was home to wannabe actors who had no money. So the workshops were *not* a lucrative way to gain income. Instead, I started to speak to people in corporate settings.

A second insight arose from the "run in better races" conversation. I thought, *"If I was a racehorse, I did not want to be a stableperson, too."* What that meant was that I needed to *work smart* and focus on doing what *I was uniquely capable* of doing. So I started to hire interns and contractors to work by the hour. I made a promise to myself that I would write my books but *not* typeset them.

We notice a difficulty for a number of people who run their own business: they burn out because they're wearing too many hats. It is better to hire independent contractors to relieve you of the burdens of bookkeeping and other tasks.

Business owners with a small budget can engage interns. For example, one of my friends recently went to a high school computer club and engaged an exceptional high school student to work on Web site-related projects.

The truth is that business owners truly need to focus on caring for current customers and gaining new customers. Once a business owner begins to work *on* the business instead of just *in* the business—the business starts to run better.

If you're a business owner and you feel overwhelmed, here is an important question: Where can you get the energy to patiently work toward healing your relationship with the offended person? Without working smart, you may be running a deficit in energy.

Pull out your personal journal and note how you might get help. Or at least how you can nurture yourself by scheduling in breaks.

The central idea about nurturing yourself

As I mentioned, getting out of debt is hard work, and you need to nurture yourself.

Here is what is important: *Find ways that do not cost money to soothe yourself, comfort yourself and put salve on your wounds.*

My clients have identified these healing actions:

- An evening walk with my spouse
- A hot bath
- Listening to relaxing music
- Playing with my children
- Going for a run

- Reading a book I borrowed from the library
- Bringing a brown bag lunch and enjoying time with a friend

Watch out for this phenomenon: *more pain equals more susceptibility to fall for bigger toys.* Have you noticed that after working extremely hard, you want more expensive vacations, more DVDs, more lattes? And have you heard yourself telling a friend, "Hey, I deserve to have … "

You can't get enough of what you don't really want. Let's face it together. *It is not really stuff that we truly want, it's feelings.* What do we really want? To feel good—plain and simple. How?

Here are the feelings we want:

- To feel comfortable
- To enjoy new sights and sounds
- To feel proud of ourselves
- To play
- To be heard (this is so valuable that I wrote a book entitled *Be Heard and Be Trusted*)
- To be admired
- To feel loved
- To feel relief from fears and concerns

My own coach suggested that I talk with my sweetheart for us to train each other in how to soothe each other. For example, my sweetheart likes when I massage her feet. That's important for me to know.

And, I like when my sweetheart massages my neck with a plastic massage tool while I'm typing *this sentence*.

Be careful to take care of yourself so you avoid feeling deprived as much as possible. For example, years ago, I only had two suits. But they were good suits. So when I wore them I felt good.

One important way to nurture yourself is to direct your attention to all the blessings already in your life. It helps to write down five details you're grateful for—just before you go to sleep each night.

> *I live in the space of thankfulness ... the more thankful I became, the more my bounty increased. That's because what you focus on expands, and when you focus on the goodness in your life, you create more of it. Opportunities, relationships, even money flowed my way when I learned to be grateful no matter what happened in my life. I keep a gratitude journal ... listing at least five things that I'm grateful for. My list includes small pleasures: the feel of Kentucky bluegrass under my feet (like damp silk); a walk in the woods ... My thank-you list also includes things too important to take for granted: an "okay" mammogram, friends who love me ...*
>
> OPRAH WINFREY

Principle

Nurture yourself and unleash the flow of positive energy to you and through you.

Power Questions

How can you nurture yourself on a daily basis? What brings relief and peace? (A hot bath, music, quiet time, calling a dear friend or something else?)

Conclusion to Chapter Eleven

In Chapter Eleven, we have covered the T.U.R.N process to help you improve your situation with creditors:

    T – Talk
    U – Understand
    R – Right-size
    N – Nurture

Remember to rehearse with friends or family members before you make a call to a creditor. Creditors want to be paid, and if you take action and start making small payments you are on the road to less stress.

In Chapter Twelve, Give It A Rest, we will cover how to bring more peace and comfort to your life by subtracting and not adding to your to-do list. With more peace, you have more strength to do what is necessary to heal your relationship with the offended person.

Let's flow forward …

12

Give It a Rest

Have you experienced this? You reach for a self-help or business book and something inside feels, "I'm just too tired to read this now."

Some people refer to this as "self-help burnout" or "self-help fatigue."

Why? The reason is often when we reach for a self-help book we're at the end of our rope and depleted of energy. It is just too painful to look at adding something more to your to-do list.

My client Martha told me about feeling overwhelmed. One Sunday, she sat down for the first time that week to enjoy a quiet cup of tea. Then her mother called with a research assignment for Martha to look up multiple Web sites. Her mother wanted Martha to pull together information and give her a cobbled-together report. Martha told me that inside her heart was screaming, "I just don't want any more work!"

Here's the good news. We're not looking for you to add something to your to-do list with this focus: Give It a Rest. Instead, in a number of situations, we're asking that you subtract something that's draining your energy.

We will use the R.E.S.T. process:

> R – Relax into it
> E – Ease through
> S – Sing
> T – Thank someone

As I mentioned earlier, the Secret Influence Process includes:

- Strengthen yourself
- Remain in a calm state of being
- Communicate your concern and kindness
- Take action with the F.A.R. methods (forgiveness, amends, regret)

And this section helps you be kind to yourself. When you make sure to renew your energy, you can be at your best during the *10 Seconds to Wealth*.

Let's step forward gently …

Relax into It

When I was snorkeling in the Bahamas, I experienced horrible cramps in my legs. I learned something quick: trying to force my way past this pain would not help anything. I had to let go and use my arms to help me move toward the shore. This gave me the lesson that some things cannot be solved with pushing, forcing and extreme effort.

If you see someone resisting your ideas, silently remind yourself to "relax into it." Ask questions and start listening. After you listen to the offended person (for example), he or she may soften a personal stance.

Seeking to relax, many people have experienced the benefits of meditation. I have found that even three minutes of quieting my mind and deep breathing on a train (or plane) transforms my outlook. I feel better!

Some of my clients have noticed that they feel on edge most of the time. A number of them have found the benefit of repeating an affirmation in their mind—and thus developing a positive, healthy mental habit. Here are examples:

- I live in a friendly universe that supports me.
- God holds me safe.
- "Be still and know I am God." (from *The Bible*)
- I feel blessed and peaceful now.

Remember that people who have some daily quiet time become graceful. Graceful people are flexible and can move in any direction. This even brings confidence. You'll start to feel that you can adapt to whatever flows into your life.

Principle

Relax into it.

Power Questions

What are three simple, brief things you can do each day so you experience some relaxation? How can you slow down and relax—and avoid trying to force things?

Ease Through

This part on "Give it a rest" is often about subtracting something. If you want to avoid having your energy drained, pick your battles. Sometimes the best thing is to say nothing. If it is not a "teaching moment," don't offer advice. A teaching moment is the rare occurrence in which someone actually asks for your help and advice. However, many times when someone asks, "What do you think?" the person is actually looking for agreement.

To avoid resistance, don't start spouting advice without asking permission first. For example, I saw an older man tell a young woman on crutches, "You shouldn't lean on those." The young woman looked up with anger.

Instead, a better approach would include the man saying, "Oh, that looks rough. I remember how a nurse told me a way to avoid some pain with crutches. Would you like to hear her helpful idea?"

If the young woman said, "No, thanks," then the interaction would have remained neutral.

If you avoid being judgmental, you can often avoid creating resistance. Then you will not need a breakthrough. Instead, you will have an Ease-through™. The Ease-through is a concept I introduced in my book *Nothing Can Stop You This Year*.

The easiest way I can illustrate the Ease-through is by having you imagine a karate move. One opens the hand and slams the palm toward a wooden board. If you take the board out (remove the resistance), you can ease through!

> *Aikido is the principle of non-resistance. Because it is non-resistant, it is victorious from the beginning. Those with evil intentions or contentious thoughts are instantly vanquished. Aikido is invincible because it contends with nothing ...*
>
> MORIHEI UESHIBA, FOUNDER OF AIKIDO

When I teach public speaking to graduate students, I show the difference between a karate blocking motion and an aikido motion. The karate block is when force meets force. Then I show an aikido motion in which the attacker is guided to miss the defender and flow past. In this way, I talk about how one can deal with tough questions.

> *You can turn a question into a gift even though it was thrown like a spear.*
>
> TOM MARCOUX

The idea, aikido is invincible because it contends with nothing, is helpful as we seek to create healing with an offended person. Hear the person out. Avoid jumping in and defending yourself.

> *If you are centered, you can move freely. The physical center is your belly; if your mind is set there as well, you are assured of victory in any endeavor ...*
>
> MORIHEI UESHIBA, FOUNDER OF AIKIDO

What is the real victory? Harmony. Closeness.

> *Let attackers come any way they like and then blend with them ...*
>
> MORIHEI UESHIBA, FOUNDER OF AIKIDO

The idea of "blending" with your opponent is a primary method when you interact with the offended person. The offended person, on some level, is expecting you to defend yourself. Don't do it! Listen. After a time, ask, "Is there anything else?"

If you agree in part with what the offended person is saying, the person does not have anything to push against.

> *To practice aikido properly, you must: Calm the spirit and return to the source. Cleanse the body and spirit by removing all malice, selfishness, and desire ...*
>
> MORIHEI UESHIBA, FOUNDER OF AIKIDO

Some of my clients express their concern by saying, "But I do have a desire. I want healing between me and my [boss, father, spouse]."

Yes. And the idea is to remove the desire for you to be proven right.

> *Strong negative emotions can cause you to experience tunnel vision ... Second, strong emotions make you vulnerable to the point that your emotions take control of your behavior ... You risk acting in ways that you will regret.*
>
> ROGER FISHER AND DANIEL SHAPIRO

This is the reason that we need you to take extra good care of yourself. We want you to build up positive "reflexes." When negative emotions rise up or even if your positive desire for healing shakes you up, practice deep breathing.

You can repeat silently to yourself: "Calm … peace … center."

The idea is to avoid resisting another person. You can also avoid creating resistance. This is the reason I developed Non-Correcting Conversation™.

The Power of Non-Correcting Conversation

When we love someone, we tend to try to help the person to avoid pain. The problem is that when we talk with them, we sound as if we're correcting the person. We mention what is not ideal ("You're not exercising enough") and then offer our opinion of what the other person needs to do.

In Non-Correcting Conversation, you ask two simple questions:

- What are you happy about? (This is about the present.)
- What are you looking forward to? (This is about the future.)

Some people you'll encounter seem to be allergic to the word happy. In those cases, you can use alternative questions:

- What is working for you?
- What are you feeling pretty good about?

When dealing with the offended person, the above questions may not help. You can use alternative questions, such as:

- Is there something else I can do now that will help the situation?
- As I'm doing _____, is that helping the situation?

The point is to help the person experience some small amount of positive results in the present.

Certainly, with family members, we want to protect them. My point is that let's make sure to have some Non-Correcting Conversations. Don't let it happen that a family member would say something like, "She's always correcting me." Instead, have conversations that inspire a family member to say, "I really appreciate how my [mom, dad, brother, sister] listens to me."

Principle

Remember to ease through; be sure to have Non-Correcting Conversations.

Power Question

With whom can you practice a Non-Correcting Conversation?

Sing

You do not need to literally sing. But that works, too. For example, as I type these words I'm listening to soothing music. Instead of singing, I started to whistle. Yes. Fortunately, no one was nearby.

> *God respects me when I work, but He loves me when I sing.*
>
> RABINDRANATH TAGORE

I'm talking about being carried away with music. Sing, sway, whistle, dance. Come alive!

Just a moment ago, I lifted my hand from the computer keyboard and moved it as if I was conducting a symphony orchestra—I'm still listening to music.

> *This is the day the Lord has made; let us rejoice and be glad in it.*
>
> PSALM 118:24

Happy people have more energy and it is each person's responsibility to increase personal energy. With a surplus of energy, you can bring benevolent energy to each interaction. You can be patient and kind to the offended person.

> *Do not ask yourself what the world needs; ask yourself what makes you come alive. And then go and do that. Because what the world needs is people who have come alive.*
>
> HOWARD THURMAN

Principle

Lift your spirits through music: sing, sway, whistle and dance. Come alive!

Power Questions

How can you make time to enjoy music? Can you include music naturally in your day? Perhaps, while doing household chores?

Thank Someone

What is one of the fastest ways to step away from feeling bad? Shift to being thankful. Thank someone. A friend, yourself, or Higher Power.

> *If the only prayer you say in your whole life is "thank you," that would suffice.*
>
> MEISTER ECKHART

For years, I have been sharing four simple words that have helped my clients and audiences make an important shift to a positive perception. These are the words: *I am grateful for.*

Pull out your personal journal and write down—in 20 seconds—ten details that you're grateful for: people, experiences, your eyesight, and more.

> *Every day you can choose to create feelings of wonder, excitement, abundance and gratitude. When you get up in the morning, take a moment to say a prayer of gratitude that you're waking to a day filled with possibilities and that you have the health to enjoy it and the freedom to choose your emotions regardless of what happens.*
>
> PEGGY MCCOLL

> *Pick three new things each day that you appreciate about your spouse or significant other and tell him or her.*
>
> MIKE ROBBINS

At each meal, my sweetheart and I hold hands and say together, "We're grateful." And, during dinner gatherings, our friends (of various spiritual paths) smile as we all hold hands around the table and say, "We're grateful."

Principle

Thank someone and you'll feel positive that you're enjoying benefits in life.

Power Questions

Who can you thank? How would you thank them and for what? What process or ritual can help you shift quickly to feeling gratitude?

Conclusion to Chapter Twelve

In Chapter Twelve, we have covered the R.E.S.T. process:

        R – Relax into it
        E – Ease through
        S – Sing
        T – Thank someone

The central idea is to avoid adding tasks to your to-do list. We are looking to subtract actions that may have led to more resistance and the draining of your energy.

Remember to find ways to enjoy an Ease-through. When you are enjoying more moments of life, you are strengthened. From a calm state of being, you'll be able to do what is necessary to restore your relationship with the offended person.

A Final Word

Springboard to Your Dreams

Thank you for your attention and efforts. As I mentioned earlier, the Secret Influence process includes:

- Strengthen yourself
- Remain in a calm state of being
- Communicate your concern and kindness
- Take action with the F.A.R. methods (forgiveness, amends, regret)

> *People who say it cannot be done should not interrupt those who are doing it.*
>
> GEORGE BERNARD SHAW

Remember, Secret Influence is to stay in a calm state of being and then transfer your positive energy to the offended person.

To heal a personal or business relationship after you've made a mistake can be an extended process. The point is to continually nurture yourself and to condition yourself so you're at your best during the *10 Seconds to Wealth*.

Let's review the essence of *10 Seconds to Wealth:*

- In 10 seconds you can close a sale … or torpedo a relationship.

- Using your Divine Gifts enables you to be at your best during the crucial 10 seconds of any interaction.

- Your building and enhancing a positive connection with people (during the 10 seconds) creates the relationships that are key for success and fulfillment.

- The strategy is to condition yourself to be at your best during the 10 seconds [methods abound in this book].

- Recent brain research notes that it takes 10 seconds for positive input to impact your long term memory. [Memorizing empowering thoughts, rehearsing effective behaviors, and writing positive details in your personal journal all help physically alter your brain so that your brain is inclined toward the positive.]

- Your preparation to condition yourself helps you overcome "default settings."

I invite you to return to these pages again and again to reenergize yourself. You will get more value each time you review the steps covered in this book.

Please visit me at TomSuperCoach.com to get free reports and my free e-newsletter, Success Secrets. And, visit my blog www.BeHeardandBeTrusted.com

Also, I work with clients one-on-one, in person and over the telephone. And I present workshops and speeches to various associations and companies.

On the next page you will find empowering audio programs and books that will help you continue your education and enhance your feelings of success and fulfillment.

The best to you,

Tom

Tom Marcoux
America's Communication Coach
Motion Picture Director & CEO, Tom Marcoux Media, LLC

Special Offer for My Readers

Bring Tom to your company, organization, conference or church and gain a 10% discount for Tom's presentation. (contact TomSuperCoach@gmail.com)

Tom's popular topics:

- 10 Seconds to Wealth: Master the Moment Using Your Divine Gifts
- Be Heard and Be Trusted
- Full Strength Marketing: Use Your Hidden Strengths
- Nothing Can Stop You This Year!
- Power Time Management
- Double Your Sales in Half the Time™
- 10 Best Kept Secrets of Persuasion Masters
- Wake Up Your Spirit To Prosperity
- Say Yes to Yourself: Reduce Stress and Increase Ease
- Empower Your Personal Brand

To view a downloadable page of these topics, go to:

bureau.espeakers.com/simp/viewspeaker5261&multimedia

Glossary

Glossary

For easy reference, here are listed all the specially defined terms used in this book.

~~~~~~~~~~~~~~~~

9-Minute Miracle Breakthrough—The process of bringing prosperity-expansion down to daily, individually-tailored steps.

Choice Market Testing™—The process by which you show a person two versions of something and ask two questions in this sequence: a) "Which one do you prefer?" and b) "What about ___ (the person's preference) grabs your attention?"

Destructive Default Setting—A pattern that includes a trigger and a reacting behavior that is set in one's childhood.

Ease into Momentum—The process of getting started by taking the pain out of the first step. Once you begin, you create momentum that carries you through the rough parts.

Easy Part Start—The process of starting a project with something easy.

Ego—The Ego is made of fear. When you are stuck in your Ego you feel small, vulnerable and fragile. A number of people, when stuck in their Ego, feel irritable and angry. Anger is fear twisted.

Emotional Leverage—The strategy that utilizes your emotions to help you get big results with little effort.

Entrepreneurial Partner—The partner who has a future-focus, a vision for a better life, tolerance for pain in the present, and is comfortable taking risks. This partner often works many hours and puts career or self-employment very high on a priority list.

False Self—Also known as the Ego. This is the part of you that is stuck in fear, like being in a cage.

Appendices   *Glossary* • **V**

Healthy Humility—To acknowledge that our Ego often clouds our perception; and we often do not know what is for our highest good.

Leverage Triangle™—This process is: Merge with your True Self, Strategize, and Act. The process is the cure for when people try new strategies and then find themselves falling back on old habits.

Martyr's Badge—This is a form of trumpeting how we make sacrifices for other people. It is a way of saying: "Look how much pain I endure. This makes me a good person." It is a way to be a hero in your own eyes. The Martyr's Badge can get in the way of inner peace and forgiveness.

Momentum Action Plan™ (MAP)—This is your roadmap to your best life. When one goes through the 9-Minute Miracle Breakthrough process, one has created a Momentum Action Plan.

Non-Entrepreneurial Partner—The partner who has a present-moment focus. Often this partner does not see or feel the vision for the brighter future. This partner, when listened to, can help the Entrepreneurial Partner avoid burnout. Also, the Non-Entrepreneurial partner is concerned about missing life on a day-to-day basis.

Personaltainment™ Branding—The process of connecting with your prospective customers so they know you and trust you quickly—and purchase what you offer. The process involves the P.E.C. Triangle of personalized, entertaining and connecting material.

Replace Inky Water Method—This is the process that uses words, body posture, an aroma, an image and music to help flush out old destructive patterns (the inky water). If you pour enough fresh water into the bucket, the inky water will flow out, leaving you with just fresh clear water.

Reverse Examples—People who are doing something that causes them to go backwards. This is the opposite of progress and the opposite of supporting the flow of grand abundance.

True Self—This is the part of you that is naturally brilliant and naturally courageous.

Bibliography

Further Reading

The following list of books and audio programs provides the reader with select landmarks in the rich literary landscape which has informed this book. Enjoy!

~~~~~~~~

Adler, Bill ⇒ Winfrey, Oprah & Bill Adler

Albom, Mitch, *Tuesdays with Morrie: An Old Man, a Young Man, and Life's Greatest Lesson,* 2002, 192p, Broadway, 978-0767905923

Alessandra, Dr. Tony, *Charisma: Seven Keys to Developing the Magnetism that Leads to Success,* 2000, 288p, Business Plus, 978-0446675987

_____, *Non-Manipulative Selling,* 2nd Ed., 1992, 276p, Fireside; 978-0671764487

_____, *The Dynamics of Effective Listening*, 2008, audio, 5 hours, 29 mins, Nightingale-Conant

Alessandra, Dr. Tony & Michael J. O'Connor, *The Platinum Rule: Discover the Four Basic Business Personalities and How They Can Lead You to Success*, 1998, 304p, Grand Central Publishing, 978-0446673433

Allen, Marc, *The Greatest Secret of All: Moving Beyond Abundance to a Life of True Fulfillment*, 2007, 128p, New World Library, 978-1577316190

_____, *The Type Z Guide to Success: A Lazy Person's Manifesto to Wealth and Fulfillment*, 2006, 160p, New World Library, 978-1577315407

Ash, Mary Kay, *Timeless Principles from America's Greatest Woman Entrepreneur*, 2008, 272p, Wiley, 978-0470379950

Bach, David, *The Automatic Millionaire: A Powerful One-Step Plan to Live and Finish Rich*, 2005, 272p, Broadway, 978-0767923828

Barron, David R. & Danek S. Kaus, *Power Persuasion: Using Hypnotic Influence to Win in Life, Love, and Business*, 2005, 108p, Robert D. Reed Publishers, 978-1931741521

Bauer, Joel et al., *How to Persuade People Who Don't Want to Be Persuaded: Get What You Want Every Time!*, 2004, 256p, Wiley, 978-0471647973

Bedell, Gene, *Three Steps to Yes: The Gentle Art of Getting Your Way*, 2002, 256p, Three Rivers Press, 978-0609807194

Ben-Shahar, Tal, *Happier: Learn the Secrets to Daily Joy and Lasting Fulfillment*, 2007, 224p, McGraw-Hill, 978-0071492393

Bettger, Fred, *How I Raised Myself from Failure to Success in Selling*, 1992, 192p, Fireside; 978-0671794378

Blanchard, Ken, & Sheldon Bowles, *Raving Fans: A Revolutionary Approach To Customer Service*, 1993, 160p, William Morrow, 978-0688123161

Bloom, Linda & Charlie, *101 Things I Wish I Knew When I Got Married: Simple Lessons to Make Love Last*, 2004, 256p, New World Library, 978-1577314240

Bowles, Sheldon, ⇒ Blanchard, Ken, & Sheldon Bowles

Byrne, Rhonda, *The Secret*, 2006, 198p, Atria Books, 978-1582701707

Campbell, Joseph, *The Hero with a Thousand Faces* (Bollingen Series, No. 17), 1972, 464p, Princeton University Press, 978-0691017846

Canfield, Jack & Mark Victor Hansen, *Chicken Soup for the Soul*, 2001, 480p, HCI, 978-1558749207

Carlson, Kristine, *Don't Sweat the Small Stuff for Women: Simple and Practical Ways to Do What Matters Most and Find Time for You*, 2001, 288p, Hyperion, 978-0786886029

Carlson, Richard, *Don't Sweat the Small Stuff—And It's All Small Stuff*, 1996, 272p, Hyperion, 978-0786881857

Chapman, Dr. Gary, *The Five Love Languages: How to Express Heartfelt Commitment to Your Mate*, 1995, 204p, Northfield Publishing, 978-1881273158

Churchill, Winston, *Never Give In!: The Best of Winston Churchill's Speeches*, 2004, 558p, Hyperion, 0786888709

Cialdini, Robert, *Influence: The Psychology of Persuasion* (Collins Business Essentials), 2006, 336p, Collins Business, 978-0061241895

Cohen, Alan, *Relax Into Wealth: How to Get More by Doing Less*, 2006, 240p, Tarcher, 978-1585425631

Collier, Robert, *The Secret of the Ages*, 2008, 164p, Wilder Publications, 978-1604591880

Confucius, *The Analects* (Oxford World's Classics), translated by Raymond Dawson, 2008, 160p, Oxford University Press, 978-0199540617

Covey, Stephen, *The 7 Habits of Highly Effective People*, 2004, 4p, FreePress, 978-0743269513

Cutler, Howard C., ▬▶ Dalai Lama, The, & Howard C. Cutler

da Vinci, Leonardo & Serge Bramly, *Leonardo: The Artist and the Man*, (Illustrated), 1995, 512p, Penguin, 978-0140231755

Dahlkoetter, Dr. JoAnn, *Your Performing Edge: The Total Mind-body Program for Excellence in Sports, Business and Life*, 4th Ed., 2007, 264p, Pulgas Ridge Press, 978-0970407986

Dalai Lama, The, & Howard C. Cutler, *The Art of Happiness: A Handbook for Living*, 1998, 336p, Riverhead, 978-1573221115

DeNoon, Daniel, "Health-Food-Store Safari," WebMD.com

Disney, Walt, *Quotable Walt Disney*, 2001, 272p, Disney Editions, 978-0786853328

Dyer, Dr. Wayne, *Inspiration: Your Ultimate Calling*, 2007, 272p, Hay House, 978-1401907228

_____, *Your Erroneous Zones*, 1993, 320p, Avon Books, 978-0061091483

Einstein, Albert, *The World As I See It*, 2006, 128p, Filiquarian Publishing, 978-1599869650

Emerson, Ralph Waldo, *Emerson: Essays and Lectures: Nature: Addresses and Lectures / Essays: First and Second Series / Representative Men / English Traits / The Conduct of Life*, 1983, 1150p, Library of America, 978-0940450158

Fettke, Rich, *Extreme Success: The 7-Part Program That Shows You How to Succeed Without Struggle*, 2002, 288p, Fireside, 978-0743223140

Franklin, Benjamin, *Benjamin Franklin: Autobiography, Poor Richard, and Later Writings* (Library of America), J. A. Leo Lemay ed., 2005, 816p, Library of America, 978-1883011536

Gage, Randy, *Why You're Dumb, Sick & Broke ... And How to Get Smart, Healthy & Rich!*, 2006, 224p, Wiley, 978-0470049310

Gandhi, Mahatma, *An Autobiography: The Story of My Experiments With Truth*, 1993, 528p, Beacon Press, 978-0807059098

Gilbert, Bill ➠ King, Larry & Bill Gilbert

Gospe, Mike, *Marketing Campaign Development: What Marketing Executives Need to Know About Architecting Global Integrated Marketing Campaigns*, 2008, 176p, Happy About, 978-1600050770

Greene, Bob, *Get with the Program!: Getting Real About Your Weight, Health, and Emotional Well-Being*, 2003, 224p, Simon & Schuster Australia, 978-0731811892

Groppel, Jack L., PhD, *The Anti-Diet Book*, 1995

Hansen, Mark Victor ➠ Hayden, C. J., *Get Clients Now!*, 2nd Ed., 2007, 256p, AMACOM, 978-0814473740

Hendricks, Gay, *The Big Leap: Conquer Your Hidden Fear and Take Life to the Next Level*, 2009, 224p, HarperOne, 978-0061735349

Hepburn, Katherine, *Me: Stories of My Life*, 1996, 432p, Ballantine Books, 978-0345410092

Jampolsky, Gerald "Jerry," MD, *Love is Letting Go of Fear*, 25th Anniversary Ed., 2004, 144p, Ten Speed Press, 978-1587611964

Jay, Robin, *The Art of the Business Lunch: Building Relationships Between 12 and 2*, 2006, 254p, Career Press, 978-1564148513

Jung, Carl, *The Portable Carl Jung* (Viking Portable Library), Joseph Campbell ed.,1976, 704p, Penguin, 978-014015070

Kaus, Danek S. ⟹ Barron, David R. + Danek S. Kaus

Kaus, Danek S., *You Can Be Famous: Insider Secrets to Getting Free Publicity*, 2009, 176p, Robert Reed Publishers, 978-1934759110

Kawasaki, Guy, *The Art of the Start: The Time-Tested, Battle-Hardened Guide for Anyone Starting Anything*, 2004, 226p, Portfolio Hardcover, 978-1591840565

Keller, Helen, *The Story of My Life: The Restored Classic*, Centennial Ed., Anne Sullivan et al. eds, 2003, 352p, W. W. Norton & Company, 978-0393057447

Kennedy, John F., *Let the Word Go Forth: The Speeches, Statements, and Writings of John F. Kennedy 1947 to 1963*, Theodore Sorensen ed, 1991, 448p, Delta, 978-0440504061

King, Larry & Bill Gilbert, *How to Talk to Anyone, Anytime, Anywhere: The Secrets of Good Communication*, 1995, 224p, Three Rivers Press, 978-0517884539

King, Jr., Martin Luther, *A Testament of Hope: The Essential Writings and Speeches of Martin Luther King, Jr.*, James M. Washington ed., 1990, 736p, HarperOne, 978-0060646912

Kiyosaki, Robert T. & Sharon L. Lechter, *Rich Dad, Poor Dad: What the Rich Teach Their Kids About Money—That the Poor and Middle Class Do Not!*, 2000, 207p, Business Plus, 978-0446677455

Klein, MA, CSP, Allen, *The Healing Power of Humor*, 1989, 240p, Tarcher, 978-0874775198

Kushner, Malcolm, *Presentations for Dummies*, 2004, 384p, For Dummies, 978-0764559556

_____, *Public Speaking for Dummies*, 2nd Ed., 2004, 288p, For Dummies; 978-0764559549

Lao-Tzu, *Te-Tao Ching—A New Translation Based on the Recently Discovered Ma-wang-tui Texts* (Classics of Ancient China), tranlated by Robert G. Henricks, 1992, 430p, Ballantine Books, 978-0345370990

Lee, Michael Soon, MBA & Sensei Grant Tabuchi, *Black Belt Negotiating: Become a Master Negotiator Using Powerful Lessons from the Martial Arts*, 2007, 224p, Amacom Books, 978-0814474617

Lee, Michael Soon, Ralph R. Roberts, & Joe Kraynak, *Cross-Cultural Selling for Dummies*, (Illustrated), 2008, 384p, For Dummies, 0470377011

Levinson, Jay Conrad, *Guerrilla Marketing: Easy and Inexpensive Strategies for Making Big Profits from Your Small Business*, 4th Ed., 2007, 384p, Mariner Books , 978-0618785919

Luskin, Dr. Fred, *Forgive for Good*, 2003, 240p, HarperOne, 978-0062517210

Luskin, Dr. Fred, *Forgive for Love: The Missing Ingredient for a Healthy and Lasting Relationship*, 2009, 240p, HarperOne, 978-0061234958

MacFarlane, Michael, *Share and Grow Rich: The Dottie Walters Effect*, 2007, 207p, Elevate, 978-1601940087

Marcoux, Tom, *10 Best Kept Secrets of Persuasion Masters*, Marcoux Media

_____, *101 Acting Secrets: Tips from A Director for Your Acting, Auditions, Movie Roles, and Self-Promotion*, Marcoux Media, www.TomSuperCoach.com

_____, *Be Heard and Be Trusted: How You Can Use Secrets of the Greatest Communicators to Get What You Want*, 3rd Ed., 2009, Marcoux Media, 978-0-9800511-4-8

_____, *Darkest Secrets of Persuasion and Seduction Masters: How to Protect Yourself and Turn the Power to Good*, 2006, 186p, Marcoux Media, 978-0-9800511-0-0

_____, *Double Your Sales in Half the Time*, Marcoux Media

_____, *Empower Your Personal Brand: Align Yourself for Promotions and Raises*, Marcoux Media

_____, *How to Heal When Life's Too Much*, Marcoux Media

_____, *Make Money through Products Power*, Marcoux Media

_____, *Nothing Can Stop You This Year!: How to Unleash Your Hidden Power to Persuade Well, Get More Done, Gain Sudden Profits, Command Intuition, and Feel Great*, 2nd Ed., 2010, Tom Marcoux Media, 978-0-9800511-5-5

_____, *Online Secrets to Build Your Brand*, Marcoux Media

_____, *Personal Branding*, Marcoux Media

_____, *Power Time Management: More Time, Less Stress and Zero Procrastination*, Marcoux Media

_____, *Say Yes to Yourself: Secrets to Overcome Stress and Change in Your Workplace*, Marcoux Media

_____, *Secret Influence to Get You Out of Trouble: How You Can Restore a Personal or Business Relationship After You've Really Screwed Up*, 2008, 156p, Marcoux Media, 978-0-9800511-3-1, www.TomSuperCoach.com

_____, *The Recession-Proof Cupcake: How to Feed Your Soul, Save a Business, or Get a Job in a Crisis*, Marcoux Media

_____, *Truth No One Will One Tell You: How to Feed Your Soul, Save a Business, or Get a Job in a Crisis*, 2010, Tom Marcoux Media, 978-0-9800511-6-2

_____, *Ultimate Make Money While You Sleep via the Internet System*, Marcoux Media, www.TomSuperCoach.com

_____, *Wake Up Your Spirit to Prosperity for Couples!: 7 Secrets to Increase Wealth, Romance, and Anything You Want*, 2006, 150p, Marcoux Media, 0-9624660-6-9

_____, *Wake Up Your Spirit to Prosperity!: 7 Secrets to Attract Wealth, Love, and Anything You Want*, 2006, 132p, Marcoux Media, 0-9624660-5-0

McWilliams, Peter, *Wealth 101: Getting What You Want-Enjoying What You'Ve Got*, 1999, 532p, Prelude Press, 978-0931580185

Melograni, Piero, *Wolfgang Amadeus Mozart: A Biography*, 2008, 316p, University Of Chicago Press, 978-0226519616

O'Connor, Michael J. *see* Alessandra, Dr. Tony & Michael J. O'Connor

Orman, Suze, *The Laws of Money: 5 Timeless Secrets to Get Out and Stay Out of Financial Trouble*, 2004, 352p, Free Press, 978-0743245180

Parnell, Aaron Lloyd U., *Living with Vitality—The Dynamic Power of Extraordinary Health*, 2007, 204p, PZQ Press Divison, 978-0615143323

Ragas, Matthew W. and B. J. Bueno, *The Power of Cult Branding: How 9 Magnetic Brands Turned Customers into Loyal Followers (and Yours Can, Too!)*, 2002, 224p, Crown Business, 978-0761536949

Reeve, Christopher, *Nothing is Impossible: Reflections on a New Life*, 2004, 224p, Ballantine Books, 978-0345470737

RoAnne, Susan, *How to Work a Room*, Revised Ed., 2007, 336p, Collins Living, 978-0061238673

Robbins, Anthony, *Awaken the Giant Within: How to Take Immediate Control of Your Mental, Emotional, Physical and Financial Destiny!*, 1992, 544p, Free Press, 978-0671791544

Robbins, Mike, CSP, *Be Yourself, Everyone Else is Already Taken: Transform Your Life with the Power of Authenticity*, 2009, 256p, Jossey-Bass, 978-0470395011

_____, *Focus on the Good Stuff: The Power of Appreciation*, 2007, 240p, Jossey-Bass, 978-0787988791

Roffer, Robin Fisher, *Make a Name for Yourself: Eight Steps Every Woman Needs to Create a Personal Brand Strategy for Success*, 2002, 224p, Broadway, 978-0767904926

Savage, PhD, Elayne, *Don't Take It Personally! The Art of Dealing with Rejection*, 2002, 242p, iUniverse, 978-0595255757

_____, *Breathing Room—Creating Space to Be a Couple*, 2001, 210p, New Harbinger Publications, 978-1572242210

Seid, Syndi, *Etiquette in Minutes*, www.etiquetteinminutes.com

Siddhartha, Guatama, *In the Buddha's Words: An Anthology of Discourses from the Pali Canon* (Teachings of the Buddha), Bhikkhu Bodhi ed., 2005, 496p, Wisdom Publications, 978-0861714919

Siegel, Dr. Bernie, *Love, Medicine and Miracles: Lessons Learned about Self-Healing from a Surgeon's Experience with Exceptional Patients*, 1990, 256p, Harper, 978-0060919832

Spielberg, Steven, *Interviews* (Conversations with Filmmakers Series), Lester D. Friedman & Brent Notbohm eds., 2000, 250p, University Press of Mississippi, 978-1578061136

St. John, Noah, *The Secret Code of Success*, 2009, 256p, Collins Business, 978-0061715747

Tabuchi, Sensei Grant *see* Lee, Michael Soon, MBA & Sensei Grant Tabuchi

Teresa, Mother, *Mother Teresa: In My Own Words*, edited by Jose Luis Gonzalez-Balado, 1997, 128p, Liguori Publications, 978-0764802003

Tracy, Brian, *Eat That Frog!: 21 Great Ways to Stop Procrastinating and Get More Done in Less Time*, 2nd Ed., 2007, 128p, Berrett-Koehler Publishers, 978-1576754221

Trump, Donald J., *The Art of the Deal*, 2004, 384p, Ballantine Books, 978-0345479174

Waitley, Denis, *The Psychology of Winning*, 1987, Nightingale-Conant, 0671520679, audio recording (also available in paperback)

Walters, Dottie & Lillet "Lilly" Walters, *Speak and Grow Rich*, 1997, 288p, Prentice Hall, 978-0735203518

Wattles, Wallace D., *The Science of Getting Rich*, 2008, 112p, Wilder Publications, 978-1604591903

Wieder, Marcia, *Making Your Dreams Come True*, 1999, 235p, Harmony, 978-0609606087

Williams, A.L., *All You Can Do Is All You Can Do, But All You Can Do Is Enough!*, 1997, 219p, Ballantne Books, 978-0449001103

Winfrey, Oprah & O, The Oprah Magazine, Editors of O, *Live Your Best Life: A Treasury of Wisdom, Wit, Advice, Interviews, and Inspiration from O, The Oprah Magazine*, 2005, 336p, Oxmoor House, 978-0848731052

_____ & Bill Adler, *The Uncommon Wisdom Of Oprah Winfrey: A Portrait in Her Own Words*, 2000, 290p, Citadel, 978-1559724197

Ziglar, Zig, *Goals—Set goals ... and reach them!*, 1988, Nightingale-Conant, audio recording

About the Author

Tom Marcoux
America's Communication Coach

Tom Marcoux helps people like *you* accomplish big dreams. As Tom says, "I help people like you *command the Wow!* in your audience. When presenting, branding, or communicating one-on-one, my coaching helps you make people feel good and *want* to follow your lead." Further, Tom helps people get more done and feel good doing it.

Tom is also a prolific author, including *Nothing Can Stop You This Year!*, he has published 10 books and 21 audio programs, with sales in 15 countries. These have included both fiction and nonfiction. Prominent among his publications is *Be Heard & Be Trusted*, 3rd Ed., which, in a prior edition, was a required textbook at Cogswell Polytechnical College. The Third edition features contributions by Jay Conrad Levinson, Guy Kawasaki, and Dr. Fred Luskin, among others.

When you want *to influence others*, join Tom's many clients who benefit from his secrets on branding. Tom is described as "the Personal Branding Instructor" by the *San*

Francisco Examiner. Helping people become more effective job candidates, he has presented to ProMatch, Project Management Institute and chapters of Experience Unlimited (affiliated with the California Employment Development Department).

Holding a degree in psychology, Tom is also a personal and professional coach and guest expert on TV and radio In addition to being featured in technology and communication magazines, he earned a special award at the Emmy Awards. For six years, he addressed the National Association of Broadcasters Conference in Las Vegas on topics like, "Online Secrets to Build Your Brand."

Tom is an award-winning speaker and corporate workshop leader (to professionals from IBM, Wells Fargo, Sun Microsystems, and Silicon Valley Bank). He is a member of the National Speakers Association.

Tom is also a faculty lecturer in public speaking, science fiction and fantasy literature and cinema, and comparative religion at Academy of Art University. He has been a guest lecturer at Stanford University, DeAnza College, and California State University at Los Angeles, among others. In addition to traditional classroom forums, he teaches online and has authored several online courses. He also presents workshops to fellow faculty at the Academy of Art University's Teacher Conferences.

In a more artistic vein, Tom has written, directed, and produced feature films, including one that went to the Cannes Film Festival market, where it gained international distribution. He performed as an actor in feature films and commercials. Presently, he is leading teams working on book-film projects titled *Crystal Pegasus* (children's fantasy) and *TimePulse* (science fiction). In addition, his audio programs and audio novels often feature orginal soundtracks composed by Tom.

When you need to enthrall audiences or effectively communicate your message to the media, engage Tom as your media coach. Tom will clarify your message, build your confidence in speaking, and craft compelling sound bites and stories for the press. Tom will help you excel!

(415) 572-6609
TomSuperCoach@gmail.com
www.TomSuperCoach.com
Blog at www.BeHeardAndBeTrusted.com

Collophon

Designed

and set by gBambo of the graphic
and cartographic atelier:

kunst+aventur

Named for the slim booklet *Kunst und Aventur* (Art & Enterprise), published in Strasbourg, France in 1440, in which Johannes Gutenberg (c. 1398–1468), a German goldsmith, unveiled his epochal mechanization of printing, vastly accelerating the pace of learning and human progress.

The text was set principally in Minion Pro, Zapf Humanist, Poor Richard, Fontin, and Gill Sans families. The body font, Minion Pro, was designed by Robert Slimbach based on classical old style types of the late Renaissance.

The design was executed in Adobe's excellent Creative Suite 5, including Photoshop, Illustrator, and InDesign.

Write kunst.aventur@gmail.com about design inquiries large or small and user feedback.
Enjoy!

Get what you really want ...

use the methods found in Tom Marcoux's books!

For special discounts, order at:
www.TomSuperCoach.com/SpecialOffer.htm

For more QuickBreakthrough resources, see
www.TomSuperCoach.com
blog at BeHeardAndBeTrusted.com

www.ingramcontent.com/pod-product-compliance
Lightning Source LLC
Chambersburg PA
CBHW070547100426
42744CB00006B/242